HIGH POTENTIAL

HIGH POTENTIAL

How to Spot, Manage and Develop
Talented People at Work

2nd edition

BY
IAN MACRAE, ADRIAN FURNHAM
AND MARTIN REED

Bloomsbury Business
An imprint of Bloomsbury Publishing Plc

B L O O M S B U R Y
LONDON · OXFORD · NEW YORK · NEW DELHI · SYDNEY

Bloomsbury Business

An imprint of Bloomsbury Publishing Plc

50 Bedford Square	1385 Broadway
London	New York
WC1B 3DP	NY 10018
UK	USA

www.bloomsbury.com

BLOOMSBURY and the Diana logo are trademarks of Bloomsbury Publishing Plc

First edition published 2014 by Bloomsbury Publishing Plc

Second edition first published 2018

© Ian MacRae, Adrian Furnham and Martin Reed, 2018

Ian MacRae, Adrian Furnham and Martin Reed have asserted their right under
the Copyright, Designs and Patents Act, 1988, to be identified as Author of this work.

British Library Cataloguing-in-Publication Data
A catalogue record for this book is available from the British Library.

ISBN:	HB:	978-1-4729-5349-0
	ePDF:	978-1-4729-5348-3
	ePub:	978-1-4729-5347-6

Library of Congress Cataloging-in-Publication Data.
A catalog record for this book is available from the Library of Congress.

Cover design by Kerry Squires
Cover image © Getty Images

Typeset by Integra Software Services Pvt. Ltd.
Printed and bound in Great Britain

To find out more about our authors and books visit www.bloomsbury.com.
Here you will find extracts, author interviews, details of forthcoming events
and the option to sign up for our newsletters.

For Neil MacRae:
Potential realized and cut short
and
Benedict Furnham:
Great potential realized

CONTENTS

LIST OF ILLUSTRATIONS

Figures

Tables

PREFACE

The intention of this book in the first edition was to be interesting, thought-provoking, and to approach some of the issues that seem to be controversial in public discourse, address the facts that would benefit people in the workplace, and to discuss topics where there is no scientific controversy on the facts. The first sentence of the preface to the first edition was: 'There is, almost certainly, going to be something in this book you object to'. The surprising reaction was that there was nothing objectionable, other than slight overuse of commas.

There seems to be a genuine groundswell in the realms of HR, management, leadership and workplaces in general that involves people making better decisions based on good judgement. It is the purpose of this book to bring the science of psychology, of business and of people to life. The goal of making workplaces better, more profitable, more productive and healthier goes hand in hand. The science firmly backs this up, and there are so many opportunities to bring it to the workplace.

The topic of what is desirable at work remains an interesting one. There are certain behaviours, activities and results that are desirable in particular times, societies and environments and not in others. There are certain things that make people successful at work that may cause difficulties in other areas of life. Similarly, there can be qualities that make someone an excellent friend, but a terrible boss. A brilliant accountant but a terrible counsellor. A sublime performer but a lacking conversationalist. The problem of potential is always a question of *what kind of potential do you mean?* Many people believe that a leader of a massive company or country is the pinnacle of achievement: Success is power.

Others believe that a very different type of achievement is the pinnacle of human achievement. Some confidently announce that art, science, military victory, spiritual awareness, athletic performance, personal power, wealth, happiness, conformity or even extreme suffering (i.e. *le douleur exquise, White House Press Secretary*) is the pinnacle of achievement. The more specific you get about particular types of achievement, the more discriminating people can be. Tchaikovsky once said of Brahms, 'what a giftless bastard'. Others will disagree.

Our purpose in this book is not to say what is valuable, socially desirable, or to say potential is a specific behaviour or accomplishment. That would be an error. Instead, we see potential as a probability or likelihood to behave in a particular way. That means high potential at work can be seen as a *high* probability to be successful at a particular type of work, and will likely lead to exceptional performance in a particular area (but not always). Potential is a bet, but not a guarantee. But it is based on an extremely important set of traits and characteristics. The probability of performance can also mean people with 'low' potential in a certain area may still perform well in that area, under exceptional circumstances – but exceptions are by no means the rule.

Make decisions based on potential, on probabilities, but leave room for people to surprise you – give people the benefit of the doubt, and the occasional opportunity to prove you wrong. Not everyone will surprise you, but it's worth waiting for the person who will. Uniformed decisions in favour of, or against, people lead to frequent errors. As we discuss in this book, there are very many factors that contribute to potential. In many cases, being 'average' is strength. Yet, as positions get more demanding, responsibilities are greater, consequences of failure become more dire, scrutiny becomes more important. Exceptionality is also abnormality – with all the implied strengths and weaknesses. The more demanding the position, the more particular the requirements.

Also, remember that the focus of this book is on potential *at work*. The characteristics one would use to evaluate an employee or boss are not the same one should use to judge the personal relationship with a partner, lover, friend, parent or child. We will describe the components of potential *at work*, while the question remains for you, dear reader, to consider the potential to do *what*.

That is, in fact, the purpose of this book: to provide a framework for describing potential at work along with some of the key attributes. These attributes are based on the best available scientific evidence and applied research. This is a framework, an efficient way of describing and thinking about potential, within a particular structure.

That being said, only one point remains before moving from the preface into the very real face of this book – and that is to recognize the contributions. Just as potential does not exist without someone defining *potential to do what,* and many others developing potential. Likewise, this book would not exist without many contributions. Heather Stewart, Lloyd Craig, Zohra Ihsan, Zac Olson, Ken Whittall, Paul Rein, Alison Lui, Matthew Griffiths, Jessica Weaving, Róisín O'Connor, Stephen Cuppello, Cherie Mandoli Jayson Darby, Kamilla Bahbahani, Cherie Mandoli, Brendan MacRae, Rebecca Milner, Sonya Bendriem Luke Treglown, Toni-Ann Murphy and John Taylor all contributed directly (whether knowingly or unknowingly) to the content in these pages.

PART ONE

POTENTIAL

1

What is potential

Things are always at their best in their beginnings.
– BLAISE PASCAL, *LETTRES PROVINCIALES*

Life being very short, and the quiet hours of it few, we ought to waste none of them in reading valueless books.
– JOHN RUSKIN, *SESAME AND LILIES*

Introduction

Every organization needs to hire able, motivated and talented staff with potential. At the same time, most organizations and anyone who has worked knows that promoting talent does not always turn into high potential. Some intelligent people turn out to be lazy. Some highly successful people turn out to be narcissistic, manipulative and, ultimately, destructive to their team and can potentially turn self-destructive. Others are hard workers who can never seem to apply themselves to the correct tasks. Talent, ability or personality history do not always turn into future potential.

Imagine a technician that is promoted to a leadership position, a salesperson who is assigned to work in the HR department. What about a scientist who becomes an activist, a politician who becomes a newspaper editor or a businessperson who becomes a politician. They may succeed, but one cannot assume success in a previous position will lead to success in a fundamentally different type of job. Success in one type of work does not always translate to potential to do something else or succeed in another field. This assumption, *The Performance Delusion* (discussed in Chapter 9), is extraordinarily common across organizations and workplaces, and stems from a misunderstanding of potential.

So the question is, how do we predict high potential? What can be done to identify potential top performers and sift out the potentially poor performers or likely derailers? This book answers that question, and provides a detailed guide to the tools, resources and knowledge that can be used to spot, manage and develop potentially high performers and make every effort to sift out those who will fail, derail or be destructive.

High potential

High potential is the ability to perform exceptionally well (at work, for a reasonable amount of time) for their own benefit and that of the organization. Having high potential is about being talented and capable of exceptional performance in the future. Potential means possessing an underlying capacity to do well in future endeavours and have the possibility of becoming even better. A person with potential is one who can grow to maximize their capacity to do well.

High potential is about achieving that which is possible: to explore and exploit personal gifts and situations; to realize talents one was born with, to continually learn and develop these talents.

However, the topic of potential can seem simultaneously enormously complex or enormously simple. It is tempting to simplify the idea of potential. Many tempters and temptresses will sell the idea of a single measure or single important characteristic of high potential. There are no magic bullets to identify potential – if there was a single magic bullet this book would be much shorter. The idea of identifying high potential is incredibly attractive. CEOs demand that their human resource staff recruit and select employees with high potential who will ensure the future success of the company. Human resource departments are tasked with identifying high-potential employees. Many consultants claim to have the secret and be able, for a generous fee, to spread their 'magic dust' over the organization.

The reality of identifying and managing human potential cannot be simplified down to one single factor. There is no *one potential* because how a person behaves (at work, their behaviour is typically referred to as performance) is affected by what they know about their job, how much they want to do the job and what the consequences are for performance and what people around them are doing. Their own characteristics are constantly interacting with their situation and surroundings (their environment). There is not *one potential* because there is no one single job description or one type of organization. If every job were identical, the components of potential would be identical.

People choose and change their work environments and it changes them. People are dynamic, in motion, moving and responding to their work group and corporate culture. High potential must be defined by considering the person, the organization and the type of work.

Purpose of identifying potential

The goal for organizations is usually to attract people who can be (very) successful in their job, and have the potential to advance into other, more challenging or demanding, positions 'up the organization'. Many corporations endorse a natural selection view: as a natural progression for people to demonstrate their own superior performance, and work their way towards new promotions and rewards. As we will see in coming chapters, survival of the fittest models can have serious consequences for workplaces. If you're lucky the best rise to the top. But if you're unlucky or careless the people with the worst and most destructive tendencies will manipulate, lie, coerce, bribe or blackmail their way to the top.

The purpose of the growing field of 'talent management' which we will discuss later is to get the best people into the right position to improve performance, and improve the overall performance of the organization. In other words, the aim is to get the *right people* in the *right roles* with the *right skills and attitudes* to deliver value to both the organization and the individual themselves. Ideally, getting the right person into the right job optimizes performance, job satisfaction and delivers the results the organization is looking for.

This is a question of both capability and context. Does the person have the right skills, abilities, characteristics? Will they fit into the organization, position and situation now and in the uncertain times ahead? Are they flexible and adaptable enough to thrive in novel situations?

In many organizations this means getting *high-calibre people* to work in a *high-performing culture*. But high-calibre people can mean very different things at different times and places. The stereotypical high-calibre person is the high-flying leader that gets promoted quickly, inspires others and leads large companies to profit. This is one common, but very narrow, conceptualization of potential. In reality potential is more difficult to pin down because it is tied to the organization, sector and person. High potential is frequently equated with leadership potential, which it is not.

Many assume the most talented, or highest-performing, people should (or want to) end up influencing, managing and leading others. This is an error. Potential is not necessarily leadership potential, and this book is not exclusively a leadership book. Leadership is a particular type of potential that requires certain skill sets and characteristics. But, as will soon become clear, it is critical to have an overarching framework for understanding potential.

2

Potential

They change their clime, not their disposition, those who run across the sea.
– HORACE, *EPISTLES*

Introduction

The most important question to ask when discussing potential is: 'potential to do what?'. Without asking this question about potential to do what, the concept of potential is too vague and non-specific to have any real meaning. The potential to be successful and the criteria for success are different between a pastor or a police officer, a manager or a motivational speaker, a CEO or a custodian. There may be some commonalities between what makes most people successful in their work, but there are also many differences. While there are some traits which are useful in most or all careers, there are always distinctions and variations. A physical attribute like height may be extremely important for a basketball player but less important for a call centre employee.

It is very necessary to have an overall framework of potential, future likelihood of success, which can be mapped onto any different career or type of work. This kind of framework can and must have the following characteristics:

1 *Important:* it deals with issues that really matter, as opposed to trivial, limited, inconsequential ideas. Psychological theories based on psychotherapeutic observation or student studies in the laboratory often run the risk of being trivial. We believe it needs to be important to people at work;

2 *Operational:* the theory allows the meaning of a concept to be clearly defined and measured. This ensures precision which is essential for usefulness.

3 *Parsimonious:* the theory should be as simple as possible, but not more so. It should be as clear and simple as possible without losing validity.

4 *Clarity:* good theories are easy to understand and apply to real situations in life and at work. The clearer the language in a theory, the easier it is to apply it to observations of people in order to understand them better;

5 *Valid:* theories should make predictions that are testable and can be objectively validated;

6 *Stimulating:* a theory should be capable of provoking others to thought and investigations. Important as this goal is, it cannot be an important criterion until the above factors have been confirmed;

7 *Contextual:* the theory should be able to state in which contexts the processes do and do not occur. That is, it is important to describe how social and cultural forces affect the processes.

Our objective is, then, to bridge the gap between science and practice. To create a measure and a model of personality and potential that is scientifically valid, useful and practical to use in the workplace. We will start with a framework for understanding potential. Then we move on to identifying the key traits and characteristics that are related to potential in Part Two.

The fundamental questions

There are three fundamental questions about potential. These questions span the full range of an employee's job tenure and the full spectrum of talent management activities. These three questions are introduced here; then they will be answered more completely and in much greater detail in Part Three. First, we look at these questions and how they relate to the concept of potential and different perspectives. While each of the concepts can be relevant to everyone in the world of work, the questions might be posed in different ways as shown in Table 2.1.

TABLE 2.1 *Three fundamental questions about potential from two perspectives*

	Leader/HR perspective	Individual perspective
1. Finding	How do I identify others' potential?	How do I understand my own potential?
2. Developing	How do I develop others' potential?	How (and where) do I develop and channel my skills?
3. Retaining	How do I keep high-potential people?	Should I stay in the same position? With the same company?

The key difference is that from a leader's or organization's perspective high potential is about finding (recruiting and selecting), developing and keeping (retaining) the right people for the organization. From an individual's perspective, the important part is finding how, where and when to practice and apply one's talents.

1. Finding (identifying) those with potential: There are talented people out there, but it is not always easy to spot them. When multiple candidates apply for a job, there are some candidates which are more capable than others and have a greater capacity to succeed. Typically finding high potential involves first attracting a pool of (hopefully!) qualified candidates, then choosing those with the greatest capacity to succeed in that role. Recruiting and then picking the best qualified, or highest-potential, person from many candidates.

At other times, finding the right person may require actively seeking out high potentials within the company or actively searching for and enticing high potentials away from other companies. The purpose is either to select the best person who is already interested in the position, or to seek out the best person and *make* them interested in the position. For employers there are two interrelated questions. First, how do you figure out who is the best person for the job with the potential to succeed? Second, how do you entice them into the job?

2. Developing those with potential. Development is an important part of any job from the very beginning. High potential is about capacity to succeed, but that capacity needs to be encouraged and actively developed to turn high potential into excellent performance. The first part of any job is developing a person's ability to fit into the job and its requirements. Any job involves learning about the tasks, the job demands, the culture at work and how to work with others. Mediocre development programs stop at a quick introduction and overview of the job – teaching the person the very basics of the job and then letting them get on with it. For some people, learning to do their job and being left alone to get on with it is exactly what they want. But many others want to learn how to do their job better (and to benefit either financially or from the satisfaction of a job well done) or to take on new responsibilities in the organization. Spotting high potential also requires spotting those who *want* to improve and develop and who has the capacity to do so.

Development should not be thought of as a process of promoting people or just sending them off to a training program. Development, at its best, is moving people into their optimal roles. For some, the optimal role can be mastering the job they do well and want to become the best they can be in that same role. Then, for some, the optimal role is constant learning and development and new experiences to develop potential in different areas. The most versatile and promotable are as important, and as deserving, of development efforts as the dependable and consistent workers.

Development efforts can be large-scale, with overall frameworks and processes, but *must* also occur at individual levels. There are many different ways people learn and develop; three important ones are listed below. These are covered in great detail in Chapter 21.

- *Experiential*: 'Stretch assignments', shadowing, outplacement, job rotation.

- *Educational*: MBA, Short course, Case Studies, Simulations.

- *Personal*: Coaching and Mentoring.

High-potential development typically involves all three.

3. Retaining those with potential: It is surprisingly common for organizations to forget that commitment to a job and loyalty to a leader or organization do not come automatically. Trust is a commitment that has to be developed mutually and earned. Staying in a company or organization is not an automatic instinct for workers, and most people do not feel obligated to stay in a company that is buying their skills based on hourly, weekly or annual labour agreements. Keeping people, especially talented or high-potential people, is an ongoing and worthwhile effort.

Retention of skilled and engaged employees is sometimes viewed as a strain, limited by time and budgetary constraints. However, it should not be viewed as a burden, but a worthwhile endeavour that makes people more productive, reduces costs such as turnover and improves the commitment of employees. Most people want to take pride in their own work and want to feel they make a meaningful or valuable contribution to a team or organization. Job satisfaction and personal achievement are important to employee retention. People who are bored, feel unrewarded, unappreciated, misunderstood or maltreated are much more likely to leave irrespective of their potential to do the job well. This needs to be done on an interpersonal, not a corporate, level. People leave or stay with managers, not companies.

Many with high potential desire, and actively seek out, development opportunities. The simple argument can be made for cost effectiveness and return on investment: hiring and development is expensive. Retention protects and secures that investment. When many talented or high-potential employees leave, it can be to a competitor's gain. Keeping a talented employee could mean transforming the high-potential employee into a talented manager, into a talented director or even a talented CEO. Or it can mean transforming a team of technicians into local or world-leading specialists who develop excellent products, provide expert services or have brilliant ideas. For a budding entrepreneur or community activist it may be about finding (and developing) the right people or group of people to match up with a vision and plan.

Retention is also about keeping those who are best for the organization. In times of hardship, retention takes on the more grim focus of deciding which employees not to retain. Retention is keeping the best and the brightest, but it is also about keeping *only* those who add value to the workplace; the kind term is 'letting people go' which sounds disingenuous because it misapplies agency. More amusingly it implies there was a time when they were not allowed to leave. As with hiring and developing certain people, it is equally important that decisions about firing are made based on strong evidence and good judgement.

What potential is

Potential is the upper (and lower and middle) possible trajectory of what a person can do. Success and performance are what a person has done in the past; potential is what the person could realistically do in the future. Figure 2.1 shows a simple representation of success and performance.

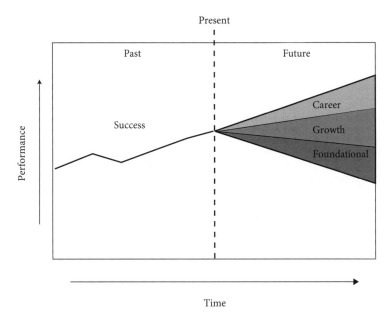

FIGURE 2.1 *Possible trajectories of potential*

Potential can be dependent on factors outside of individual control. Internal characteristics are not the sole determinant of performance but they are foundational. People can get caught up in office conflicts, power struggles, economic conditions or other factors through no fault of their own. Even internal characteristics like intelligence and personality are, to a certain extent, influenced by a person's environment and upbringing. Furthermore, opportunities, good fortune, development, mentors, career and life events can be unpredictable and drastically affect a person's potential.

Potential is not a guaranteed path, but really is a *probability* of following a certain trajectory. It is variable, contextual and an interaction between internal and external factors. It is a range of possible trajectories. More information about the contributors to potential helps to narrow down and predict a specific, probable trajectory of career potential. More information leads to more accurate estimates. An uppermost limit of potential always exists when an optimal combination of the right traits mixes with the right environment and opportunities. A potential 'floor' exists – where even very intelligent, talented people may end up if deprived of education or opportunities to develop and hone skills.

Key points

The lessons from giftedness (Subotnik et al., 2011) can be translated into understanding potential:

1 **Potential reflects cultural and organizational values.** Those with potential to be top performers in any domain reflect value judgement about what performance is useful, instrumental and similarly what performance is undesirable. Organizations that value a specific type of behaviour make those who behave in that way have higher potential. It also reflects what types of jobs and work add social, cultural, community or economic value.

2 **High potential eventually leads to specific outcomes.** By the very nature of defining potential, there will be measurable outcomes. Those with high potential have a high probability of performing well, and likely performing better than others with lower potential. Thus, potential must be defined as having high potential to do x. For example, it could mean having a high potential to be successful as a CEO.

3 **Potential is specific to certain jobs and domains.** Defining potential means defining the job, and the domain. While there can be overlap between high potential in different domains, potential to be successful in one area does not translate directly into potential to be successful in another. Just because someone is a high-performing mathematician does not necessarily mean they are a high-potential public speaker or leader.

4 **Multiple factors influence potential, including biology, psychology, social and cultural groups.** We discuss this throughout subsequent chapters. But there is no single, simple measure of potential. Characteristics like intelligence, personality traits, experience and opportunity all interact to influence potential.

5 **Potential is relative.** High potential exists only relative to moderate and low potential and validity. Potential is high because it is related to the greatest probability of success, or probability of the highest performance. The highest and lowest potential is, by its very nature, rare.

Types of potential

The best framework for understanding potential has been provided by Silzer and Church (2009a), who developed a framework of potential that can be used for any number of different jobs or job demands. It is broad enough that is universally useful for understanding potential at work, but also offers the flexibility to incorporate different types of performance, understand different types of work or to use different assessments and measures in a talent management process. These three dimensions are well defined enough to be testable, while being broad and adaptable enough to be practical.

Career dimensions

Career dimensions of potential are specific attributes that lead to success in specific occupations or jobs. The best example of a career dimension of potential is a specific skill that can be demonstrated at varying degrees to a specific task. For example, mechanical knowledge is specific to being a mechanic. Accountancy training is specific to being an accountant. Knowledge of the human anatomy is a skill that is specifically useful for being a surgeon but may not be necessary for other jobs. Career dimensions can be learnt and developed through experience: experience is essential for career dimensions.

One must be cautious when using career dimensions as a measure of potential, because by their very nature, they are specific to specific jobs or tasks. The absence of a particular career dimension of potential does not necessarily mean a person does not have any potential. Career dimensions can be learned and taught. People go to university, college or training programs to learn career dimensions. The career dimensions of potential can be learned from scratch, or developed and improved. Sometimes people switch jobs or careers and have to start learning the career dimensions of potential in that role. For example, even the most culinarily challenged person *may* be able to learn to cook if they chose to become a chef.

Career dimensions of potential can vary greatly in difficulty and complexity. When these are specific skills, they can take anywhere from a few hours to learn (in the case of a cashier) to years (an airline pilot or brain surgeon). Career skills can be complex, such as aircraft engineers who are responsible for building and repairing engines. However they can be exclusive to specific jobs, and have limited transferability to other jobs.

Career dimensions of potential are very important when hiring new employees. Career dimensions are typically the first (and sometimes only) consideration during hiring. In fact, career dimensions are one of the most common measures employers use: CVs ask for previous experience and credentials. Asking about previous credentials is appropriate and makes sense when the positions are very similar (e.g. you need someone to do a job right away, and be able to perform well right away). But this is not always the most effective method. Always ask the question: What do you want this person to be able to do in the long term? The key question about career dimensions is, 'what do we need the employee to be able to do?' In other words, what skills, education and expertise do we want? Career dimensions can be acquired and developed, whereas this is less so for other dimensions. Career dimensions are the most trainable, so it's often about asking whether to hire the talent or develop it in-house.

Growth dimensions

Growth dimensions of potential are aspects that affect development and career improvement. They moderate potential to improve and succeed and are relatively stable over time. Growth dimensions can interact with environments or situations; for example, those who learn quickly from training have higher growth dimensions of potential. Growth potential can be a combination of internal characteristics and can also be situational factors. For example, a person who is very interested in a particular area may be more focused and learn faster. An encouraging and supportive teacher or mentor can further improve the person's growth. Intellectual curiosity is perhaps the simplest and best marker for growth along with motivation and determination to succeed.

Growth potential can partially be identified ahead of time. For example, interests, propensity to learn, adaptability and ambition can all be identified and selected for (which will be discussed in much greater detail in Part Two). An individual's growth potential is only a partial component that interacts with the situation. So, an individual with growth potential is unlikely to thrive in an environment with poor leadership, or when not given the opportunities to learn and develop. Capability needs opportunity.

Growth potential is important for identifying potential because the greatest gap between current performance and potential is bridged or inhibited by growth potential. Growth potential may promote success in certain environments but may not be realized in others, whereas toxic situations and damaging leaders can distort growth potential and make people develop unethical or undesirable attributes, which will be discussed in the future chapters on dark side traits.

Foundational dimensions

Foundational dimensions of potential are fundamental, stable characteristics that predict success across the range of careers and types of work. Foundational dimensions are consistent across time and so are excellent at predicting short- and long-term potential. Foundational dimensions are those attributes that contribute to success in any career, job or time. Intelligence is the prime example of a foundational dimension of potential because it is generally and consistently useful. Conscientiousness, too, is an excellent example of a foundational dimension because it generally predicts potential across nearly all types of work and job tasks.

Situational factors will have only limited effects on foundational potential. Foundational dimensions are quite stable across the adult lifespan, and can be changed only with serious intervention.

Potential to do what?

One of the best reasons to use and build on Silzer and Church's dimensions of potential is because it is the most broadly applicable and best framework currently available to understand and assess potential. It is a broad enough conceptualization of potential to be applicable to potential to do any job or type of work. But it is also specific enough to be applied to a specific potential and assess potential in a specific and measurable way. The specific question, *potential to do what?* is as much of a question for you, the reader, to consider. Thus it can be applied to policy and strategic planning in a multinational organization; a specific position in a small company; or even your own work, career or business.

If someone has high potential to be successful in a particular job, direct experience may be ideal if the intention is to hire someone who will be able to perform well at work immediately. Low growth potential can be undesirable if the purpose of recruiting is to develop a talent pool of future leadership talent. Yet, if the objective is to find talent, and a strong, consistent performer who wants to stay in the same job, that is a very different type of potential. Much is made of growth potential, which is of course important, but it risks neglecting people with valuable talents whose value is not identified, because they don't fit into a limited description of high potential.

It is easy to forget the contributions of someone who does the same job, for a long time. But, there are many roles in an organization which are valuable, jobs which are most easily overlooked when they are done well. Not everyone needs or values rapid promotion, ever-increasing responsibility and great rewards. For some success means balancing work life with personal or family commitments – and there are many jobs for which high potential and success can mean consistent performance and reliability.

PART TWO

THE STYLE AND CHARACTER OF POTENTIAL

3

Intelligence: Capacity for learning and growth

Talents are distributed by nature without regard to geneologies
– FREDERICK THE GREAT

I fear nothing so much as a man who is witty all day long
– MADAME DE SEVIGNE

Introduction

Intelligence is an excellent predictor of success, and a fantastic indicator of high potential. In general, highly intelligent people tend to learn faster, process and make use of information more quickly. They tend to perform better in training and, in general, tend to be more successful at work. If there was only one test used to select employees, a test of intelligence would be a pretty good choice. However, this does not mean intelligence automatically and solely makes people successful at work.

The picture is more complex, and the next two chapters address the questions such as: Are all high-potential people 'super-bright' wunderkinds? Or are the high potentials of average intelligence but having amazing motivation and the ability to spot opportunities? Can you use energy and drive to compensate for lower intelligence? Do high potentials use what ability they have differently than others? Are people with talent highly curious and try more than others to learn and grow? Is it that you just need to be 'bright enough' and, if so, what is 'enough'? Does this vary from job to job? And what does smart, bright, intelligent actually mean?

Intelligence is an innate ability that makes some people good at solving problems, understanding complex situations and making use of new information more quickly than others that is so appealing to some and appalling to others.

Intelligence is also a basic attribute linked to survival. The fundamental ability to perceive patterns, understand circumstances and adapt behaviour to survive and thrive is not even limited to humans. Some people are just naturally quicker, sharper and more insightful than others. They seem to have better judgement; they learn faster; they have a wider knowledge base. We all lie on some continuum from very low to very high intelligence.

An important question about intelligence is to what degree it influences high potential at work. Is it possible to be talented without being very (generally) bright? Can people practice or learn to become more intelligent? Is there evidence that gifted children turn into gifted adults? Can we find potential high flyers at school and university by giving them intelligence tests? Is intelligence, alone, enough?

The answer may seem surprisingly straightforward. The simple answer is that intelligence is (quite simply) the best, most valid, predictor of job performance. Intelligence does predict job performance: more intelligent people tend to perform better than their less intelligent counterparts. Even more importantly, the more challenging or complex a job is, the more important intelligence is to success. This is because as problems at work become more complex, intelligence becomes an even more useful attribute in adapting to difficult or new circumstances.

Even though intelligence testing sometimes gets bad press, the reality is intelligence testing is a valid way of predicting high potential. Despite negative portrayals of intelligence testing, it is valid across many jobs, criteria, nations and cultures. Many people and media sources are deeply sceptical about the use of intelligence tests. The advantage is that over a century of research into intelligence has remarkably consistent findings. It was the famous Sir Francis Galton who was the first clear advocate of intelligence tests. He believed that intelligence was a single general ability, that it was largely inherited and that it could be best measured in terms of the speed of problem solving and other related mental processes: he was absolutely correct.

Although experts still cannot agree on a *precise* definition of intelligence, there is consensus about its importance to success in general and to success in the workplace. There are two key themes common to most expert definitions of intelligence:

a The ability to learn from experience: Learning from past experience is important to succeeding and even important for basic survival. For example, people who learn quickly from training can use it to improve their performance at work. Those who can't seem to learn how to improve their performance at work based on past experience struggle to perform well.

b The ability to adapt to the environment: Learning from the environment, what's going on around you, makes people more responsive and adaptable in changing surroundings.

The current debate about intelligence is not *whether or not it exists* but about the precise *nature* of its inner workings. Intelligence is a concept that is both valid and useful in general and in understanding high potential at work.

Nature or nurture?

There are a number of factors that can influence intelligence, especially the intelligence of children as they grow up and develop intelligence. But there is also a fixed component that is determined by genetics. Intelligence is partly determined by nature, partly by nurture. Genes can provide an advantage: some people just process information more quickly because their brains are biologically wired to be more efficient at processing information, and use fewer resources to accomplish the same task. Intelligence is located in particular areas of the brain and works as a network of interactions in a 'small-world' network of connections within the brain. So intelligence involves efficient and uninterrupted connections. More efficient connections that use fewer of the brain's resources (like glucose and oxygen) help to create more 'intelligent' brains (Deary et al., 2010). Some people are just genetically 'gifted' with higher intelligence.

But, biology is not destiny. Estimates suggest intelligence is somewhere between 30 per cent and 70 per cent genetic, and intelligence is not just about the structure of the brain, it's about how you use it. There are different ways to solve any problem and this is equally true of the brain. Different connections and methods of processing information can be used to solve the same problem. People may be born with natural advantages or disadvantages. However, the environment and lifetime experience affect intelligence. Environment, education, socioeconomic status, health and a range of other circumstances affect how intelligence develops.

Intelligence has been shown to affect so many areas of life and achievement. Discussion of intelligence has found its way much more than many other psychological concepts into the realm of public discourse. It is ironic that one of the most well-researched and well-validated concepts in the psychology of performance is one of the most publicly contested. There are controversies about intelligence, which will be discussed later in this chapter.

Over a century of testing, re-testing and validation shows intelligence is both valid and useful. It influences almost all aspects of life and behaviour; it is valid across times, places and cultures. Of any single measure taken at one point, it is the best predictor of success at a later point. It is also very consistent across the lifespan. A forty-five-minute test of intelligence on an eleven-year-old predicts nearly two-thirds of the variation in intelligence in a 79-year-old (Deary et al., 2010).

> Intelligence is a very general mental capability that, among other things, involves the ability to reason, plan, solve problems, think abstractly, comprehend complex ideas, learn quickly and learn from experience. It is not merely book learning, a narrow academic skill, or descriptive of test-taking smarts. Rather, it reflects a broader and deeper capability for comprehending our surroundings – 'catching on', 'making sense' of things, or 'figuring out' what to do.
>
> (Gottfredson, 1997b, p. 13)

The multiple intelligences debate

There is an enduring debate about intelligence and whether or not there are multiple types of intelligence. The idea is that there are many different 'types' of intelligence beyond the ability to learn from your experience and environment. Cattell (1987) suggests that there is a difference between crystallized and fluid intelligence. The analogy refers to states of matter – fluid can take any shape, whereas solid crystals are rigid. Fluid intelligence is the ability to process and react to new information as it flows into the stream of perception, to adapt quickly to new situations as they arise. It includes the ability to understand relationships, deal with unfamiliar problems and gain new types of knowledge. Crystallized intelligence is already obtained; it is structured knowledge and skills that have been built up by experience. It is the ideas and knowledge that have solidified in one's brain, the foundations and building blocks that you accrue through a lifetime of learning. It could be a way of doing things; it could be the lyrics of a song or poem that still rise to the mind unbidden; the proper way of doing things in a profession.

Fluid intelligence peaks before twenty and remains constant, with some decline in much later years. Crystallized intelligence, on the other hand, continues to increase as long as the person remains active. Thus, a schoolchild is usually quicker than a pensioner at solving a problem that is unfamiliar to both of them. Although this is one of the generalizations that work on average, it will not necessarily always work when comparing any two individuals. Crystallized intelligence is more related to experience, so it is cumulative. Years and decades of experience provide significant advantages when compared to the new student or trainee. Although *what* you have learned (crystallized intelligence) is influenced by *how well* you learn (fluid intelligence). This is why some people take much longer to 'pick things up'.

Other factors, like personality, do play a part – introverts like to read, study and learn, while equally bright extroverts like to socialize, have fun and experiment (see Chapter 4). But people can learn from either books or people. Introverts, who like learning on their own, often do better at tests of crystallized intelligence. Self-evidently, motivation is important; a highly motivated adult will learn more efficiently and effectively than an adult less interested in learning. Take the following examples of questions testing crystallized and fluid intelligence.

A Memorize the following numbers, and repeat them in order from least to greatest:

600, 5, 8, 47, 1.

B Underline which adjective does not belong with the others:

Tall, tan, young, thin, lovely

The former is a measure of fluid, the latter of crystallized intelligence. Question A is possible to complete without specific prior knowledge, but it does require ability to store, organize and retrieve information. It would be possible to test Question A in any language, or even with someone who could not read or write. Question B requires knowledge of a particular song ('the

Girl from Ipanema' is tall and tan and young and lovely – no mention of her circumference). To show how a question like this could be even more culturally biased, consider which of these is the odd one out: Banker, Knight, Miller, Reeve, Cook.[1] This question requires very specific knowledge of Middle English literature: knowledge which is particularly tied to the socioeconomic status, and the type of education. It is measuring knowledge in a very specific domain. Crystallized intelligence is something that one would (could) study for.

Furnham (2008a) notes that intelligence is: 'a basic building block for the differential psychologist. It is, quite simply, the most easily and reliably measured individual difference variable with the best reliability and validity' (p. 180).

The idea of innate ability along with the measurement and use of innate cognitive ability is controversial. It is not unusual for media sources to describe completely valid conclusions about intelligence as 'discredited'.

There is a serious disconnect between the information in scientific journals and textbooks, and that in the realm of public discourse. The evidence from psychology and neuroscience clearly shows intelligence exists, it can be measured, and those measurements can be used to predict success in education, training and work (Gottfredson, 1997a). Because of the controversy, there is a perfectly understandable tendency for people who are responsible for hiring, assessing or developing potential to err on what they feel to be the side of caution. Unfortunately, this is an error.

Another popular myth is that there are multiple types of intelligence. The idea is that while some people may have low intelligence in terms of their capacity to learn from experience and their environment, someone who has low intelligence might have some sort of musical or aesthetic intelligence. This is an error. There are not multiple types of intelligence that relate directly to abilities like musical talent or appreciation for nature.

The confusion surrounding multiple intelligences tends to be a problem of mislabelling. Other concepts like values or learning styles or abilities are sometimes mislabelled as 'types' of intelligence. Educators often like to use the idea of 'multiple intelligences' because it helps to identify different talents or types of potential in their students. It can be well intended, designed to make everyone feel good about themselves.

The problem with the idea of multiple intelligences is that it muddies the water because it's not always clear that when people use the term, they are not actually talking about intelligence. Intelligence is about reasoning, planning, mentally organizing information – capacity to learn and adapt to surroundings. The idea that there are 'multiple' intelligences was popularized in Howard Gardner's 1983 book *Frames of Mind: Theories of Multiple Intelligences*. The book outlined what he believed to be seven or eight or nine or ten separate and unique types of intelligence.

Gardner's idea was that there are distinct types of intelligence and each operates independently. However, this theory has been largely unsupported by scientific evidence. 'Naturalistic intelligence', for example, is supposed to be a preference for natural environments, and feeling connected with nature. This is clearly a value or a preference, but it is unrelated to intelligence. It is a preference, not a fundamental method of processing, storing and managing information. That's not to say there is anything wrong with that preference, and knowing that characteristic might help to identify potential. But it is simply not a part of intelligence. These kinds of multiple intelligences are scientifically unsupported. Intelligence, as an independent and clearly defined construct, is useful and good at predicting behaviour, performance and achievement in education and at work.

Nettlebeck and Wilson (2005) dismiss Gardner's theory: 'A person doing well in one domain tends to do well in others' (p. 615). This is an underlying, foundational cognitive process: intelligence.

The concept of multiple intelligences is unhelpful because it makes it easier to confuse intelligence (cognitive ability) with learned abilities and preferences (naturalistic, existential). To assess potential, we need to clearly define

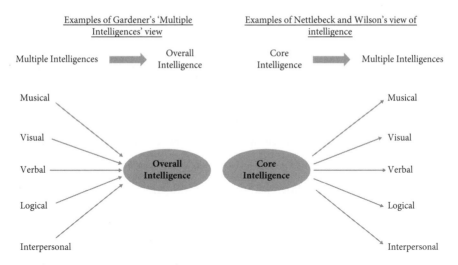

FIGURE 3.1 *Theories of multiple intelligence*

potential – and subsequently we need clear-cut, valid concepts to measure factors that contribute to potential. It is easy to see why the idea of 'multiple intelligences' may be appealing, with as many as ten types of intelligence; most people will be above average in at least one area – everyone has a particular aspect they can personally feel proud of. Everyone is special! The problem is that when put up to the lens of scientific scrutiny, multiple intelligences are not actually valid or useful; they are counterproductive and misleading.

What intelligence is not

It is perfectly understandable to be cautious about testing in the interest of fairness, ethics and only using good tests. Unfortunately, the misconceptions about intelligence mean that investing intelligence is avoided for the wrong reasons: controversy in the media or in public beliefs does not necessarily mean there is scientific controversy. Because there are misconceptions it is particularly important to describe what we *don't* mean when we talk about intelligence.

Misconceptions quickly lead to mistakes, so we will review some of the common misconceptions about intelligence. Fortunately they lead nicely into a discussion about why intelligence is so useful in understanding potential.

The first key point is that when we say intelligence we don't mean a particular skill or talent. Intelligence is *not* talent; Intelligence is not something that you can learn like a musical instrument; it is not an ability that starts from *no* ability and is cultivated to a certain level. People are born with a baseline level of intelligence. No one is born without *any* intelligence; it's not something that you pick up as you go along. People are born with a certain capacity to learn, and an innate speed of learning about problems, coming up with solutions and understanding what is going on around them. Intelligence is influenced by the environment and experience, but is also rooted in genetics and physiology.

Intelligence can also be used to predict performance, but concerns are often raised about using intelligence tests in the workplace. This misconception stems from people who confuse the difference between intelligence *tests* and the overall *concept* of intelligence. Specific tests or measures like the intelligence quotient (IQ) test have been singled out for criticism. There are limitations to IQ tests of overall intelligence, but that does not mean general cognitive ability (intelligence) as a psychological construct and measure of individual differences does not exist (a century of cumulative evidence suggests that it does).

> Intelligence is best defined in terms of multiple domains configured within a hierarchical structure that accounts for different degrees of commonality among, and specificity between, those domains. IQ, on the other hand, has until fairly recently amounted to little more than an average outcome from an abridged range of those domains.
>
> (Nettlebeck and Wilson, 2005, p. 613)

In other words, IQ is a quick and dirty method for estimating intelligence. It's not perfect, but it does work.

Individual characteristics aside, another widespread misconception is that intelligence is a measure of cultural value. Some people say that intelligence is a measure of what urban, capitalist, white, neoliberals (insert objectives ad infinitum, ad absurdum) value. It is possible to test cultural knowledge, but intelligence is not cultural. It is a fundamental attribute not limited to nations or cultures. Intelligence is not even limited to species; it is possible to test animals for intellectual properties. We can measure and compare intelligence in people, chimpanzees, dolphins, cuttlefish, rats and many more.

Intelligence occurs because of the way the brain works, and the way certain structures of the brain are connected. It is easy to see the connection between intelligence and culture because an 'intelligent' brain tends to be good at adapting to physical and social environments. Intelligence helps people learn what is true, appropriate and useful – consequently, intelligent people may adapt more quickly to any culture. It is absurd, based on both evidence and understanding of intelligence, to suggest that the concept of intelligence is tied to a certain culture.

Giftedness in children

There is a thorough literature about gifted children. Giftedness is essentially used as a synonym for intelligence in this case. The findings of this research show intelligence in children also has consistent and important features (Brody, 2005). This makes it a good place to discuss the role of intelligence in success and potential. Research with gifted children shows they possess the following attributes:

- **Advanced Understanding.** They show complex understanding about how things work, or they show very advanced development within a specific skill area. For example, they demonstrate sophisticated understanding of things like early reading or mathematics without having been directly instructed. Or they show rapid development when provided the opportunity in arts.

- **Advanced Vocabulary.** They have a vocabulary much more mature and sophisticated than other children their age. They enjoy playing with words or other means of symbolically representing in their world.

- **Mature Thinking.** They demonstrate exceptionally *mature thinking* on tasks that are complicated. They tend to learn very quickly and rapidly pick up new information or ways of doing things, or perceive hidden meanings.

- **Memory.** They excel at activities related to memory, above and beyond what one would expect at the given age level.

- **Older Children.** They seek children older than themselves as playmates and enjoy especially creative imaginative play scenarios.

- **Self-management.** They show a high degree of managing their own progress and development of their own learning. They are able to learn independently.

- **Variability.** They show a great deal of variability between very sophisticated thinking and behaviour in other ways that indicate they are still young children.

- **Variety of Experiences.** They demonstrate and express a high need for a variety of different experiences. They seek out new and different opportunities to learn and seem to delight in novel problems to solve.

There are four distinct clusters of characteristics of gifted children.

1 **Ability.** Gifted children are described as observant, inquisitive and smart. They learn quickly, have a large and impressive vocabulary. They enjoy intellectual challenges and seek them out. They also tend

to be well-co-ordinated, dextrous, athletic and energetic (i.e. have advanced psychomotor skills). They can also show impressive visual, spatial, auditory skills. It is often their advanced vocabulary that makes them stand out as possessing intelligence and knowledge beyond their years, and which most clearly marks them out as different.

2 **Creative Thinking.** They are innovators, improvisers, independents and original thinkers. They enjoy coming up with several solutions to standard problems and thinking creatively about different ideas. They put extra effort into creative solutions, even when it is not necessary. They do not mind standing out from a crowd with different or novel ideas. Unlike many adults, they tend to be quite uninhibited about their creative products and express interest and confidence in the process.

3 **Social Intelligence.** This means they are expressive, self-confident, popular and able. They show good social judgement and are able to predict the consequences and implications of their judgements and actions. They often assume responsibility in social settings which is then accepted by others. This attribute means they are more likely to get elected or appointed to positions of leadership by their peers and their teachers.

4 **Task Commitment.** They are able to concentrate easily and remain focused on tasks. They actually enjoy taking on challenging projects and are committed to seeing them through to the end.

Not all gifted children grow up to be talented adults but most talented adults were once gifted children. There is a strong connection between intelligence and performance at all ages. Intelligence often has a compounding effect as people get older too. The gifted children who take on difficult tasks and persist in their endeavours are rewarded with success (or failure, and experience). Being identified as gifted often means they get more opportunities to learn and succeed and take more on themselves.

Are we all getting smarter?

There seems to be a tendency for countries as a whole to increase average intelligence levels over time. There is strong evidence that intelligence at a national level can increase gradually over time. So what could be behind this gradual drift up in intelligence?

It was an American political scientist working in New Zealand, James Flynn, who gave his name to the 'Flynn Effect'. He noticed two things when he inspected famous and respected IQ test manuals: First that every so often the norms which describe typical scores for different age, sex and race groups seemed to change. Over time, intelligence test scores drift higher. The conclusion seemed to be that either the tests were getting easier or that we as a species were getting brighter – or perhaps both. Teasdale and Owen (2008) found intelligence test scores increased by a few points every decade since the mid-twentieth century, but gains in intelligence may have plateaued in developed countries.

There is impressive evidence from developed nations showing that intelligence gradually drifts upward over time in the overall population. But there are other reasons that could explain these results. The central question is, why? Are we really becoming more intelligent?

There are two possibilities: either test scores are changing or people really are getting smarter. There is much research to suggest the Flynn Effect does indicate a real rise in intelligence. Gradual improvements in education, nutrition, the labour market and parenting styles could all explain increases in intelligence. Similar effects have been found across nations and generations. A comparable effect can be found with height. Height has gradually increased in developed nations because of nutritional, medical and generational differences. Box 3.1 explains the possible reasons for intelligence to increase at a national level.

BOX 3.1 POSSIBLE CAUSES OF THE FLYNN EFFECT

Education. In many countries, subsequent generations spend longer at school and with better facilities. Schooling is compulsory and people from all backgrounds learn more, get better quality instruction and participate in a richer intellectual environment. Intelligence is related to learning, so as education improves and is more accessible, scores improve.

Nutrition. People are now better nourished particularly in childhood, which reduces the incidence of physical and psychological underdevelopment from nutrition. Poor nutrition stunts physical and intellectual development, reducing intelligence. There are fewer people who cannot learn because of deprivation and fewer who are unable to concentrate or properly develop because of insufficient nutrition. Consequently, the average intelligence score rises.

Social trends. We are all now much more used to timed tests and performing against the clock. Testing has become much more widespread in schools and at work, and people are familiar with tests and testing and so do better overall. This is a possible explanation that would suggest while scores are rising it may not represent a change in the underlying concept of intelligence.

Parental Involvement. The idea is that parents provide richer home environments for their children and express a greater interest in their children's education than they used to. They have higher expectations and get involved more. They encourage intellectual development in their children and understand its importance in the contemporary labour market. The trend to have smaller families where parents invest more in their children may also be an important factor.

Social Environment. The world is more complex and stimulating. Modernization and new technology mean people have to manipulate abstract concepts more, which is essentially what intelligence tests measure. Greater access to study tools, information and resources provides advantages that were once unimaginable.

The Flynn Effect suggests environmental, rather than genetic, causes of change in intelligence. While it is perfectly conceivable to argue that brighter people seek out more stimulating environments for themselves and their children which further increases their intelligence, it raises the old arguments about nature and nurture. Thus, for the Flynn Effect to work environmental effects can work both ways. A rich environment combined with sustained early effort can increase intelligence. Equally, poor polluted environments and when people are disinterested in personal development can have detrimental effects on intelligence.

Another question that has arisen is whether the Flynn Effect has begun to taper off: that is whether there is now a decline in the increase seen. This means the next generation will not score higher than this generation. It is possible those abilities have plateaued, or that generational changes are artefacts (of chance) instead of consistent trends.

4

Intelligence at work

So it is that the gods do not give all men gifts of grace – neither good looks nor intelligence nor eloquence.
– HOMER, *THE ODYSSEY*

Nothing doth more hurt in a state than that cunning men pass for wise.
– FRANCIS BACON, *ESSAYS*

Introduction

If intelligence is such a robust construct with a strong relationship with performance, it logically follows that it would be useful to understand intelligence in the workplace. Intelligence tests can be misused, misunderstood and misinterpreted. Intelligence tests are not a guaranteed test of potential, but are a good indicator. An intelligence test that takes only an hour or two can be much more effective than lengthy interviews or observations (Nettlebeck and Wilson, 2005).

The bottom line is that intelligence tests measure a general ability that is related to success and performance. They are valid, but they are not perfect. Neither are home pregnancy tests 100 per cent accurate nor condoms 100 per cent effective, but that does not mean they should be discarded completely when they are the best tools available for a specific purpose. This is comparable to medical diagnostic tests in both validity and application. In medicine, the greater the significance of diagnoses, the more tests that are need to be performed. Further tests lead to further information, and a furthered capacity to make informed decisions.

The more important the decision-making is for identifying potential and the greater the consequences of making an error, the more important it is to test and precisely measure the predictors of potential with a wider variety of tools. That doesn't mean that a single test (such as IQ) should not be used; it means the greater the consequences of the decision, the more sensitive or rigorous the testing should be. A highly valuable, strategic position should consider a candidate's intelligence, but it should also consider a host of other factors like work history, personality, abilities and other relevant characteristics.

Intelligence is relatively stable across life and career spans. This does not mean intelligence cannot be changed, just that it is not easy to influence as other, more variable factors like motivation. Adults who have a higher level of education tend to have higher levels of intelligence. Income and organizational level are also associated with higher intelligence. Yet, it could just be that intelligent children stay in school longer, then go on to find better jobs and get promoted more quickly. Or it could be that the intelligent young person knows the social and cultural importance of education to the labour market (as well as the value of learning new skills and meeting other intelligent people).

What education and training does is to provide the intelligent young person with relevant knowledge, inculcate specific modes of thought and self-discipline. Education is certainly desirable, but an employer would struggle to drastically alter the intelligence of employees. Standard training practices can improve skills and competencies, but are not going to have drastic effects on intelligence. The only drastic changes in intelligence that occur at work tend to be the by-product of industrial accidents – like head injuries.

Nettlebeck and Wilson (2005) provide excellent suggestions for using intelligence testing. First they argue tests can be used to identify certain types of 'exceptionality': spotting the exceptionally best or exceptionally worst. Second the intelligence tests can pinpoint the source of certain difficulties, such as why a person is slow to learn. They do, however, warn that assessment should always involve assessing other traits and characteristics, intelligence alone should not necessarily be the sole basis for decision-making. They conclude: 'Our support for these tests is contingent on two provisors. First, they must be consistent with current hierarchical, multifaceted theory that includes a general ability. Second, the child's cultural background must be the same as that within which the tests were developed' (p. 626). This advice applies equally to testing adults at work.

Intelligence and performance

Intelligence is intimately associated with reasoning, problem solving, adaptation and learning – all the characteristics that are necessary to perform well at work. So intelligence can be used to predict performance (and potential) at work.

Scientific research has shown that, quite consistently, cognitive ability accurately predicts job performance across all jobs, particularly complex jobs. Intelligence is more important to work as a medical physicist than as a store clerk. It is more important for the CEO to be intelligent than for a team supervisor. However, intelligence is desirable for both, and would be likely to improve performance for both. Many believe that intelligence is the single best predictor of (senior and managerial) work performance; all recent research points to the predictive power of cognitive intelligence and hence the importance of using these tests in selection.

In the UK, Bertua et al. (2011) reviewed research from the UK investigating intelligence and performance. They combined the results of 283 separate studies and results from over 80,000 people. The results show tests of intelligence are very strong predictors of success both in training and in work. The relative importance of intelligence varied between professions; the

TABLE 4.1 *Success in performance and training in different occupations*

Occupation	Job performance	Training success
Clerical	0.32	0.55
Engineer	0.70	0.64
Professional	0.74	0.59
Driver	0.37	0.47
Operator	0.53	0.54
Manager	0.69	–
Skilled	0.55	0.55
Miscellaneous	0.40	0.55

following two charts show the relative validity (ranging from 0 to 1 with 1 being the greatest predictor) of intelligence for predicting success in different positions. It shows that intelligence is a better predictor of success for more highly skilled professions, but also that intelligence is a strong component of success for most professions and training.

It is clear that intelligence is a greater contributor to success in some occupations than in others. Jobs that are more complex, more ambiguous or have more day-to-day variation can require greater intelligence for high performance. Intelligence also tends to be of greater importance to success in training, than in work.

Ones et al. (2005) provide an excellent comprehensive and relevant review of the current conclusions on intelligence.

- Based on data of well over a million students they conclude that intelligence is a strong, valid predictor of exam success, learning and outcome at school and university regardless of the speciality or subject considered;

- Training success at work, as measured by supervisor ratings or job knowledge acquired, is predicted by intelligence and the more complex the job, the more powerfully it predicts performance;

- Intelligence tests predict performance outcomes across jobs, situations and outcomes – that is, validity is transportable across occupational groups and is cross-culturally generalizable;

- Tests of specific types of intelligence tend not to be any more useful than tests of general intelligence;

- Intelligence predicts job performance well because it is linked to the speed and quality of learning, adaptability and problem-solving ability;

- Intelligence tests are predictively fair to minority groups, but can have an adverse impact that is a sensitive political issue;

- In short, intelligence is one of the best, if not the best, predictors of success in applied settings.

Their conclusion is that, internationally, intelligence measures are among the best predictors of work performance. Despite differences in tests used; measures and definitions of job performance and training; differences in unemployment rates, cultural values, and demographics, intelligence still wins out as the best individual difference psychometric measure to predict performance and high potential. Indeed the results are strikingly similar to earlier data coming out of America (Hunter, 1986; Hunter and Hunter, 1984; Viswesvaran et al., 1996). They conclude that because of the predictive validity

TABLE 4.2 *The importance of intelligence to performance and training performance*

	Performance	Training
GMA (Overall Intelligence)	0.62	0.54
Verbal	0.35	0.44
Numerical	0.52	0.48
Spatial/Mech	0.51	0.40
Perceptual	0.52	0.25
Memory	0.56	0.43

of intelligence at work across cultures one can easily conceive of a scientifically feasible general theory of personnel selection. They also point out: 'tests of specific abilities such as verbal, numerical, spatial-mechanical, perceptual, and memory failed to demonstrate higher validity than intelligence measures. It is thus prudent to reiterate the main practical implications of this finding that intelligence tests predicted these two criteria most successfully' (p. 594).

Gottfredson (2002) believes it is vitally important for personnel psychologists and managers to understand the role of intelligence at work. In a wonderfully clear and important synthesis, she outlines the real importance of *g* (or general intelligence) at work (Gottfredson, 2002, pp. 44–46). This is well worth repeating in full:

Major Findings on *g*'s Impact on Job Performance a Utility of *g*:

1   Higher levels of *g* lead to higher levels of performance in all jobs and along all dimensions of performance. The average correlation of mental tests with overall rated job performance is around 0.5 (corrected for statistical artefacts);

2   There is no ability threshold above which more *g* does not enhance performance. The effects of *g* are linear: successive increments in *g* lead to successive increments of job performance;

3   (a) the value of higher levels of *g* does not fade with longer experience on the job. Criterion validities remain high even among highly experienced workers. (b) That they sometimes even appear to rise with experience may be due to the confounding effect of the least experienced groups tending to be more variable in relative level of experience, which obscures the advantages of higher g;

4   *g* predicts job performance better in more complex jobs. Its (corrected) criterion validities range from about 0.2 in the simplest jobs to 0.8 in the most complex;

5 *g* predicts the core technical dimensions of performance better than it does the non-core 'citizenship' dimension of performance;

6 Perhaps as a consequence, *g* predicts objectively measured performance (either job knowledge or job sample performance) better than it does subjectively measured performance (such as supervisor ratings).

Utility of *g* Relative to Other 'Can Do' Components of Performance

7 Specific mental abilities (such as spatial, mechanical or verbal ability) add very little, beyond g, to the prediction of job performance. *g* generally accounts for at least 85–95 per cent of a full mental test battery's (cross-validated) ability to predict performance in training or on the job;

8 Specific mental abilities (such as clerical ability) sometimes add usefully to prediction, net of g, but only in certain classes of jobs. They do not have general utility;

9 General psychomotor ability is often useful, but primarily in less complex work. Its predictive validities fall with complexity while those for *g* rise.

Utility of *g* Relative to the 'Will Do' Component of Job Performance

10 *g* predicts core performance much better than do 'non-cognitive' (less g-loaded) traits, such as vocational interests and different personality traits. The latter add virtually nothing to the prediction of core performance, net of g;

11 *g* predicts most dimensions of non-core performance (such as personal discipline and soldier bearing) much less well than do 'non-cognitive' traits of personality and temperament. When a performance dimension reflects both core and non-core performance (effort and leadership), *g* predicts to about the same modest degree as do non-cognitive (less g-loaded) traits;

12 Different non-cognitive traits appear to usefully supplement *g* in different jobs, just as specific abilities sometimes add to the prediction of performance in certain classes of jobs. Only one such non-cognitive trait appears to be as generalizable as g: the personality trait of conscientiousness/integrity. Its effect sizes for core performance are substantially smaller than *g*'s, however.
Utility of *g* Relative to the Job Knowledge

13 *g* affects job performance primarily indirectly through its effect on job-specific knowledge;

14 *g*'s direct effects on job performance increase when jobs are less routinized, training is less complete and workers retain more discretion;

15 Job-specific knowledge generally predicts job performance as well as does *g* among experienced workers. However, job knowledge is not generalizable (net of its *g* component), even among experienced workers. The value of job knowledge is highly job-specific: *g*'s value is unrestricted.
Utility of *g* Relative to the 'Have Done' (Experience) Component of Job Performance:

16 Like job knowledge, the effect sizes of job-specific experience are sometimes high, but they are not generalizable;

17 In fact, experience predicts performance less well as all workers become more experienced. In contrast, higher levels of *g* remain an asset regardless of the length of experience;

18 Experience predicts job performance less well as job complexity rises, which is opposite the trend for g. Like general psychomotor ability, experience matters least where *g* matters most to individuals and their organizations.

Intelligence and high potential

There is no single list of characteristics of what makes high potential; it is essential to ask the question, *potential to do what?* Despite countless books, articles and discussions about high potentials, there is no universally agreed definition of high potential or what makes someone 'talented'. However, nearly all of the companies and researchers in this area include as part of their definition something that hints very clearly at intelligence. Some talk of analytic strengths, successful intelligence, cognitive ability, smarts or capacity to learn from experience. These are all typical terms that indicate they are probably looking for intelligence, and may be a 'politically correct' way of skirting the controversies that continue to surround intelligence testing.

Intelligent people learn faster. They quickly notice patterns and analyse issues well. They tend to be more curious and have a broader base of knowledge. They make fewer errors and remember things better. It is hardly surprising, then, that intelligence is seen as a fundamental component of talent. But intelligence is not enough.

Intelligence is *necessary but not sufficient*. It is difficult to conceive of a person that is identified as high potential but is not very bright. But, how bright do they need to be? When is being bright enough? Do they have to be smart enough to get into MENSA? To some extent this depends on the sector where the high flyer works. Some sectors require more intelligence than others.

We have all known the super-bright classmate at school and university who turned out to have a very average career. Were they just unlucky, unable to exploit their high intelligence, or simply not motivated to do very well?

What data is available suggests the following. The high-potential employees usually score between one and two standard deviations above the norm on IQ tests. It is an attribute to be in the top 30 per cent, but there are not great advantages to being in the top 5 per cent or 1 per cent. A modest advantage is helpful, but top performers do not need to be geniuses, and genius alone is not sufficient for top performance. The academic careers of many high-potential people are not necessarily marked by great achievement. Some did very poorly because they were not motivated by school work but by something in later life or work that sparked their passion, motivation and channelled their intelligence, and they had the right personality traits to bring their vision to fruition. This is often true of entrepreneurs who never found their passion in formal education, but found a way to apply their intelligence and talents later in life.

High potentials are driven; highly motivated; ambitious and competitive. And usually they are above average in intelligence, but not necessarily the most intelligent. Studies that track thousands of children across generations show that exceptional intelligence is not necessary to succeed and that above-average intelligence is usually 'enough' (Shurkin, 1992).

Conclusion

In some areas of endeavour it would be impossible to conceive of a high-potential person as someone who is not very clever. The noble scientist, the imaginative engineer, the brilliant doctor. Brighter people learn more and learn faster. They see patterns, trends and mechanisms before others. Yet, as we have pointed out, the high potential need to be 'bright enough' to succeed and to realize their potential.

The potential salesperson may have a very different intelligence profile from the high-potential physicist. Yet, as we have pointed out, the high potential needs to be 'bright enough' to succeed and to realize their potential (as laid out in Figure 4.1).

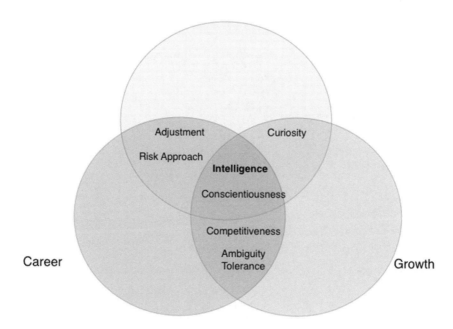

FIGURE 4.1 *Dimensions of potential (revised).*

5

Overview of personality

When we see men of worth, we should think of equaling them; when we see men of a contrary character, we should turn inwards and examine ourselves.

– CONFUCIUS

It is native personality, and that alone, that endows a man to stand before presidents or generals, or in any distinguish'd collection, with aplomb – and not culture, or any knowledge or intellect whatever.

– WALT WHITMAN, *DEMOCRATIC VISTAS*

Introduction

To predict high potential employers need to understand the consistent patterns that affect how people are likely to think, act and work. Personality is a general and consistent way of acting, thinking and feeling. People who have consistent patterns of being responsible, ambitious, reliably good planners can be said to have high conscientiousness. This is often an asset in the workplace when people need to be reliable, ambitious self-starters. Conversely, those who are impulsive, spontaneous, poorer long-term planners can be said to have low conscientiousness. This may be a red flag for employers who need employees who are reliable at planning and organizing themselves.

Stress in varying levels is a common component to most jobs too. Understanding consistent patterns in how employees respond to stress can be very useful to understanding and assessing employee potential. Someone who is emotionally reactive, sensitive to criticism and easily take offensive could be described as having low adjustment. They may struggle or flail in high-stress positions. The steely-nerved, less emotionally responsive people who seem to be immune to stress can be described as having higher adjustment. They may deal much more effectively with high-stress tasks and jobs. The key to these personality traits is they are consistent, fairly predictable and unlikely to change.

Personality traits are both interesting and extremely useful to understand at work because they are consistent over time and help us understand how and why people behave in certain ways (Carver and Scheier, 2000). If we can understand someone's personality and their specific personality traits, we can get a good indication of how they are likely to think and react at work today and in the future. Some people are more likely to get stressed or angry and crumble under pressure. Others tend to be good at longer-term planning and discipline. Certain people are more predisposed to exploring new ideas and learning new things.

Personality (sometimes colloquially described as temperament) is used in conversation to mean anything from a generally pleasing disposition, that person has a lovely personality to more subtle undertones. A 'forceful personality' can imply someone who is assertive, belligerent or commanding. A 'personality' can even refer to a specific character and way of acting that goes along with an image that may be real or contrived. In psychology, personality describes *persistent patterns that underlie thinking, feeling and behaving*.

A personality profile case study

There are many ways personality can be useful for individuals in their own words; take the example of a personality profile developed in the latter part of

2016 to try to understand a world leader's personality and how it might impact their future performance. This profile uses the High Potential Trait Indicator (HPTI) which is the topic of the next chapter.

Conscientiousness, 18, Low
This person was very consistently rated as having extremely low conscientiousness. Someone with low conscientiousness is often unprepared undisciplined and unreliable. If they are ambitious they are often driven to react to external circumstances instead of internal motivation and they typically lack self-discipline.

Low conscientiousness can be very challenging in a leadership position, and with increasing jobs demands they often struggle to manage their own responsibilities or the people they work with.

Adjustment, 30, Low
This person was rated as having very low adjustment. People with low adjustment tend to experience a lot of emotional swings and have difficulty controlling their emotions, particularly negative emotions. Combined with low conscientiousness, this is the characteristic profile of someone who makes a great deal of mistakes while their mistakes fuel anxiety and can descend into a vicious spiral.

High adjustment would be extremely important for any leader, particularly when the position is very stressful.

Curiosity, 34, Moderate
The experts suggested this person had relatively low curiosity. Those with lower curiosity are less likely to seek out new information or try new approaches to problems. They tend to seem stuck in their ways and they are less likely to listen to the opinion of others or seek out experts.

Low curiosity is a red flag for any position that demands learning quickly and listening to the respective experts.

Risk Approach, 29, Low
This person's risk approach score was rated as moderately low. Risk approach in the HPTI denotes a constructive, and considered approach to risk, along with a willingness to take on interpersonal and work problems. Lower scores tend to indicate a more instinctual, reactive approach to risk either avoiding the problem or lashing out instinctively.

This is a concerning level of risk approach in a senior leader because it often leads people to make poor decisions instinctually or to avoid the most difficult problems.

Ambiguity Acceptance, 69, Optimal
Our experts rated this person as having high ambiguity approach. The higher levels of ambiguity acceptance typically indicate someone who thrives in a complex environment, with many different factors at play. Sometimes they can be seen as vague when they have lots of big ideas which do not fit together well or are difficult to link.

This level of ambiguity acceptance is a promising trait in a leader.

Competitiveness, 88, Excessive
The experts' evaluations of this person suggest extremely high levels of competitiveness. It's extremely rare to see competitiveness levels this high. This level of competitiveness is characterized by a desire to always be seen as the winner or the best.

This is a dangerously high level of trait competitiveness to have in a leader who sometimes needs to work as a team player.

Note: This was a profile developed from the views of ten experts, based on this person's behavioural patterns, but was not personally interviewed.

The previous example should serve to demonstrate how personality profiles can be useful in assessing people's suitability for a job. But it should also serve as a warning that there are many other factors to consider, for example, whether or not a leader will be successful. Do they have a history of success or failure? Do their values align with the organization? Are they intelligent enough for the job? Do they have dark side personality traits that might indicate potential derailment? These are all important to consider in combination with personality profiles.

Yet, personality traits are so useful because they are enduring characteristics that are consistent over time. This can be deliberate psychological intervention with professional or extreme life-changing events. But drastic personality change is exceptionally rare. This is true scientifically, but also true in the informal use of personality. Whereas someone can be *moody* or *in a mood* (meaning a noticeably quick change in a person's behaviour), moods and emotions are transitory and not personality. To describe someone as having 'taken on a different personality' is an accusation of falsehood or deception, the implication being deceitful or disingenuousness.

Personality describes the fundamental, consistent aspects of how a person thinks and reacts emotionally, and how those reactions influence their behaviour. *Thus, personality is the public self, presented to the world.*

A few of the scientific definitions are included below. While the specifics differ slightly, more than half a century of scientific research has consistently demonstrated personality traits to be a useful way of understanding people's behaviours and indicating how they might act and behave in the future of their life and their work.

> *Personality is a dynamic organisation, inside the person, of psychological systems that create the person's characteristic patterns of behaviour, thoughts and feelings* (Allport, 1961).
>
> *Personality is that which permits a prediction of what a person will do in any given situation* (Cattell, 1965).
>
> *Personality is a stable set of tendencies and characteristics that determine those commonalities and differences in people's psychological behaviour (thoughts, feelings, actions)that have continued in time and that may not be easily understood as the sole result of the social and biological pressures of the moment* (Maddi, 1989).

The way people define personality can vary. But the fundamental components of personality are that:

- Personality traits directly affect people's behaviour and their performance at work. They strongly influence the way people work individually, the way people interact with teams and groups, and how they work within an organization;

- Personality traits are relatively stable over time, meaning they are unlikely to change very much from day to day, month to month or even year to year. They can vary a bit, but do not blow around like tumbleweeds and move wherever a breeze pushes them, they are more like willows in the wind which can bend and sway gently in response to the environment – but are still firmly rooted into a strong and unshakeable foundation;

- The personality of a person can, and must, be separated into its specific and fundamental traits which exist on a continuum. Every separate trait applies to every person, even though people can show varied and different levels of each particular trait. Furthermore, each of these fundamental traits interacts to create a bigger personality portrait.

Traits and states

The distinctness and importance of personality is best highlighted by comparing *states* and *traits*. Traits are enduring and consistent; they are very difficult to change without significant psychological intervention. The consistency of traits is rooted in the biology of the brain. Reactivity to stress, for example, is a personality trait that governs how people perceive and react to stressors.

Some people are physiologically 'wired' to feel more acute reactions to stress, they tend to worry more, about more things, and have more trouble shaking off that worry. Their threshold is lower, so they feel negative emotions more frequently and keenly. Some people are born and wired to feel stressors more acutely. Or, childhood environments can affect how a person perceives and consistently reacts to stressors.

States, unlike traits, are the reaction to a particular environment or event. A state happens at a specific time, may be triggered by a certain event, thought or activity. States have a start and an end, but they are transitory. Anxiety, for example, is a state that can change in reaction to external situations and internal personality traits. Some people may appear to constantly be anxious. People may feel anxiety in reaction to real or perceived concerns. For example many people become anxious when entering the company of a snake or spider. A moderate level of concern may be appropriate when in close proximity to a venomous creature. However, some people become anxious when even thinking about reptiles or arachnids. Events, emotions, thoughts or memories may trigger the feeling of anxiety. Anxiety is a state that can come and go, but almost everyone will experience varying degrees of anxiety at some point in their life.

There are underlying physical and chemical processes in the brain that explain both traits and states. A state like anxiety is a transient biochemical response. A state is a rush of chemicals that comes and goes along a pathway in the brain. It can rush past or linger like a bad houseguest. The personality trait, however, is essentially hard-wired into the various structures of the brain. The state can be the pathway for the biochemistry that accompanies a state – blocking the path or laying out a welcome mat.

There are actual, physical structures and connections in the brain that determine the frequency and intensity of those biochemical responses, and what can trigger them. Personality traits are regulators between the brain and the environment. Reactivity to stress acts like a dam; lower reactivity to stress is like a higher, stronger dam, keeping stressors at bay. But there is a limit to the height of the dam, and with too much water, too much pressure it becomes unbearable. So personality traits are mediators; they have certain, consistent levels, and when we know those levels we can better predict, behaviour, performance and potential.

Traits exist on a continuum, with most people being 'average'. Figure 5.1 shows how populations are normally distributed. Most people score

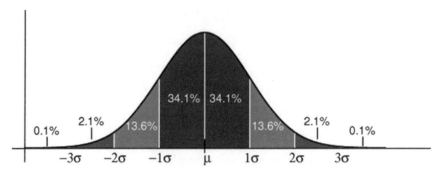

FIGURE 5.1 *Standard Deviation, the average and the exceptional.*

somewhere in the middle, these are *average* scores. Fewer and fewer people have traits further from the average. There are a few, exceptional, people who are most and least reactive stress. The extremes are the rarest.

That is why extreme personalities can appear monolithic, imposing and memorable or deplorable. They are unusual and distinctive when compared to the normal and the usual. The extremes of personalities can be useful given the right time, place and position, but there is a fine line between the right balance in extremes, and too much of a good thing. Extremes can be useful in certain circumstances but can turn toxic in the wrong environment, or when pushed in the wrong direction (this will be discussed more in Chapter 13, discussing derailment).

Although people can be affected by situations and environments, situations are not unchangeable mandates. External situations and environments interact with the internal personality traits. Traits are facets of personality that exist in a clear, testable way in every single person. Everybody will exhibit each of the traits somewhere from low to high. Personality traits crystallize in early adulthood, and change very little for the rest of a person's life except in exceptional circumstances. Thus, a person can be described using a limited number of traits that are equally applicable to every single person. The key research in personality research has been to find out what is the best, most efficient and most valid way of describing personality.

Example models of personality

Historically one of the main differences in types of personality theories has been between type and trait theories. *Type* theories put people into different categories, where personality types can be categorized in the same way people can be categorized by location of birth. Person A was born in one country; Person B was born in another. Person A has this type of personality; Person B has another. A typical example of this is 'Type A' personality, as compared with 'Type B' personality. Table 5.1 briefly outlines the Type A and Type B personalities. This is provided as a useful illustration about personality research, although it is important to note that theories about Type A/B personality have largely been discredited.

TABLE 5.1 *Comparison between Type A and Type B personalities*

Type A	Type B
Ambitious	Relaxed
Competitive	Collaborative
Very reactive to stress	Low reactivity to stress
Proactive	Reactive
Organized	Disorganized
Rushed	Casual

TABLE 5.2 *The differences between traits and types*

Trait theory	Type theory
Concerned with universals possessed in different amounts	Concerned with preferences which are perhaps inborn or learnt
Involves measuring	Involves sorting
Extreme scores are important for discrimination	Midpoint is crucial for discrimination
Normally distributed	Skewed distribution
Scores mean amount of trait possessed	Scores indicate confidence that sorting is correct

In type models of personality, each person has a 'type' which corresponds with a category and that type comes with a set of attributes. But, as can be seen in Table 5.1, type models tend to combine too many characteristics into one 'type'. This is limiting because, for example, not everyone who is proactive and organized is competitive, and the reverse is equally true. *Trait* theories describe people based on measured quantities. Instead of someone being of a single type, they exhibit a certain *level* of the trait. So if someone has a trait they can be 'a little', 'a lot', 'extremely' or other quantities of that trait. Types describe people as either or; traits describe *how much*.

MBTI

The most widely used personality test is the Myers-Briggs Type Indicator (MBTI). There is a huge industry promoting and selling MBTI which contributes to its popularity. However there is limited evidence to suggest MBTI predicts performance or potential. Some studies have found general connections between a person's MBTI type and their perceptions, but no clear behavioural link has been found. Despite its popularity, there is little evidence linking MBTI personality types with performance.

MBTI can be useful inasmuch that categories can be clearly defined and consistently described (although Furnham, 2008b shows how different MBTI usage manual defines personality types very differently). But types are easy to understand and each type can have an archetype that is easy to identify with. It can also be helpful at work, because it makes it easy to discuss personality with colleagues: You are this type, so am I, I understand you, let's be friends.

The Myers-Briggs model of personality has been criticized because the scores of people on MBTI personality 'types' show a normal distribution. This means people are cut off at the exact middle point of the distribution, the cut-off point between two different people is where there are the most people who are most similar. The greatest number of the most similar people are deemed to be completely different because of artificial categories. If there were different

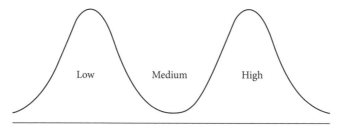

FIGURE 5.2   *Bimodal distribution we would expect from 'type' models.*

types, we would expect people to score in two distinct and discrete groups. In reality people at one end of the scoring distribution are less similar than people in the middle (Costa and McCrae, 2006). For the MBTI model to be valid we would expect the distribution of scores to look like Figure 4.4, but in fact they tend to look like Table 5.2.

The big five

Psychometric researchers, using the trait approach, first settled on three and then five dimensions of personality, now called the 'five factor approach' (FFA) or 'five factor model' (FFM), or simply the 'Big Five'. There is now broad agreement from many sources that the Big Five is a strong, useful measure of personality. Researchers have found impressive evidence, across various different languages, of the emergence of similar factors which are analogous to the Big Five (Goldberg, 1992). What they have not done, however, is to look at the association between personality traits and work outcomes. There are vigorous critiques of the FFM, which are described later in this chapter, but these have not reduced its popularity among personality researchers.

The Big Five argument from some personality researchers suggests we are now confident that we can parsimoniously describe a person's personality using five factors called domains. The domains can also be described at a more detailed level (in terms of facets). These personality characteristics are pretty stable over time: by a person's mid-twenties what you see is what you get. But

| FACTOR DEFINERS | | | |
| **Low** | | **High** | |
Perceived Positives	Perceived Negatives	Perceived Positives	Perceived Negatives
Conscientiousness Easy-going Lenient Flexible Spontaneous Relaxed Considerate	Careless Unmotivated Impulsive Lax Idle Disorganised	Disciplined Self-motivated Organised Determined Logical Persistent	Obsessive Perfectionistic Rigid Inflexible Indecisive Critical
Adjustment Sensitive Responsive Perceptive Passionate Emotive Expressive	Emotional Irrational Neurotic Self-conscious Moody Compulsive	Controlled Peaceful Even-tempered Self-confident Composed Emotionally stable	Indifferent Unresponsive Distant Serious Aloof Cold
Curiosity Focused Traditional Dependable Sensible Reliable Indifferent	Closed-minded Conventional Disinterested Suspicious Unadventurous Obstinate	Innovative Creative Open-minded Attentive Interested Inquisitive	Unpredictable Inconsistent Eccentric Easily-distracted Unfocused Intrusive
Risk Approach Cautious Careful Vigilant Supportive Obliging Harmonious	Avoidant Risk-averse Hesitant Reactive Passive Apprehensive	Bold Tactical Proactive Candid Courageous Self-assured	Confrontational Imposing Reckless Blunt Insensitive Arrogant
Ambiguity Acceptance Deliberate Orderly Consistent Methodical Straightforward Precise	Predictable Stubborn Fussy Inflexible Blinkered Simplistic	Tolerant Versatile Analytical Resourceful Adaptable Considered	Unclear Erratic Illogical Abstract Vague Confusing
Competitiveness Cooperative Amenable Accommodating Modest Undemanding Easy-going	Unenthusiastic Timid Satisfied Submissive Quiet Apathetic	Goal-oriented Ambitious Striving Driven Assertive Eager	Ruthless Aggressive Antagonistic Unyielding Harsh Hostile

FIGURE 5.3 *Descriptors of high and low HPTI traits*

it is acknowledged that with determined effort people can change at least their behaviours if not their personalities. These traits are biologically based and there is evidence of considerable heritability of these traits.

More importantly, a person's traits are powerful predictors of their behaviour. Personality influences choices in careers, partners and lifestyle. It therefore must be very important to understand personality. The 'Big Five' traits are described below. The table below shows in the first two columns the finer grain analysis of the five types. It also shows something of the advantages and disadvantages of being very 'high' on each trait.

Although the Big Five model has been widely researched and used, it is not perfect. Jack Block (2010) sums up the key remaining, unsettled, issues with the Big Five model of personality. He raises key areas of concern with current research on the Big Five, like problems about the descriptive nature of the Big Five and how they were developed. The model looks at traits in isolation, but does not provide a more comprehensive or dynamic understanding of personality as a whole system. Anyone interested in the more nuanced criticisms of the Big Five would be highly recommended to read Block's (2010) article.

Testing personality

Testing personality is a complex and hotly debated area, and the bottom line is that the validity of personality testing depends both on the test and how it is used. The validity of personality tests in predicting future work performance depends on (a) the test, (b) the criteria and (c) the population sample used to validate the test. The tests are most useful and accurate when a good, well-validated test is used and the criteria are clear, well measured and theoretically related to the trait that is measured. Furthermore, those using the test need to understand how to use it and why.

As a result of 100 years of research and discussion the underlying structure of personality traits are becoming clear. Different jobs require different personality traits, and different combinations of personality traits. For example, successful managers tend to be low on neuroticism (i.e. very low reactivity to stress), moderately open to new ideas and methods, and very conscientious. Although they are foundational traits, they are useful across nearly all careers.

Personality is most frequently assessed by asking people to respond to a list of questions because this is the most convenient, accessible and cost-effective method. Personality can also be assessed by interview, assessment centre, references or peer ratings or observing behaviour. Personality inventories are self-reports and not tests, so they can be faked. People can, if they are intelligent and intend to deceive, fake a personality test by giving what they believe to be desirable answers.

Although faking and deception is possible, the vast majority of people are honest, and provide accurate responses. Furthermore, when personality tests are used as in a way that benefits those taking the tests (e.g. to provide insight, development and learning opportunities) people tend to be more honest.

The main advantages of personality testing are:

- **Numeric Information.** Tests convert abstract concepts into numbers which make comparisons between individuals simple and clear. In interviews, different questions are asked of different candidates, and the answers are often forgotten or not properly analysed.

- **Explicit and Specific Results.** Tests give explicit and specific results rather than the ambiguous coded platitudes that are often found in references. A valid score makes for much clearer thinking about personal characteristics than terms such as 'satisfactory', 'sufficient' or 'high-flyer'.

- **Fair.** Tests are *fair* because they can eliminate corruption, favouritism, old-boy or Oxbridge networks or other self-perpetuating biases. They can measure key traits that are desirable or undesirable based on pre-determined traits that con be demonstrably tied with performance.

- **Comprehensive.** Tests cover all the basic dimensions of personality and ability from which other behaviour patterns derive. They go deeper than just behaviour, into patterns of thinking.

- **Scientific.** Tests are empirically based on theoretical foundations; that is, they are reliable, valid and able to discriminate the good from the mediocre and the average from the bad.

Conclusion

Personality is one of the keys in understanding how and why people perform well or poorly at work. However, tests need to be well tested and scientifically validated. Those using tests must be knowledgeable and experienced. Furthermore, tests of personality to predict performance must be tested and validated in the workplace and optimized for use in the workplace. The next chapter discusses the High Potential Trait Indicator (HPTI) which is more specific to a workplace context and identifying high potential.

6

High-potential personality traits and leadership

You can tell the character of every man when you see how he receives praise.

– SENECA

Curiosity is one of the permanent and certain characteristics of a vigorous mind.

– SAMUEL JOHNSON, *THE RAMBLER*

Introduction

Personality traits help to select high potential in all types of work. But understanding high-potential personality traits is particularly important for leadership. One would hope people grow into their jobs, and some do, but the same is not true for leadership. Leadership doesn't build character; it amplifies it.

The previous chapter discussed personality and some of the different ways it has been measured. This chapter discusses a specific measure of personality traits that was specifically designed to be used in the workplace and to identify high-potential talent and leadership potential. Previous research such as Teodorescu et al. (2017) has found that this specific measure of personality traits at work, the High Potential Trait Indicator (HPTI), strongly predicts both objective measures of career success like pay, and subjective measures such as employee satisfaction.

In the *European Business Review* Furnham (2015) explains how the HPTI can be used to help companies win the 'war for talent'. By understanding and assessing the personality traits that predict employee potential to succeed in the workplace, companies gain a competitive advantage in spotting, managing and developing top talent at work.

Linking the concepts of high potential and personality are challenging, but based on what we know about personality can be done:

- *First:* Personality is relatively stable from early adulthood onwards. It cannot be learnt or taught, so is not primarily a career dimension of potential. It is an important constant, so it is a useful *early indicator*;

- *Second:* Personality is rooted in neurological structures. Brain structure and biochemistry are linked to personality. Although it is not as simple as specific personality traits exist in certain 'areas' of the brain. This is still an area of ongoing research;

- *Third:* Personality traits interact to influence behaviour moods and thoughts. Although each is described individually, they are not (to use the statistical term) orthogonal. When considering two personality combinations, a 'High A, High B' compared with a 'High A, Low B' can manifest very differently in the workplace. Although the two are similar in 'A' and different in 'B', and may be compared as such, there are important differences between personality traits. Interactions create unique patterns of thoughts and behaviours;

- *Fourth:* Some personality traits may be better suited to certain careers, but no personality trait is exclusively required for a job, task or career in the same way as knowledge or experience.

Thus, an overall model of potential must account for both the highly variable elements of high potential (like learning the right skills), to the very stable characteristics like intelligence. Career dimensions of potential are too occupation- or position-specific for a general measure of success; growth and foundational dimensions of success lend themselves to generalizable measures, such as high-potential traits using the HPTI.

The *HPTI* is a six-factor model of personality traits, which is based on how people think and behave at work. The HPTI was specifically designed to measure personality traits that affect success at work, and the capacity for high performance and leadership capacity.

We revisit the HPTI throughout this book, and will provide profiles of individuals and teams to show how personality traits and the HPTI can be used to give businesses more information to make more informed decisions about personnel and gain a competitive advantage. In this chapter we explain the traits in detail, and then the specific examples show how to use personality assessment in specific contexts like leadership team development and multi-rater assessment, and identify leadership potential in subsequent chapters.

The traits

There are six HPTI traits, each of which is helpful for predicting potential, but again it is important to ask the question 'potential to do what?'. We explain each of the traits in detail, and map the personality traits onto Silzer and Church's (2009a) model of potential. We also discuss what thoughts and behaviours tend to be related to each personality trait.

Conscientiousness

I have always observed that a man's faults are brought forward whenever he is waited for.

– NICHOLAS BOILEAU

Conscientiousness is a foundational trait of success, essential for leadership and is one of the core personality traits that is an asset in almost any job or type of work. It is rare to see the word 'conscientiousness' explicitly on a job description, but when you see words like 'self-motivated', 'disciplined', 'organized', or 'punctual', the job description is essentially asking for conscientiousness. Conscientiousness is characterized by self-discipline, organization and ability to moderate one's own impulses (Costa and McCrae, 1992; Teodorescu et al., 2017).

People who are conscientious prefer to make (and commit to) schedules and plans. They like to have goals and objectives to work towards in both the short and long term. They usually can motivate themselves to start, continue and complete the goals they set. The conscientious worker tends to be punctual, organized and meets deadlines. Conscientiousness is a very strong determinant of people's success at work. Of all the personality traits, conscientiousness has been most consistently associated with strong performance and success in almost all areas of work across types of work and different tasks (Barrick et al., 2001; Linden et al., 2010; MacRae and Furnham, 2017b). This feature makes the conscientious worker stand out from less conscientious colleagues.

Conscientious workers will almost always be conscientious throughout their entire work life and conscientiousness tends to increase slightly as people get older (Costa et al., 2008). Except for a few exceptional circumstances, young conscientious workers tend to turn into older conscientious workers. Thus, hiring someone with high conscientiousness indicates that the person is likely to work hard during a training period to learn the appropriate skills, will be a diligent worker and will strive to do the best they can at their job. A consistent trait such as conscientiousness is fundamental to how a person behaves and performs at work. It is a foundational dimension of potential. If the objective is to hire someone with reliable performance, conscientiousness can be a good indicator of long-term behaviour.

Conscientiousness is useful in most occupations. However, it is important to remember (and this is true of all personality traits) that high conscientiousness is not always essential to every job or task, and conscientiousness does not always translate directly into performance. Average conscientiousness is more than enough to do most jobs fairly well. High conscientiousness is useful, but not necessary, to be successful in every position.

There are benefits to having low conscientiousness, although not all of them are related to work. One example from a person with low conscientiousness explained the benefits: 'I'm easy-going, adaptable, and things in the future don't worry me too much because I'm just not thinking about them yet. I'm not too stubborn or fussy, so I have more fun!'.

Conscientiousness alone is not *always* required in the workplace, because its effects can be suppressed or enhanced by the quality of leadership or the effects of conscientious colleagues. The effect of motivation is also important to consider. People who have low conscientiousness may have trouble planning, organizing and self-motivating *but once they are motivated they can be very hard workers*. They may struggle in positions where they are responsible for long-term planning, making goals and have strict schedules without help. But in jobs where they are skilled, and are externally motivated to do the work, they can excel. Motivation can come from compensation, interest, excitement or deadlines – but the motivation needs to be sparked. Low-conscientiousness people often have trouble both getting started with work, and stopping. Once they are engaged and interested, they can work tirelessly,

Adjustment

'My life was even then gloomy, ill-regulated and as solitary as that of a savage. I made friends with no one and positively avoided talking, and buried myself more and more in my hole. At work in the office I never looked at anyone, and was perfectly well aware that my companions looked upon me, not only as a queer fellow, but even looked upon me – I always fancied this – with a sort of loathing. [...] Of course, I hated my fellow clerks one and all, and I despised them all, yet at the same time I was, as it were, afraid of them. In fact, it happened at times that I thought more highly of them than myself. It somehow happened quite suddenly that I alternated between despising them and thinking them superior to myself.'

– DOSTOYEVSKY, NOTES FROM UNDERGROUND
(II – A PROPOS OF THE WET SNOW)

Adjustment can essentially be thought of as a person's reactivity to stress. (Costa and McCrae, 1992; Wille et al., 2012). Everyone has a different threshold of stress they can tolerate, as well as different things that make them feel stressed. Some people worry about deadlines, others worry about public speaking, some people don't like conflict while others worry about their pay. The core component of this is the level of stress that someone can tolerate. Think of adjustment as a dam that can hold back a certain level of stress, and when the dam bursts, the stress becomes overwhelming. Some people have high barriers, seemingly immune to all but the most stressful situations, while others seem to lose their cool at the drop of a hat.

People with low adjustment tend to have recurring, negative and sometimes irrational thoughts or emotions. The lower the adjustment, the more negative and the more irrational the negative thoughts tend to be. People who have low adjustment find relatively minor challenges or stressors overwhelming.

People with low adjustment worry about what they just said, what they did, and can become irrationally preoccupied with the most minor things. They may worry about what their colleagues are thinking about them, saying about them or are not saying about them. Low adjustment exacerbates nearly all negative thoughts and can get in the way of more positive emotions. Adjustment is important in the workplace because it is related to nearly all measures of performance at work. In a meta-analysis Barrick et al. (2001) found higher adjustment was associated with improved performance and better teamwork in many occupations. Wille et al. (2012), in a fifteen-year longitudinal study of final-year undergraduate students, found conscientiousness was significantly associated with higher employability and lower work–family conflict.

Very low adjustment is essentially an oversensitivity to stressors; people with very low adjustment can become preoccupied with very minor mistakes, or even believe something is wrong when there is nothing wrong. These are people who interpret silence as disapproval, praise as disingenuous and minor errors as crippling embarrassment. Extremely high reactivity to stress can be crippling when people avoid finishing work for fear of failure and spend more time worrying than working.

Conversely, people with high adjustment do not become preoccupied with negative emotions. They will not spend unnecessary time ruminating and will not be as plagued by self-doubt. This applies to all types of work, but is especially important in demanding or leadership positions. More demanding positions present more stressors which are much more difficult for people with low adjustment. Levels of adjustment can be seen as, essentially, the threshold of stressors it will take to make a person worry.

Adjustment is also a foundational element of potential. Low adjustment means being acutely aware of stressors, and regularly experiencing negative emotions even when there is no obvious reason to feel that way. People with low adjustment feel more intense and more frequent negative emotions in response to increasingly minor stressors.

Stress is a natural response to difficult or threatening situations accompanied by adaptive physiological responses. However, the stress response can become overly sensitive to problems, difficulties or everyday challenges (MacRae and Furnham, 2017a). This can turn a normal biological system into a major barrier to performance at work. The basic example of a stress response is to confront (fight) or avoid (flight) the source of stress. In the workplace, people with low adjustment may seem argumentative or avoidant. When someone with low adjustment is self-aware, this emotional reaction can help to pinpoint the source of stress, and to initiate the reaction. At best, this results in finding a solution to deal with the stress. At worst, this creates an overwhelming sense of worry that inhibits work performance.

In extremely demanding careers, such as leadership, reactivity to stress presents an interesting, but crucial, consideration. More demanding positions present more stressors, more problems and demands. And, challenging times can present unique and great challenges for people. When people appear to be able to sufficiently cope with the stressors of their current position, and time, it does not automatically mean they will be able to manage stressors piled on by a more demanding position.

Curiosity

If we do not plant knowledge when young, it will give us no shade when we are old.

– LORD CHESTERFIELD

Curiosity is openness to new ideas, experiences and situations. People who have high curiosity are more receptive to ideas, thoughts and emotions. Curiosity is related to seeking out new experiences and ideas, and willingness to test novel techniques or approaches. Curiosity has been modestly associated with attributes such as creativity and intelligence (Hogan, 2012).

Curiosity at work, as an HPTI trait, is focused on openness to new ideas, methods or approaches of *doing the work*. Curiosity also represents adaptability and flexibility in the workplace to perform multiple tasks, explore new ideas and continually learn. It also includes elements of reflectiveness, creativity and innovation (Silvia et al., 2009). In the HPTI, openness focuses on this as it is manifested at work.

Judge et al. (1999) conducted an analysis from three American longitudinal studies with 530 participants and found that openness was moderately associated with job satisfaction, occupational status and extrinsic career success. Linden et al. (2010) confirmed that openness was associated with improved performance and learning outcomes. Barrick et al.'s (2001) meta-analysis of personality and job performance found that openness was moderately associated with training proficiency, but was less related to performance than conscientiousness or adjustment. Openness is more a growth dimension of potential than foundational.

Those with high curiosity are more likely to look for new information, and be interested in training or development opportunities. Curiosity alone, though, is not sufficient to be successful in training. It can help people find new opportunities and be open to new opportunities, but more is required to succeed.

Ambiguity acceptance

It is no doubt, an immense advantage to have done nothing, but one should not abuse it.

– ANTOINE RIVAROLE

Ambiguity is a significant and enduring part of most jobs. Large groups, complex organizational structures, poor planning and guarded communication are only a few of the factors that create ambiguity. While some people cannot stand ambiguity, 'I just hate when people send mixed messages'. Others thrive in situations and interactions.

There is a great deal of uncertainty in the business world. Things are very rarely clear; there are not enough facts and details; even legal and scientific processes are not always clear. Most of us would like to live in a stable, orderly, predictable and just world. Some people seem very threatened by ambiguity and uncertainty. They take to simplifying, ordering, controlling and rendering more secure, both the external world and the internal world. Order is imposed upon inner needs and feelings by subjugating them to rigid and simplistic external codes of conduct (rules, laws, morals, duties, obligations, etc.), thus reducing conflict and averting the anxiety that would accompany awareness of the freedom to choose among alternative modes of action. It is therefore a great advantage to be able to feel comfortable and confident making decisions in a situation which is unclear and ambiguous.

Ambiguity acceptance (frequently referred to as Tolerance of Ambiguity, 'AT' in the psychological literature) describes how an individual or group processes and perceives the unfamiliar, the complex and the incongruent (Furnham and Ribchester, 1995). However, this trait, on the 'high end', is more than just *tolerating* ambiguity; tolerating implies subjugation or forbearance. As a trait, high ambiguity acceptance means enjoying and thriving in ambiguous situations.

Those who are accepting of ambiguity perform well in new or uncertain situations, adapt when duties or objectives are unclear and are able to learn in unpredictable times or environments (Furnham, 1994). McCall (1998) suggested from extensive qualitative evidence that adapting to ambiguity is an essential trait of high flyers. Herman et al. (2010) found ambiguity tolerance involved four facets: valuing diversity, challenging perspectives, unfamiliarity and change.

There are inevitable drawbacks to being too accepting and tolerant of uncertainty. That tolerance may mean that a person does not strive enough to get clarity when it is indeed possible to achieve. Further they may be loath to suggest or impose rules, laws and processes which bring stability to a situation. They may be overly reliant on informal networks to getting information as well as over-reliant on intuitive thinking. The danger is essentially being so tolerant of uncertainty, flexibility and change that appropriate attempts to seek clarity are ignored. This can be very problematic in a regulated environment.

As every other personality trait, levels of the trait may fit with different job roles. High ambiguity tolerance is useful for roles that involve large amounts of mixed information, and different unclear paths. There are some jobs where low ambiguity tolerance is helpful. People with lower ambiguity tolerance like to have clear instructions, job descriptions, tasks with specific success criteria and tangible outcomes. Every good leader knows the value of the high conscientiousness, low ambiguity acceptance employee who takes a task, needs to understand the process and the outcome, then gets it done consistently and properly.

People with low ambiguity acceptance thrive in well-defined job roles, but may struggle when they feel managers, customers or colleagues are unclear. High-level leaders may benefit from higher ambiguity tolerance because leadership positions invariably involve different accounts of the same events, varying projections of internal and external conditions and mixed information. Yet, even leadership is not that simple. Most leadership teams involve a number of different positions, from the strategic leader (usually the CEO); high ambiguity acceptance is an asset, whereas operational leaders can make use of lower ambiguity acceptance.

Risk approach

Courage is what it takes to stand up and speak; courage is also what it takes to sit down and listen.

– WINSTON CHURCHILL

Waste no more time talking about great souls and how they should be. Become one yourself!

– MARCUS AURELIUS

Risk approach is the capacity to consider and choose options, even when faced with negative emotions like fear, worry or sadness. Risk approach involves overcoming the initial instinctive or reactive response, and choosing the best option even when it is the most challenging or demanding. Hannah et al. (2007) suggest the courageous (high-risk approach) individual uses positive emotions to mitigate fear of interpersonal conflict or reprisal to confront the behaviour. Thus, the capacity to overcome negative emotions and be responsive instead of reactive is risk approach, but could also be described as courage.

There are various types of courage: moral courage to stand up against forces of corruption, dishonesty and criminality. It often takes considerable 'stand-alone' or 'whistle-blower' courage to point out to those in power unacceptable, immoral or illegal behaviours occurring in the workplace. Interpersonal courage involves confronting people in various settings like bullies, passive-aggressive or under-performing individual who can psychologically hurt people. Third, there is physical courage which some jobs call upon in work situations. People greatly admire the brave, honest leader prepared to stick his or her head above the parapet.

Fredrickson's (2001) *broaden and build theory* of positive psychology proposes that negative emotions restrict an individual's potential range of actions by creating overwhelming impulses to act in a certain way. Fear may create a strong drive to avoid what is evoking the fear, which then restricts the perceived range of responses. Therefore, courage can be expressed in many situations, including calculated risk taking, interpersonal confrontation, problem solving or moral fortitude. It may be difficult to discuss a performance issue with a colleague, but with courage, it can be discussed calmly and rationally (instead of avoidance or aggression).

Courage is not always about action; sometimes silence is courageous when confrontation would be counterproductive. However all these courageous behaviours have the same underlying cognitive mechanism of broadening the range of potential responses (Norton and Weiss, 2009). They found self-report measures of courage predicted actual courageous responses in a fear-evoking situation. Unchecked fear restricts the potential range of responses, and typically leads to behaviours like avoidance or contrived ignorance, whereas courage is exhibited as the willingness to confront difficult situations and solve problems in spite of adversity. Those with high courage are more likely to stand for their own values when others disagree and are more likely to persist in spite of opposition. This is not because they are obstinate, but the reverse. The courageous person has the capacity to consider every option instead of reacting immediately; they choose the option that fits with their values, the companies' objectives or what is appropriate given the situation.

Courage interacts with situational factors and is therefore clearly a growth dimension. A work environment that allows a courageous individual to rise to challenges may lead to success and improvement. However, a work environment that does not provide opportunities for new challenges or difficulties would not bring out the potential inherent in the courageous personality trait.

The opposite, 'low courage', in this sense is not cowardice; it is instinctive reactivity or excessive caution. Courage interacts with other traits – conscientiousness is the prime example. Those who are highly courageous but with very low conscientiousness may choose what they believe to be the best option, but without specific objectives or long-term planning in mind. Thus courage without conscientiousness can appear at best to be reckless reactivity, thrill seeking and at worst to be aggression or bullying.

Competitiveness

If victory is to be gained, I'll gain it!

– CAPTAIN JAMES LAWRENCE

Competitiveness has been left for last, because it is the easiest to misunderstand. When we discuss our trait competitiveness, it means *adaptive* competitiveness, a drive for personal (or group) recognition, improvement and performance. Competitiveness, in the sense of constructive competitiveness, is not about domination or aggression. Those are the most extreme cases of the traits, and many of the most problematic behaviours arise from a combination of high competitiveness and high stress reactivity.

Good competitiveness is the drive to accomplish a goal, to bring out the best in individuals; it indeed helps them understand about themselves. Bad competitiveness is winning at any cost: it sneers at the outmodish negativity of the old aphorism 'It's not whether you win or lose, but how you play the game.

Competitiveness is domain-specific. Thus one may be highly competitive on the sports field, but not in the family, in the classroom but not a work. Nearly all are competitive but some are team-based and some individualistic.

Certainly, competitive individuals tend to be ambitious, achievement-oriented and dominant. But like everything else moderation is a good thing. The hyper-competitive individual might be masking all sorts of inadequacies. But so might the hyper-cooperative individual who is unable to make a decision, go it alone or challenge the group. Hyper-competitiveness has its downside. It is associated with poor interpersonal relations and things like road rage and accidents. On the other hand competitiveness can bring out the best in people. It can make them go that extra mile to put in that extra special effort which can bring about results.

Competitiveness as a personality trait focuses on a strong desire for individual and team success. It may be a drive to be the best leader, and knowledge that the best leader is not necessarily the most aggressive or domineering helps. Competitiveness is not just personal ambition. Trait competitiveness can be channelled into focusing on team or organizational success (Wang and Netemeyer, 2002). For example, being recognized as one of the best employers, the greatest productivity, the highest sales or an impressive philanthropic record.

For some personality traits, such as conscientiousness or openness, very high levels of the trait may be useful. Competitiveness has a lower threshold at which maladaptive behaviours can occur. But many high-performing people find outlets for their most competitive desires, either in individual sports,

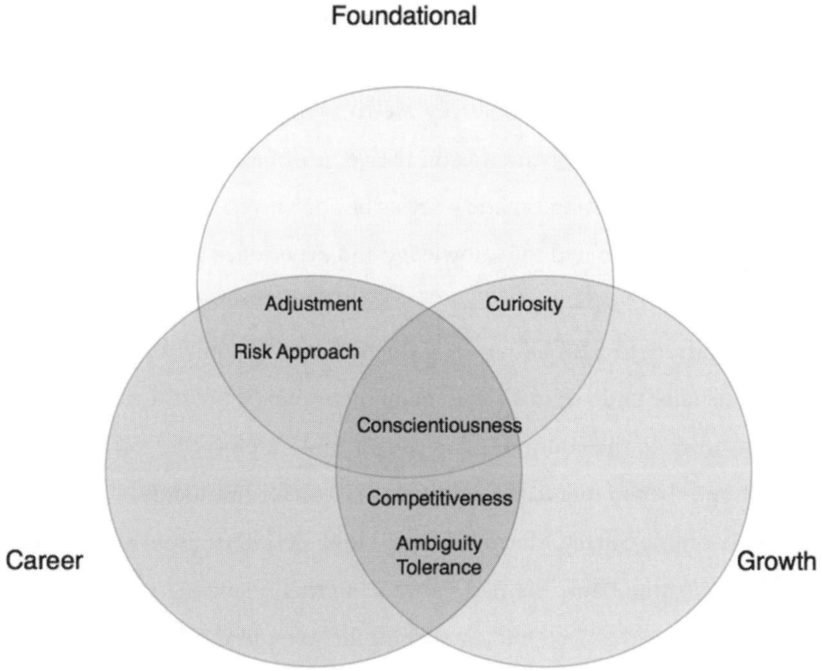

FIGURE 6.1 *Dimensions of potential and high-flying personality traits.*

video games, gambling or in competitive pet events. Indeed, the competitive can find innovative ways to make nearly anything a competition. Yet, when competitiveness is contained and channelled appropriately, then the person with high potential can focus on the more constructive elements of their competitive traits at work. See Figure 6.1 for description of how these fit into the dimensions of potential.

As Peter Jones (Farleigh, 2007) goes on to say

There is, however, a key difference between tennis and business. Business is not about winning at all costs. In business you are trying to find ways where you both benefit, rather than winner takes all [...] I want my business colleagues to walk out of the room thinking that they are really happy, while I'm thinking the exactly the same. (pp. 8–9)

Case study: High-flying exemplar

Lloyd Craig was brought into Surrey Metro Savings Credit Union in 1986 by the board when the company was on the verge of bankruptcy. It was a small, local credit union that had made a series of poor investments, and needed to bring in a leader who had the knowledge and experience to turn the company around. Under Lloyd's leadership, Surrey Metro Savings grew from $500 million of assets to $2.7 billion in sixteen years. Not only did the company grow financially, under Lloyd's leadership the company become one of the best places to work in the country, rated fourth-best employer to work for in the country, and the top financial institution to work for in Canada.

Before joining Surrey Metro Savings, Lloyd describes experience working for the Mercantile Bank. He had various international assignments, but was really thrown in the deep end, managing his own branch in California. He describes the feeling of being thrown in the deep end in a challenging role: 'You have to do this. You were sent down to do this – it's just you'. And he did it. Lloyd describes that early experience that was clearly challenging, but also career-shaping. He describes this position as a key learning experience, learning to make deals, learning to manage people and really beginning to thrive when forced to rely on his own abilities and values. His success led to a series of promotions, where he moved from managing assets to managing people – the transformation into a leader.

Lloyd's HPTI traits (MacRae 2014, 2016) show some of the key attributes, those attributes that change little over a lifetime. He is conscientious and courageous. When faced with challenges he plans and steps up to meet those challenges. He takes risks, and has his history and that of his company that showed they were measured, effective and successful.

Lloyd managed a merger between Surrey Metro Savings Coast Capital Savings in 2002, more than doubling the assets of the company. Under his leadership, Coast Capital then grew from $6 billion in assets in 2002 to

$12.9 billion in 2009. Lloyd has been a leader not just of business, but also in charitable works. He was named National Champion of Mental Health in the Private Sector, by the Canadian Alliance on Mental Health in 2008. He continues to be active in charitable work even in his 'retirement'. While he has all of the key personality traits one would expect of a high flyer, his values suitably match.

The key message is that high potentials have the right personality, but also strong values. Success and leadership must be constructive, not destructive.

Optimality and too much of a good thing

Abnormality is partly a statistical concept. You can be abnormally outgoing or abnormally clever. Being unusually high or low on any criterion always has consequences. The issue is now called 'the spectrum hypothesis'. It means that extreme normality is abnormal. By definition people at extremes are rare/few and therefore not typical. Nearly all human characteristics are normally distributed from creativity to conscientiousness when tested; the range of scores can be graphed and look like Figure 6.2. There are a few exceptionally conscientious perfectionists and exceptionally slovenly and disorderly. Most people are fairly conscientious, slightly disorganized but are somewhere in the middle: average.

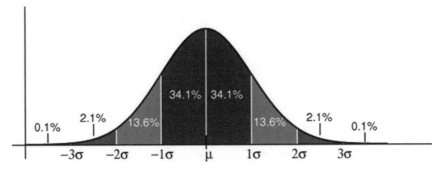

FIGURE 6.2 *Standard deviation, normality and exceptionality.*

Even factors thought to be beneficial and healthy can occur at extremes. Healthy high self-esteem becomes narcissism; out-of-the-box creative thinking becomes schizotypal; sociable, optimistic extraversion becomes impulsive hedonism. Many people believe there is a linear relationship between a 'virtue' and success. The more, the merrier. However, it is clearly apparent that leaders can be too vigilant too tough, too hardworking. Selection errors occur because of linear, rather than cut-off, thinking. Too much of a good thing becomes a bad thing.

Nearly every human characteristic is normally distributed. Most of us (68 per cent) are within one standard deviation of the norm. Virtually all of us (97 per cent) are within two standard deviations. However very few are in the very top category, over two standard deviations above the norm. They are rare by definition: at the far extreme of the spectrum. There are usually costs, as well as benefits, to extremes on either side.

It seems, in general, that it is better to strive for optimality not maximality, so that one does over-rely on strengths which then become weaknesses. Hence the idea of neither too much nor too little.

Figure 6.3 shows the HPTI traits with the perceived positives and negatives for high and low scores on each trait.

7

Emerging trends in personality testing

O! For a Muse of fire, that would ascend
The brightest heaven of invention.
– SHAKESPEARE, *KING HENRY V*

I love fools' experiments. I am always making them.
– CHARLES DARWIN

Introduction

People have been trying to test personality for centuries, not always with a great deal of success. In the eighteenth and nineteenth centuries (Nezami and Butcher, 2000), phrenology was a popular pseudoscientific technique that attempted to measure personality by feeling various lumps and bumps on a person's skull. It turned out to be bogus, but some scepticism about techniques and methods of measuring personality remains to this day.

More valid and scientific measures of personality emerged in the early twentieth century. Although the popularity of personality testing seems to rise and wane between decades, the overall trend has been for personality testing to become more widespread, more valid and useful – particularly in the workplace. Personality testing in the workplace is no longer just a science; it is a multibillion dollar (USD) industry (The Economist, 2013).

Now, scientifically valid personality testing is commonplace at work that can be used for specific purposes like selection, development, retention, identifying leadership potential or a range of other uses.

Now there are new methods, technologies and platforms being adapted for personality testing. Some of these have been used and studied for longer periods of time, like patterns of social media use to predict personality traits, while others like 'gamification' (attempting to conduct psychometrics in a 'game format') are in earlier stages of development.

The web and social networks

Switching to the internet has been argued to provide quicker, cheaper selection and assessment with wider access for many people. It saves time and travel costs, even leading to the possibility of 'same day offers'. Organizations thus now make job offers (recruitment advertisements) on their website. Electronic application forms can be used to collect data and do a simple first-filter. Thus those without certain qualifications may quickly be rejected; software can be written to do a matching task between answers to questions and the 'ideal' profile. But, not everyone has access to the internet. There are geographic, age, educational, ethnic, income and gender differences that are associated with internet access. This has equity and legal implications.

Electronic methods have similar complications and limitations to in-person methods. Participants are equally likely to engage in practices such as faking (social desirability), impression management as well as omissions and commissions of information. Chapman and Webster (2003) have pointed out that the new assessment technologies, predominantly on the web, are changing assessment and selection processes. They can potentially: improve efficiency; enable new screening tools; reduce costs; standardize the HR system; expand the applicant pool; promote the organizational image and increase applicant convenience.

However, there are also unintended and uncontrollable effects that arise from internet selection. Thus, the use of the internet does expand the applicant pool, but may increase the number of under-qualified and out-of-country applicants. It is easy to be flooded with inappropriate applicants. There is also the loss of personal touch that both assessor and assessed value and respect. There are also concerns about cheating if tests are used – and online testing is a field unto itself. Finally, there are still concerns about adverse impact which means that certain groups simply do not have access to the technology.

But can one do good assessment via the internet? Does this exclude certain groups? Are the results different from pen and paper tests?

Yes. The answers are as complex as the questions. But the important thing to remember is the stable, foundational traits do not change. The internet and information technology can affect values, culture, social interaction – but foundational characteristics remain the same. Even in a seemingly variable world, the cultural and mediums change, but there are key elements, psychological traits that are as true and consistent now as they will ever be.

Social network evaluation

The use of social networking websites (SNWs) has boomed over the past decade. Facebook was started in 2004, as a small, digital way for university students to connect online. As of Spring 2017, Facebook reported that it had over 2 billion active users. Facebook is the largest social networking site, and has the broadest user base (there are many niche social networking services). Over 90 per cent of American college students are on Facebook (Wilson et al., 2012).

The advantage of SNWs for assessing potential is that the social networks have large amounts of information about people interacting, posting information about themselves, photos, and other information Social networks are designed to be interactive, so there can be a rich amount of interpersonal communication and behaviour (Skowron et al., 2016). Many users post their information publicly, so it is easy accessible. Furthermore, SNWs have a standardized format, with biographical information in one section, posts of 'real-time' events, thoughts, and behaviour. Then, photos are organized in a specific section, and are easily organized based on who 'tagged' as appearing in the photos.

Because people are behaving and interacting, and posting (in some cases) a large amount of information about themselves, it is a good way of evaluating characteristics such as personality traits that are shown in how people behave (Chorley et al., 2015; Shen et al., 2015). Research has found, for example, that extraverted people tend to have more Facebook 'friend' connections with other people (Karl et al., 2010). Other research by Amichai-Hamburger and Vinitzky (2010) found that people with lower conscientiousness were more likely to post more questionable or controversial behaviour like sexual activity or drug taking.

Kluemper et al. (2012) found that assessors could determine personality traits quite accurately from analysing people's Facebook profiles. They found that independent evaluations of personality were actually better predictors of performance than when people evaluated their own personality. Kluemper and colleagues found that when accounting for intelligence, the independent ratings of people's personality based on their Facebook profile predicted performance: 8 per cent for openness, 6 per cent for conscientiousness and 4 per cent for emotional stability.

Other online platforms have attempted to quantify performance online, using standardized calculations instead of human judgement. Klout, for example, is a website that combines all of a person's or businesses' social network activity (from a range of sources including Facebook, Twitter and various other social media). It gives a score, ranging from zero to 100, judging how influential the individual is in social media, as well as how influential the person is in key areas, such as business, fashion, politics and television.

There are, however, problems with assigning a specific number to a person's influence – particularly when the formula for generating the number is not disclosed. It means that although we have a general idea of how the number is determined, it's impossible to know exactly why specific actions, behaviour and connections are weighed in to contribute to the number. As SNWs grow in both numbers of users and the magnitude of information shared, we will see many more companies quantifying, packages and selling bundles of this information, and making judgements based on the information collected. These, of course, are interesting indicators but should be interpreted cautiously.

While expert assessments can be useful for making hiring decisions, one should always be cautious about using ratings like Klout, which is equally true of using headhunters or assessment centres without proper understanding of their function. While there are certainly some jobs where a strong online presence and social media influence is desirable, actual evidence about its utility and validity may not be readily available for measures and calculations that are private property. There are also drawbacks to using information from SNWs. Privacy concerns are a key and recurrent theme in digital media and online communication. While some have little concern for keeping their information private online, others feel information they post online should be private, secure and do not (paradoxically) want it to be used by companies or organizations. Although there has not been extensive research on the topic (yet), early studies show that as Facebook has grown, and privacy issues have been a matter of personal and media attention, people are putting less personal information online. For example, a large study of 4,000 students by Gross and Acquisti in 2005 found more than 50 per cent of students publicly displayed their home address, and over 40 per cent showed their phone number. One study showed only 10 per cent showed their home address (Fogel and Nehmad, 2009). Another study showed about one-third of students had recently revised their privacy settings (Dey et al., 2012).

Although some people are becoming more concerned with privacy, it is still common for people to have completely open, public profiles with detailed personal information, photos and regular, personal, updates. Some researchers such as Ferwerda and colleagues (2015) found that Instagram profiles, photos and the filters applied to photos could be used to predict personality traits. These methods can still be useful for recruiters, but there are still a few key points to consider:

- There may be significantly different characteristics, values and personality traits that mean there are differences between those who have open, public profiles and those who have closed, or private, profiles;

- While some people may be unaware, or unconcerned with sharing their information publicly, some may also deliberately use social networks for positive self-presentation. Narcissists are particularly prone to positive self-presentation and aggrandisement. It is quite easy to set up a public profile to make one appealing to prospective employers;

- Different social networking sites have very different purposes, which lead to very different behaviour. The primary reason people use Facebook is to connect with friends (Wilson et al., 2012), whereas other SNWs are intended for dating, sharing mutual interests, or may be deliberately for self-presentation to prospective employers or colleagues, such as LinkedIn. Just like in the real world, social context and environments affect behaviour;

- While some may not make efforts to make their information private online, they may dislike employers trying to find personal information about them online;

- The more employers, or other interested parties, use Facebook to gather information about people, the more concerned people can become with protecting their privacy online. This may result in people providing incorrect or misleading information, more positive self-promotion and/or restricting public access to their information. This may create difficult situations where the more useful or valuable data is, the less likely users are to share it publicly.

Of course, this final point highlights a major limitation to profiling people based on their online social presence. It is a paradox inherent to measuring any type of human behaviour: The more aware people are that they are being monitored often means, they are more likely to then change or censor their own behaviour. More recent research shows that as social media becomes ubiquitous, more and more people are making their own profiles limited, private or abstaining completely from posting personal information. Private and sanitized profiles are much more difficult are much more difficult to use to access personality.

Big Data and personality profiling in elections

Alongside the surprising (to many) election results in 2016 of the British referendum to leave the European Union and US presidential election, some said Big Data and digital personality profiling were determining factors in the results. Big Data is the accumulation of vast datasets which can be used to connect a wide range of variables, create complex models and (supposedly) create predictions (Chamorro-Premuzic et al., 2016).

Speculative articles, with less-than-convincing titles like 'The British data-crunchers who say they helped Donald Trump to win: Are Cambridge Analytica brilliant scientists or snake-oil salesmen?' (Wood, 2016) 'A lot of people are saying Trump's data team is shady' (Lapowsky, 2016) had less-than-convincing evidence that Big Data and online personality assessments were the deciding factor in those 2016 election results.

Yet the superficial arguments are both interesting and worth noting, backed up by limited (but by no means definitive) empirical evidence.

There is some evidence that 'liking' or endorsing certain products, pages or messages on social media can help understand and predict different things about people. A study by Kosinski et al. (2013) found that a person's likes on Facebook could predict a great deal about that person, with a surprisingly high degree of accuracy. They found that within a sample of nearly 60,000 Americans they could predict whether a person was homosexual or heterosexual with 88 per cent accuracy, whether the person was African-American or Caucasian with 95 per cent accuracy and whether the person was a Democrat or Republican voter with 85 per cent accuracy. These findings were based exclusively on that individual's Facebook 'likes'.

Then they found they were able to use those same likes to assess a person's personality traits with about 50–75 per cent accuracy (slightly less convincing numbers). The idea, and sales pitch, of Cambridge Analytica was that voters could be targeted based on an automatic and online analysis of their personality traits. Specific messages could be targeted towards people with specific personalities.

The business case is that audiences can be targeted based on what would appeal to their particular personalities. For example, the pitch of Cambridge Analytica is that 'For a highly Neurotic and Conscientious audience, you're going to need a message that is both rational and fear-based: the threat of a burglary and the "insurance policy" of a gun is very persuasive.' And, 'for a Closed and Agreeable audience, people who care about traditions and habits and family and community, talking about these values is going to be much more effective in communicating your message' (Nix, 2016).

The pitch sounds both incredibly Machiavellian and very clever. The question is, does it really work? Does this approach have the potential to sway consumers, shoppers and even the electorate? There may be some truth to it, but when one considers the hard scientific evidence it seems to be a claim that is 'all hat and no cattle' as a segment of the American electorate might say. There is good evidence to suggest online data can be used to profile individuals (Park et al., 2015) but there is no hard evidence behind the speculation that it can be used to sway election results.

While personality traits are useful, measurable and related to a host of behaviours online and offline, they are not an immutable prophecy or destiny.

Conclusion

New digital forms of personality tests are certainly a promising and useful business tool which have come a long way over recent years. They are useful in a workplace setting for spotting, managing and developing talent. Personality tests are one of the most useful and informative tests in the workplace. And, there are novel and innovative ways of testing personality which can complement self-report questionnaires. But be sceptical of silver bullets or speculation about personality tests being used extraordinarily effectively for propaganda or thought control in the future. As Goldwyn-Meyer said, famously quoted by Margaret Thatcher, 'never prophesy, especially about the future'.

8

Experience: The most brutal of instructors

Men are wise in proportion, not to their experience, but their capacity for experience.

– JAMES BOSWELL

For age, tho' scorn'd, a ripe experience bears,
That golden fruit, unknown to blooming years:
Still may remotest fame your labours crown,
And mortals your superior genius own

– METAMORPHOSES, OVID, BOOK 6, PARAGRAPH 4

Introduction

Not everything can be learned in a classroom or by watching online instructional videos. Many with a great deal of 'real world' experience argue that there are certain things that cannot be learned in a classroom using slideshow presentations. You cannot learn to ride a bicycle or to swim by watching an instructional video. One does not become an elite athlete simply by reading fitness magazines. The question then becomes: *What is best learned through experience, and what is the best way to learn about management and leadership? Can it be taught, and, if it can, how?*

Experience is an essential part of development and training from earliest learning. Even children and very young students benefit from experiential programs tailored to their ability levels, and capacity for learning (Subotnik et al., 2011). Providing opportunities for those who excel to further hone and develop their skills improves performance, and increases confidence and motivation from an early age. This is equally true of adults in the workplace.

There are two key reasons why work and personal experience is so important to understanding and spotting potential. First, gaining experience (or failing to gain experience) affects the trajectory of potential over time. Second, experience, or a lack of it, can easily compound over time. It is difficult to catch up, so those without experience may fall behind and find it difficult to compete with their more experienced peers.

One can have a *virtuous cycle*: gaining knowledge, insight and skills from experience make it easier to gain more. The most experienced workers are more likely to be given opportunities to gain even more experience. 'To him who hath, shall more be given'. Equally one can have a *vicious cycle* where little experience leads to fewer offers to gain experience and hence a serious lack of growth. The question is twofold: first whether people volunteer for, and put themselves forward for activities that provide rich experiences; second, what opportunities are available.

Those with salient, early experience related to their future career, and those who demonstrated success and achievement early tend to lead to more varied and high status achievement. Those who take part in community, school or work competitions (be they musical, athletic, debating, artistic, or hold some other talent or interest) gain experience and achievement in those areas. Further, they learn all the so-called soft skills of networking, influence, and persuasion that generalize to all aspects of the workplace. This is why extracurricular activities are often studied so intently, because they provide insight into the person's energy, motivation and passion and experience.

Furthermore, employers look for experience: those with motivation and flare to seek out and excel at a variety of experiences. It is not uncommon for job requirements to be something like: 'requires 3/5/10 years' experience in a similar position'. Many young people or new entrants to the labour market describe a very common trap: they can't get a job without experience, but it is the job that gives them experience.

Unlike many of the foundational traits, like personality and intelligence, employers and employees are jointly responsible for offering and making the most of opportunities for experience. You might not be able to change personality very much, but you can fairly easily provide very useful, even life-changing, learning experiences. It is essential for developing high potential, but developing the experience that is really necessary for growth into truly high potential requires continuous effort and engagement from both the employee and the employer or leaders.

Ten thousand hours of experience

The rule of thumb popularized by Malcom Gladwell is that it takes 10,000 hours of work (or, about ten years) to master anything. The 10,000 hours rule states that, whatever your ability, build or aptitude, you (or anybody else) can show expert talented performance with (as little as) 10,000 hours of coached, motivated and structured practice. The magic ingredient is the power of practice: the more practice, the quicker and more skilled people become at a task.

The idea is that practice not only makes perfect, it makes talent. So if you practise yet you don't succeed in winning an Olympic Gold, appearing at the Carnegie Hall or starting a successful company, it is not that you simply don't have the talent, but rather that you have not practised enough or have not practised in the correct way. The argument is that you make your talent.

Certainly it seems quite reasonable to assert that practice is an essential component to elite, expert or excellent performance: be it on the sports field, in the examination hall or in the office. This is necessary, but hardly sufficient. A good coach, hard work and a good practice schedule all aid success; but are they enough for real success?

Unfortunately, practice in most areas has limitations that cannot be overcome by anyone and everyone. Consider athletes: sprinters, swimmers, pole-vaulters and basketball players. All may (and in some cases must) be born with physical advantages. They are remarkably similar for each sport and often somewhat different from the normal population. The sheer amount of practice cannot finally explain the very real and manifestly apparent differences between elite or expert performers. Take ten random people, put them through the same well-designed, but gruelling, 15- 20,000-hour practice programme and one is a star, another barely managed to finish. Even 100,000 hours cannot teach the 5'1" high jumper to outperform the 6'2" high jumper. That is latent talent.

Talent is not innate or fixed. It is potential that needs shaping. The seed is important but so are the soil, the fertilizer and the nutrients.

The other consideration is that some people learn faster than others. 10,000 hours is neither simple nor easy to obtain, but comes more naturally to the motivated, dedicated and conscientious. As was mentioned in Chapter 3 when discussing 'giftedness', some people stand out as being incredibly self-motivated and excellent at driving their own performance forward. They are 'naturals', and they take to practice eagerly while others are loath to practice. Even when putting in maximum practice some people are constrained by natural limitations in physiology, morphology (shape) or capacity (intellect).

This does raise the essential point that few high performers achieve their success entirely by themselves. Most high performers are more than willing to share credit for their achievements with friends, parents, partners, colleagues or mentors. Take out the parent, the teacher or the coach and their motivation to practice dwindles. It's the opposite of 'falling among thieves'. Stay in the right crowd and the motivation to succeed develops. Take them away and the idea of the 10,000 hours to ensure success becomes deeply demotivating.

Different skills also place different demands on an individual's assets. These are necessary but not sufficient to become talented. People differ enormously in their passions and capacity to invest in their talents. Some people would prefer to spend time with their friends and family than practicing alone or with a coach. Others enjoy the practice but do not aspire to great heights; they treat it more as a hobby or a pastime. And there is absolutely nothing wrong with either of these preferences. But outside influences can help people overcome their performance plateaux by only so much.

Thus it can be argued that talent is not a genetic endowment. It is not something that only needs to be 'discovered' within, but neither is it something you can acquire by willpower and practice alone. The desire to be talented or a high flyer is not enough. Hard work, indeed 100,000 hours of practice, will not suffice. Neither will foundational potential. You get into the talent group by effort and ability. The less ability, the more effort is required. But there are minimum thresholds for both; experiences build upon foundations, but beware of building too much on weak foundations.

The real question about experience is not about whether or not it is important, but about what, how and when it is advisable to provide work experiences. What does experience teach that is important at work? But first, what kind of experience really matters?

Active experience, engagement, deliberate practice

All experience is not made equal. Experience to improve and realize potential needs to be deliberate, purposeful and focused. Practicing to achieve mastery is not mindlessly repeating the exact same thing over and over; it is mindfully and deliberately practicing in order to develop insight, expertise, and to broaden (instead of narrow) focus and ability (Colvin, 2008).

Repetition can help people to master a specific task. This is something that most people who drive a car would be experienced with. The constant repetition and experience turns it into an unconsciously directed activity. Experienced drivers can change gears, street, use buttons and controls on the steering wheel, pay attention to traffic lights and traffic, effortlessly amongst other things.

Most people who drive will be familiar with the feeling of losing lengthy periods of time, lost in thought or conversation. Likewise, one can switch back into being conscious of one's driving, especially in difficult conditions like bad weather or unfamiliar road. It's a relatively difficult and complex task that with experience can be automated and pushed to the back of the mind.

To broaden the metaphor, at work, driving the same car on the same journey every day does not help to increase skill or to develop potential. A daily commute will never be the kind of practice required to win the Indianapolis 500 or Monaco Grand Prix. It can help to make the task more automatic and feel easy, but that is not the same as deliberate practice. If the objective of practice is to become exceptionally good at a single task that varies little, then basic repetition can be useful. Take Ivo Grosche from Germany's achievement; he holds a world record for 'most garters removed with teeth in one minute' (Guinness World Records, 2013). This is an achievement, of sorts, that would require constant practice on exactly the same task. Of course, there are fairly narrow, limited applications of this skill.

Deliberate practice in particular is essential for turning high potential into high performance. Experience is necessary for everything from starting a new job, acquiring a skill such as playing a musical instrument, learning a new language or learning the best ways to get a job done. Everyone starts with limited (or no) skill and knowledge in a particular domain. Learning a language is a process of acquired knowledge and experience. It is entirely possible to learn the basics of a language from a book, and mental rehearsal. The words can be practised, and the grammatical rules can be memorized. Yet it is impossible to become fluent in a language without speaking that language with other people.

Languages are a process of mutual communication, so they can vary by region (dialects); they can vary depending on who you are talking to or the social situation. Fluency in a language is like expertise in a skill. The expert public speaker can gauge the audience, establish rapport and modify the presentation accordingly, just like the native speaker of a language will be more able to pick up the subtleties of another's speech, phrasing and linguistic particularities to improve communication. This has to be done by practice, practice and more practice. The more varied the practice, the more adaptable the talent. New and different situations broaden the experience and deliberate, effortful practice leads to greater improvement.

This applies to any work. Different skills or positions at work vary in complexity and difficulty, but (nearly all) require practice. Many people who begin a job after a long period in education or training are initially frustrated because of seemingly trivial problems in the workplace. There can be excessive paperwork, challenging colleagues, delays, bureaucratic and political delicacies, and difficulties that seem entirely unnecessary. These are difficulties that were not present in the same way in the training or education because the practice didn't involve many of the difficult day-to-day (or, sometimes, exceptional) circumstances.

Mastering a skill requires deliberate practice and the broadest range of experience and opportunity to practice. Talent and ability can plateau at a certain level when people reach a certain level of performance. Then they either stop looking for new ways to improve, or their work does not give them opportunities to continue to improve their performance. Some managers and leaders may feel that once performance reaches a satisfactory level, their responsibility to improve the employee's performance is finished.

Ericsson and colleagues, when discussing deliberate practice, describe a classic, early example of practice and skill development in Morse code operators during the late nineteenth century. After improving their performance to certain levels, the Morse code operators could not improve further. Practicing the exact same task in the same way only improves it up to a certain level, but not beyond. Research half a century later showed that the plateaus in Morse code operator skills were not always inevitable; new, improved training techniques could help people exceed these skills plateaus.

The key message is that repeating the same task will improve performance on that task to certain levels – but only to certain levels, and only in that domain. No amount of practice working as a Morse code operator will make that person a better tap dancer. This may seem silly, but consider a common situation in development: the highest-performing Morse code operator is rewarded with a promotion, and is made the line manager. But, why? Managing and motivating people are as similar to being a Morse code operator as tap dancing.

A further consideration of practice and learning is that skills, knowledge and experience are relative. A top-performing student may be the most knowledgeable in their peer group, but that is not the same as being a top performer. Formal education is a specialized environment, with specific sets of tasks to master along with general competencies. The most successful student can feel like an expert in the field upon graduation and may get annoyed when seemingly unnecessary complications make getting 'the real work done' more difficult.

True high potential requires learning to practice and master skills in many environments. The best experience teaches people how to do their job, improve their performance wherever they are and whatever the obstacles. A public speaker is not good at their job if they are exceptional when speaking to their own mirror, but cannot speak to larger groups or in unfamiliar places. But this highlights the role of experience.

The true expert will have real experience with the delays, the extra paperwork, the shiftless colleagues or the bureaucratic hindrances. High performance means learning the systems, adapting to their demands and gaining the new skills when required. The non-experienced employee (who has learned the basic skills, but has not learned them in the real world) sees their skill set as separate from the obstacles that keep them from doing their job well. The experienced worker knows how to get their job done while working within the immediate problems and systematic barriers because that is part of the job. Experience leads to expertise because the expert has learned how each of those problems can be solved or bypassed.

Three types of job

Furnham (2012) argued that the path of management and leadership is usually a journey through these three types of jobs. Not everyone continues the journey. Not everyone wants to or should. It can be a journey from specialist education and training to corporate strategist, if desired. This can be true of individual career paths, and careers within large organizations. Small business leaders and entrepreneurs typically find themselves doing some combination of the three types of jobs.

The technical job

To acquire their technical skill may involve years and years of intense and demanding education and training followed by a long period of apprenticeship.

Many CEOs are trained accountants and engineers. Some start life in marketing; others in research and development; and a few in human resources, as technicians, salespeople or tradespeople. They acquire skills as they move around and up the organization, usually as a function of their own ability and ambition.

Most people are selected on their technical knowledge and skills, and leadership positions should be no different. They require a unique skill set.

They may be relatively easy or difficult to acquire. They may require years of training or it can be achieved in a matter of weeks.

Technical jobs are evaluated primarily on skills and knowledge. These often take many years to acquire through learning, training and experience: this might be done through the apprenticeship model, such as that of carpentry or academics; the teaching model or the experiential model. A newly trained doctor or driver, accountant or actuary, cook or carpenter must acquire the skills and experience to do the job well.

Thus a young 'certified', 'chartered', 'qualified' lecturer, lawyer or land surveyor attempts to get a (good) job after qualifying. They hope for a job that is interesting, well paid and one that offers the possibility of progress and promotion. A certification serves as a recognized description of a complex skill set. It is shorthand for supposed competency.

Over time, demonstrated success is typically rewarded with offers of promotion. There are essentially two types of promotion. The first is to be made a senior 'X' such as a senior train conductor, a senior house doctor, a senior lecturer. Rewards and greater prestige typically accompany the promotion along with more money and more difficult tasks. Or it may be just a reward for years of work with essentially no differences in work tasks. Technical people are recognized for their ability, skills and knowledge and, through experience, are asked to do more complex, difficult and demanding tasks within the same area.

However, there is a second, very different type of promotion. This involves supervision. It is the transition from managing one's own abilities to managing other people. It means doing less of the task oneself and more monitoring, motivating and engaging others. Whilst supervisors often do a great deal of 'the task' themselves, their newly promoted role is supervisory. In essence, others report to them who require help, guidance, and instruction. The exasperated customer or disgruntled employee often demands to 'see the supervisor'.

The managerial job

This job becomes managing people. It is the job of supervisors to get the best out of those that work with, and for, them. They need the ability to plan, organize and control but more than that they need the ability to engage staff. Job satisfaction, commitment and engagement are, to a large extent, a function of a supervisor. These will be discussed in greater detail in Chapter 22, Retention.

For many the problem is 'letting go'. Supervisory jobs are much less 'hands on' and more 'hearts on'. It is about helping, aspiring and supporting others to do the task. It is about achieving goals with and through others. Hence the importance of interpersonal skills and learning how to work with and among many people and groups.

The time between moving from a technical to a supervisory job may be long or short depending on the job itself, the individual's ability and ambition as well as company policy. Some organizations have very clear ideas about how to develop people, such as moving people around organization to get an understanding of how it all works, learning about systems as well as people. Other organizations or environments such as those of unions base promotion and pay on aspects such as the length of tenure instead of ability or potential. How to give a technical person the best experience to become a good leader is an important task for many organizations.

The strategic job

Promotion from a supervisory-interpersonal-management job is also a recognition of a particular kind of effort, ability and potential. The third type of job is strategic planning job. This is usually thought of as a 'broad-level' job. At this stage a person, often a senior or possibly a general manager, relinquishes direct supervision, and manages both people and systems at a larger scale.

The task moves on to direction giving. Strategy is about the future. People at the strategic level have to learn to 'read the signals' from the future. What is coming down the line? What are the opportunities or threats to the company? No organization can afford to stand still and become complacent. 'Third-level' top, strategic jobs are about the future.

This involves looking more outward than inward. Strategists need to look to the future as well as the present and they need to look around them at competition. Changes in technology, in customer expectations and in population as well as laws can mean a successful organization can potentially 'go-under' overnight.

The strategist job is to plot the journey to the future. It is partly an analytic and partly a planning function. But perhaps more than anything else it is a job that requires the leader to sell his/her plan, motion, vision and values; a brilliant strategy that no one understands or believes in is essentially a failed strategy.

Strategists need to align and motivate their staff often through charismatic speeches and clear documents. They need to inspire the confidence of all their staff. They need integrity and most of all to be inspirational to communicate their strategy and make sure others are behind it.

The question we can glean from all this is: *What experiences can teach technicians to manage people and systems? How does different experience influence potential?*

Direct and indirect applications of experience

Useful experience can be broadly classified into two different categories. First, there is active, competency-focused experience. This is about developing a single skill (or related set of skills). Practicing a musical instrument or a single piece of music alone can improve the skill playing that instrument, and ability to play that piece of music. Whereas rehearsing the same piece of music in an orchestra involves playing in concert with other musicians, playing a solo piece in front of an audience involves developing a stage presence, establishing a certain level of rapport while playing the music – and while some people can master a skill, they cannot always apply it to broader successes. This is specifically, or loosely, related to the career. It involves building up and advancing skills that can be directly practised, used and applied, for example, interpersonal skills, computer programming, writing, musical ability. Experience provides a deeper understanding, knowledge of contexts, and allows the skills to be used and applied more broadly, skilfully and elegantly.

Second, there is the very different, contextual experience that is not about practicing a specific skill, but about learning how to really use and apply skills within an environment, situation or context. This can be loosely or completely unrelated to the specific job or career. But it broadens perspective and allows one's intelligence of knowledge to be applied in different situations. Contextual experience is about using either already available skills optimally in a certain workplace or among a group, or unrelated experience and learning seemingly 'useless' information that turns out to be useful in the future.

Serial entrepreneur Duncan Bannatyne provides an example of this:

For example, it was because of a skiing accident that I established Bannatyne Health Clubs. My injured leg needed strengthening, but my nearest gym was a 25-minute drive away. As I rebuilt the muscle I began to calculate the figures and became determined to build a health club of my own to service the people of my area. We now have more than 60 throughout the UK. I set up Just Learning, a chain of day-care centres, because I needed a nursery for my kids in Darlington but all the centres had waiting lists – clearly there was a demand to be met. So I built my own. [...] I was able to reuse my basic principles about human resources and staff development as I graduated from one business to the next. (p. 45, Farleigh, 2007)

This is a great example of using general, seemingly unrelated knowledge and experience to come up with business ideas. An entrepreneur may benefit from knowledge of the local community, first-hand experience with what people need, from hobbies and related service. This is true not only for entrepreneurs or leaders, but in any job. A broader perspective and greater understanding of a wider range of issues will improve potential. A narrow and focused approach that deliberately ignores outside or differing information can seriously limit performance.

9

The performance delusion

Love of bustle is not industry.
– SENECA

Deliver me, O Lord, from the errors of wise men, yea, and of good men.
– ARCHBISHOP ROBERT LEIGHTON

Introduction

When we talk about experience, the most straightforward way to measure it is based on past performance, qualifications and achievement. Performance is regularly equated with potential. Morgan McCall, who offers insight into the importance of experience in development, focuses on the role of experience in determining potential. He says of what determines potential, 'One of the first conclusions to be drawn is whatever "it" is, it is ultimately determined by performance' (p. 6, McCall, 1998).

It may be true that potential is ultimately determined by performance, but we need ways of estimating who is likely to perform better (higher potential), and who will benefit the most from which types of experience. Hindsight is difficult to apply to selection procedures. It is important to distinguish exactly how performance is being evaluated and potential is being defined.

It is true that performance, in the end, should be how results are evaluated. A programme aimed at identifying potential should ultimately be evaluated by the performance of those identified as high or low potential. If those identified as high potential end up being low performers, something has gone wrong. Yet, this should not lead to the conclusion that past performance is the only predictor of future performance.

The performance delusion is a mismatch between the skills or characteristics being evaluated in the context of performance and the conceptualizations of potential. In other words, assuming someone who will perform well at one thing will perform well at another task can be a huge mistake. The most common example of the performance delusion is the mismatch between technical or specialist skills with leadership skills. When someone is good at his or her job, be it a nurse, accountant, mechanic or professor, the best performing people in their current position tend to be considered the most viable for promotion to manage and lead their colleagues.

An example in practice

Take nursing for example, which is a skilled, challenging and specialist occupation. However, when looking for nurse managers, the available talent pool is screened for the highest-performing nurses. Those who have the record of strong and consistent performance, dedication, affability and interpersonal skills appear to be the best candidate to be a nurse manager. Yet, they are fundamentally different jobs, despite both having the term 'nurse' in the job title. It's like mistaking an ophthalmologist for a proctologist. The results may be unpleasant. Table 9.1 shows extracts from real job descriptions of nurses and nurse managers.

Promoting the highest-performing nurse to the position of nurse manager, based on the job description of a nurse, is the performance delusion exemplified.

TABLE 9.1 *Example job descriptions for nurses and nurse managers*

Nurse	Nurse manager
Writing patient care plans	Maintains nursing policies and procedures
Observing and recording conditions of patients	Initiating, co-ordinating and enforcing policies and procedures
Checking and administering drugs and injections	Recruiting, training, orienting and training nursing staff and auxiliary staff
Responding quickly to emergencies	Maintaining annual budgets, scheduling expenditures
Maintaining patient records	Coaching, counselling and disciplining employees
Advocating on behalf of patients	Developing and interpreting philosophies and standards of care
Communicating with and relieving the anxiety of patients and their relatives	Communicating with patients and developing multidisciplinary team strategies

It is easy to believe that the highest-performing person in one job will be the best able to take on what is seen to be a higher 'level' position. Yet, in actuality, it requires a fundamentally different set of responsibilities. The reason this assumption is so widespread is because some of the foundational traits that lead to good performance in some positions lead to strong performance in others. For example, those who are intelligent can be adaptable and quick learners. Those who are very conscientious tend to be better at long-term planning, organization and goal setting. These traits will lead to improved performance in most jobs. But the performance delusion is equating other characteristics that can lead to high performance (such as conscientiousness) with the actual skills and expertise that lead to high performance in the prospective position.

For a nurse, the key responsibilities include establishing rapport with patients, helping patients plan their care, checking progress, monitoring and administering treatments, working with patients about health issues, routine and administrative tasks, along with other responsibilities. Whereas a nurse manager is responsible for hiring and evaluating other nurses, managing budgets, monitoring service quality, coaching and disciplinary actions. These are entirely different skills, although the positions are clearly linked. Of course, knowledge about what makes a good nurse and first-hand responsibilities of nursing are excellent qualifications, and will be useful to the nurse manager, but (alone) are not very good indicators of a high-potential nurse manager. Much of the experience that makes for a high-performing nurse does not transfer directly to predicting high potential to succeed as a nurse manager. Evaluating potential in the two different jobs requires evaluating potential to gain very different types of experience, and then use very different sets of skills.

The greater the overlap between performance on Task A and Task B, the better past performance is at predicting future performance. If potential means the potential to do a similar job, at a similar level with similar results, then yes, current performance is a good indicator of potential. However, especially when looking at high potential, promotion or additional assignments typically involve very different positions that require new skills, experience and characteristics.

The greater the similarity between two positions, and the more skills transfer between the two, the better past performance will be an indicator of future success. The more overlap between Job A and Job B, the better performance is a predictor of success. However, when looking at high-potential people and promoting people, typically the purpose of a promotion is to move people into new jobs, with new and different responsibilities, and more complex or very different demands.

The solution

Instead of measuring past performance overall, it is much more effective, and more appropriate, to make a list of the current responsibilities, and prospective responsibilities to compare how the two overlap.

TABLE 9.2 *Example of performance review for current and potential performance*

Responsibility	Current performance	Current	Prospective
A	Good	✓	
B	Satisfactory	✓	✓
C	Excellent	✓	
D	Unknown		✓
E	Unknown		✓
F	Good	✓	
G	Acceptable	✓	✓
H	Excellent	✓	
I	Satisfactory	✓	
J	Unknown		✓

Table 9.2 shows that current performance is good or excellent, in many areas. But those areas of performance are not responsibilities that are important to the prospective position. Although the person's current performance would generally be considered good, that performance cannot necessarily be compared to prospective performance. The responsibilities of the new position are largely unknowns, and the responsibilities that are similar to the current position are the person's lowest-performing areas.

If the person is already excelling in some of the key areas of the prospective position, and has the capacity to learn the remaining areas from experience, then the promotion may be a good idea. If the person's current performance is much higher in the skills that are essential for the current position, but shows little potential of learning from experience in the areas necessary for the potential position, it may be a challenging transition (to say the least). In both cases, it is useful to look at foundational traits such as personality and intelligence. In some cases, it can be as simple as an honest conversation. Many people who are performing well and have self-awareness know if they do not want to or will not be suited to positions when they have a clear and honest description of the other position – particularly when it comes from a trusted manager or colleague.

Promotions to new and very different types of work also create challenge(s) for the employee who receives promotion. People may, justifiably, become frustrated, confused or defensive when most of their skills and experience from the past position are not useful for the new job. The fewer the skills that are transferrable to the new position, the more frustrating it can be to go from a top performer to struggling with the demands of a new job.

It takes resilience (emotional stability) and perseverance (conscientiousness) to develop and deliberately practice a whole new set of skills. This can be particularly challenging when the person's pride and satisfaction with their work came from their ability in certain areas – if those are skills they no longer get to use, the person can feel disappointed and even resentful of the responsibilities. This is particularly a concern when people are thrown into a new position with limited help or support. The importance of mentoring and supported learning and development will be discussed in Chapter 10.

This is one of the reasons many promotions that come from the best intentions can be misguided. Leaders, who are looking to promote a team leader or manager, may look to members of the team as the talent pool. Especially at lower levels of management, hiring externally from someone who has no experience of the business, and may not have a relationship with other employees, does not seem a very desirable option. Furthermore, for many good reasons, many people prefer to promote from already available talent pools – so that they can choose based on previous experience and knowledge of the person's performance. Whether conscious or not, many people involved in selecting employees prefer to select a person they feel they already know and are comfortable working with.

The performance delusion and disengagement

The performance delusion represents a problem that happens in many different sectors and for different types of roles. High performers in one role do not automatically or necessarily transform into high performers in another type of role. This happens quite often because of poor development pathways, poor career planning or simply just neglect.

MacRae and Furnham (2017a) use the example of a group of high-performing physicians. Although their job is extraordinarily challenging and demanding, they also report very high engagement in their work. Their work is engaging because they are making excellent use of their extremely specialized skills. Even though the job is challenging and demanding, it is also stimulating and engaging. The group report enjoying a feeling of mission and purpose in their work; it is a challenging but rewarding use of their talent and energy.

Specialized jobs often provide these opportunities because the job balances the optimal level of being both challenging and rewarding. The *feeling of engagement* can be described as *flow*. Transylvanian psychologist called Csíkszentmihályi (2008) wrote a book titled *Flow*. People feel best when engrossed in some challenging activity. During flow they lose track of time because the work is enjoyable, feel more capable, more sensitive and more self-confident even though the activities may be challenging. The activity was its own reward: intrinsically motivating. Flow lifts mood and banishes distraction and creeping dispiritedness. So what are the preconditions of flow?

Csíkszentmihályi identified the following factors as accompanying an experience of flow:

1   Clear goals, expectations and rules are discernible, and goals are attainable and align appropriately with one's skill set and abilities. The challenge level and skill level should both be high;

2   Concentrating, a strong focus on a specific field of attention (a person engaged in the activity will have the opportunity to focus and to delve deeply into it);

3   A loss of the feeling of self-consciousness, the merging of action and awareness. Being and doing lose the distinction;

4   Distorted sense of time, one's subjective experience of time is altered. The activity is more important than the time it is taking;

5   Direct and immediate feedback (successes and failures in the course of the activity are apparent, so that behaviour can be adjusted as needed);

6   Balance between ability level and challenge the activity is neither too easy nor too difficult; 'The Goldilocks Zone';

7   A sense of personal control over the situation or activity;

8   The activity is intrinsically rewarding, so there is an effortlessness of action;

9   A lack of awareness of bodily needs (to the extent that one can reach a point of great hunger or fatigue without realizing it);

10 Absorption into the activity, narrowing of the focus of awareness down to the activity itself, action awareness merging.

Vallerand et al. (2008) see flow as the consequence of (harmonious) passion. Thus for flow to be experienced at work a person needs a clear goal in mind, reasonable expectations of completing satisfactorily the goal in mind, the ability to concentrate, being given regular and specific feedback on their performance, and having the appropriate skills to complete the task.

This flow is an essential component of keeping employees engaged. Conversely, when someone is promoted from a position where they felt a sense of flow into a position where they do not, problems are likely to emerge. There are all sorts of reasons this happens, from overoptimistic employees, inexperienced managers or a misunderstanding of different types of potential (The Performance Delusion).

It's not something that is always immediately recognized either. People may try to work their way 'up' the career ladder for years or even decades, seeing it as the only valid high-potential trajectory. Some people realize it immediately after a promotion; others take much longer to realize that they were happiest and most engaged in their technical or specialist role. Many people would rather do a job they are good at and love, than to supervise other people doing that job (MacRae and Furnham, 2017a).

The performance delusion can quickly lead to disengagement, whereas keeping people in the roles they have highest potential in can keep people highly engaged. For some, flow is experienced in a leadership role, while for others it can be in a technical, sales or teaching role. This is where stretch assignments, job shadowing or other developmental experiences can be very helpful. Often, gaining that experience provides insight about what that position really involves. This is discussed in greater detail in the next chapter, about how to avoid this problem, gain experience and, very importantly, how to learn from failure.

10

How to gain experience

The secret of success is constancy to purpose.
– BENJAMIN DISRAELI

Work helps us to preserve us from three great evils – weariness, vice and want.
– VOLTAIRE, *CANDIDE*

Learning from failure

'The most interesting thing about any technique is how and where it goes wrong' (Perry, 2013).

Do you learn more from failure or success? Do you learn more from others' 'war stories', 'cock-ups', disasters and error or successes, triumph and victory? Research shows people learn valuable lessons from failure. Error management training (Keith and Frese, 2008), as it is referred to in the HR jargon, tends to be helpful. This involves making mistakes and learning from them, or learning from the mistakes of others. It is argued that errorless learning promotes happy, quick and seemingly effortless skill acquisition. But error exposure training teaches people how to react more effectively in unexpected situations. People remember error exposure training better.

There are various arguments in favour of focusing on failure:

- *First*, it helps understanding. Errors illustrate underlying principles clearly;

- *Second*, errors are seriously memorable: they tend not to repeat these errors if they are aware of the cause and the effect from it, and can reflect upon the errors in a supervised environment;

- *Third*, errors underline the message of thinking before acting, of being attentive, being 'all there'. It helps to concentrate the mind, identify problems and generate sensible solutions.

But, what of 'war stories'? This is when people tell hyperbolic or embellished stories based on true events. Old soldiers talking of lost battles, accident-emergency people telling of serious mistakes; managers talking of disastrous products or shambolic mergers and acquisitions.

One study looked at the training of firefighters. Some learnt with case studies that described errors and their consequences while others had errorless versions. They also varied the complexity of the scenarios from simple to complex. The different groups were later measured by the number of appropriate alternative actions they could generate when given a unique and novel scenario. They also were evaluated on the problems they could identify in realistic scenarios. Results showed the groups who learned from errors had higher performance later: stories of others errors, particularly complex problems, clearly helped people learn lessons.

Everyone makes errors and mistakes throughout their career, although the visibility and consequences vary greatly. Few organizations or people, except the most histrionic, want their mistakes to become public. People, groups and organizations miscalculate, overextend, miscommunicate, err and fail. It happens in every organization at every level. A single failure should not usually be career-ending. High-potential people, like those with lower potential, do make mistakes; the difference is in how that failure is dealt with.

High-potential people make mistakes, and then learn from the mistakes. They take responsibility, reflect on the error and consider what they would do if the similar situation arose again. They learn from each experience of failure how to get a different outcome from a similar situation. Lower-potential employees and managers are more likely to make the same mistake over and over again, because they either do not take responsibility for their part, or do not understand why things are going badly.

High-potential people have the intelligence, the problem-solving and reasoning abilities to understand where things went wrong, the self-awareness to understand their part in it and the emotional stability and fortitude to realize that failing at a task is entirely different from failing 'as a person'. The high-potential person has the motivation to continue, and seek more experience, to put things right and do it better next time. They also need supportive leaders and colleagues who they can speak openly and honestly about why things went wrong, get help fixing the problem or moving past it. Even the most motivated, intelligent person with all the right personality traits, with the best intentions, can become a scapegoat – so, although internal factors are important, individual characteristics alone are not always enough to overcome adversity.

Experience is important, particularly in the learning and development of high potentials. However, experience does not always have a direct or immediate connection with performance and potential. Experience is accumulated over time, but may not show immediate benefits. Take, for example, an employee who has a personal interest in social media runs a small blog in her spare time, or is active on Facebook, Twitter, Pinterest and various other sites: she has spent years of interacting with people in the context of social media, has a general knowledge of how each of the systems work, knows the etiquette for different platforms, has a few businesses that she really likes to follow on social media and has seen some examples of when businesses use social media badly. This hobby may never have affected her work before, or may have slightly diminished her performance when distracted by a sly tweet or two during the workday.

Now, suddenly, her boss has gone to a social media workshop, and decides the small, local business needs to launch itself into the world of social media. Now, her experience as the only person at work with any knowledge of social media is a huge advantage. She takes on new responsibilities, her performance improves because it's another responsibility and one that she enjoys, and is knowledgeable about. That's why wide-ranging experience is so important to success, and bringing together teams of yet wider-ranging experience and a broad base of knowledge.

Internships and apprenticeships

An internship is the middle-class, white-collar equivalent of the apprenticeship and is typically less structured and unpaid. It is about practical training but without formal learning outcomes. Typically, students might do a summer or even longer stint with an organization in the private or public sector. The demand seems to have exploded and well exceeded supply, though some organizations are noticing the enormous benefits of having an intern: unpaid, available and ambitious workers. So what is the role and function of the intern? Who is the internship good for? What do the intern and employer really want from the exchange? And who, when and where are these fuzzy expectations clarified?

Certainly it is obvious that some things cannot be very well taught in a classroom setting. Classroom learning and training has its place, but some skills seem best acquired and honed in the work environment. Book learning and test writing is one thing; the ability to understand and how to use a skill among colleagues, clients and customers is quite another. Intelligent and experienced employers know this. Students complain that they can't get a job without experience but they can't get experience without a job. So, one solution is that internships provide experience, but what sort of experience and for whose benefit?

Universities tumbled to this concept years ago with the 'sandwich course'. The language teachers knew this all along; people learn best when in the country of the native speakers during informal and unstructured conversations. But the same may be true of other things. So you do a four-, not a three-year, degree, the third of which is essentially an internship organized by the university. There are benefits and criticism of internship programmes. The key question is really who benefits. A good internship program has three benefits:

- *First:* it develops young or emerging talent;
- *Second:* it helps employers find suitable workers;
- *Third:* it creates pathways from training to employment.

In this sense the internship is a sort of selection and probationary period all wrapped up into one. The politically savvy employer has usually learnt a simple lesson: Select for attitude trained skills, *not* the other way around. The problem is getting enough accurate data at the interview. You simply can't keep up the pretence of being a motivated, enthusiastic, 'keeny' for weeks while on the internship.

Thus the question is what companies need to think through when they offer an internship. Who do interns report to, and why? What sort of experiences they offer over what period of time: is there a well-thought-through syllabus/path that they follow? What is the outcome of the internship in terms of references, evaluations? Many interns complain about being underworked and supervised; being given menial work by someone who neither wants the task of supervision, nor knows what the company wants. Both parties need to clarify expectations. Forbid that the whole thing becomes regulated by some ghastly bureaucracy full of form-filling, compliance-demanding, 'nyet' oriented officials paid from the public purse. But does it seem a good idea that there is a forum where buyers and sellers may discuss what they offer and expect?

Apprenticeships, on the other hand, tend to be well- structured with clear learning outcomes and required skill development. Many apprenticeships combine standard in-school book learning and lecturing with practical experience. Apprenticeship programmes (when done well) are far better developed than internships, and the programmes involve relationships between governments and employers: the idea is to get people into good training programmes that will then lead into a job. Thus apprenticeships can combine standardized learning outcomes with experience with specific employers, workplaces, colleagues, equipment and technology. The Germans, Austrians and Swiss are widely regarded as having the gold standard apprenticeship programmes. The programmes don't just teach skills, but help people become experts, and provide a clear and well-organized transition from training into the workplace. For detailed information about apprenticeships and national differences, the Organization for Economic Co-operation and Development produced an excellent series of reports detailing best practices and recommendations in different countries: *Learning for Jobs OECD Reviews of Vocational Education and Training*.

Types of experience

Talented leaders with a record of success consistently report the value of experience. A broad range of experience in varying settings is fundamental. Studies across different organizations in different sectors across different corporate and national cultures, even different time epochs, reveal the same story. Talented leaders mention six powerful learning experiences.

Early work experience

The early work experience can vary broadly between people. There is no common job, or specific experience. The key similarity is an experience that seemed to teach a lifelong lesson. The experience could be an early part-time job, volunteer work experience, or practical work at school or university. The early experience is positive for some, where they enjoyed the work, found a lifelong passion, or learned skills that benefit them for the rest of their life; for others it is a tedious or frustrating summer job.

For some it was the unadulterated tedium or monotony which powerfully motivated them to avoid similar jobs in the future. The key similarity is the person learned some sort of important lesson, or gained personal insight from the experience. It could be a leader or colleague that inspired them, taught them skills or outlooks that they carried forth into future work. Or, it could have been an awful job experience that taught them what kind of work they did not want to do, what kind of person/employee/boss they did not want to be, or simply inspired them to work harder to never have to be in the same type of position. It should not be surprising, after reading the characteristics of potential like intelligence and conscientiousness, that potential high flyers will take any experience (positive or negative; success or failure) and use that experience to improve the chances of future success.

The experience of other people at work

This is something those with high potential will learn from. It is typically an immediate boss or mentor, but could also be a colleague or peer. As with the early work experience, they could be remembered as good or bad. The best and the worst are the most memorable, and both teach lessons. The good teachers and leaders teach through examples, provide exemplars of behaviours that lead to success. They also may provide feedback, advice and support. The worst leaders or role models also teach lessons to those who are willing to learn. They teach those with high potential how they don't want to be treated, and provide a reminder of how not to treat others. They model negative behaviours, or provide examples of behaviours that inhibit one's own success or organizational success.

The lesson from this is that a key aspect of developing employees is to ensure strong leaders can also act as mentors for those with high potential. It is also, to some degree, the responsibility of those with high potential to seek out people they can work with and learn from. High-potential employees should be aware of the development opportunities in the organization, and be aware of managers, bosses, teachers or colleagues who are willing or interested in mentoring others. For the high-potential employee it is a balance: be interested and receptive, but not too pushy and demanding.

Short-term assignments

Project work, standing in for another or interim management; this takes people out of their comfort zone and exposes them to issues and problems they have never confronted, so they learn quickly. For some it is the lucky break: serendipity provides an opportunity to find a new skill or passion.

First major line assignment

This is often the first promotion, foreign posting or departmental move to a higher position. It is frequently cited as important because suddenly the stakes were higher; everything becomes more complex, novel and ambiguous. There were more pressures and they were ultimately accountable. Suddenly the difficulties of management became real. The idea, then, is to think through appropriate 'stretch assignments' for talented people as soon as they arrive.

Hardships of various kinds

It is about attempting to cope in a crisis which may be professional or personal. It teaches the real value of things: technology, loyal staff and supportive head offices. The experiences are those of battle-hardened soldiers or the 'been there, done that' brigade. Hardship teaches many lessons: how resourceful and robust some people can be and how others panic and cave in. It teaches some to admire a fit and happy organization when they see it. It teaches them to distinguish between needs and wants. It teaches about stress management, as well as the virtues of stoicism, hardiness and a tough mental attitude.

Management development programs

Some remember and quote their MBA experience; far fewer, some specific (albeit an expensive) course. One or two quote the experience of receiving 360-degree feedback. More recall a coach, either because they were so good or so awful. This is bad news for trainers, business school teachers and coaches.

To the extent that leadership is acquired, developed and learnt, rather than 'gifted', it is achieved mainly through work experiences. Inevitably some experiences are better than others because they teach different lessons in different ways. Some people seem to acquire these valuable experiences despite, rather than as a result of, company policy.

Experiential learning takes time, but timing is important. It is not a steady, planned accumulation of insights and skills, but some experiences teach little or indeed bad habits.

Three factors conspire to defeat the experiential model. First, both young managers and their bosses want to short-circuit experience: learn faster, cheaper, better; hence, the appeal of the one-minute manager, the one-day MBA and the short course. Second, many HR professionals see the experiential approach as disempowering because they like to be 'in charge' of the leadership development programme. Third, some see experience as a test, not a developmental exercise.

Conclusion

Experience must be deliberate, targeted and provided to the right people at the right time. There is no substitute for good experience combined with support from excellent teachers, mentors and coaches. Yet experience alone is not enough. Most people will never be Olympic athletes, Nobel Prize winners, multinational CEOs or groundbreaking artists; there's nothing wrong with that. Certain individuals who are intelligent, motivated and guided by strong mentors, colleagues and peers benefit more from experience, and this is the focus of Chapter 10, Development. Although not everyone (by definition) will become a top performer, nearly everyone can benefit from experience. Different types of potential require different types of experience. The leader and strategist need a broad base of experience, while the technician or subject matter expert requires more targeted, consistent experience (see Figure 10.1 for updated dimensions of potential).

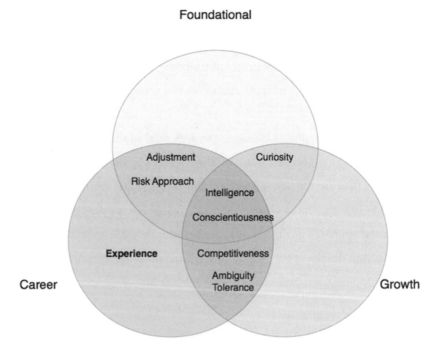

FIGURE 10.1 *Individual differences and dimensions of potential.*

11

Workplace culture
and values

In order that people may be happy in their work, these three things are needed: They need to be fit for it. They must not do too much of it. And they must have a sense of success in it.

– JOHN RUSKIN, *PRERAPHAELITISM*

It is not enough to good: one must do it the right way

– JOHN, *VISCOUNT MORLEY OF BLACKBURN*

Introduction

Some of the most useful, reliable and interesting psychological concepts are factors that are universal not just in humans, but are factors that can also be measured in animals. Intelligence, for example, is one of the most accurate predictors of workplace performance and leadership potential (MacRae and Furnham, 2014). One researcher estimated dogs' intelligence to be about on par with a 2-year-old child (Coren, 2009). Chimpanzees are a bit smarter (Hermann et al., 2010), and some crows can solve problems that elude most children under 5 (Cheke, 2012).

Why is this important? It's a useful comparison because concepts that are widely applicable, even beyond humans, can help to demonstrate the validity of the concept. Things like intelligence and culture that prove to be evolutionarily useful (like problem solving, language and culture) tend to develop across many different types of animals. And it matters to this chapter because *culture* is something that exists not just for humans, but clearly exists for other social animals as well. Apes, chimpanzees, some species of bird and even certain types of fish and whales exhibit culture.

When saying that chimps and birds demonstrate culture, we don't mean painting, art or great intellectual achievements. Nor do we mean how sociologists might talk about culture, including things like political discourse or national cultures and identities. By culture, we mean information that can be socially transferred that influences overall group behaviour (Laland and Hoppitt, 2003).

Example of cultural stability

Research with primates provides a useful example of culture, and how it can be remarkably consistent and stable between groups. Sapolsky (2006) explains how troops of baboons can develop and maintain distinctively aggressive or cooperative cultures, with clear differences between groups. Some baboon troops have authoritarian and violent cultures where high-status males are aggressive towards one another as well as inflict physical violence on innocent bystanders and others in the troop who have lower status or physical strength. In the aggressive cultures of baboons, social status is essentially determined by physical strength. Winning fights improves social status while losing a brawl diminishes social status. It's not difficult to extend this example to the workplace – many people can relate to the experience of management being a troop of aggressive baboons.

Affiliative troops of baboons are friendly, more cooperative, and show more prosocial behaviours (for baboons, this is grooming). In these groups there is less aggression overall, and the baboons who lose fights are less likely to be subsequently violent towards smaller baboons or the female baboons. These types of groups have more prosocial interactions between males and females, and are more tolerant of changes in social status. They also show dramatically lower level of 'bullying' behaviours – aggression that does occur is usually between those of similar status, instead of frequent aggression from the highest-status individuals towards the lowest-status individuals.

The most interesting finding from this animal research is that baboon troops can show consistent culture, even when no members of the original group remain (de Waal, 2004). Cultures where bullying is normal perpetuate and encourage the behaviour. Cultural differences can and do persist independently of any and all members of the group. The overall norms and acceptable behaviour within the group is learned by younger and new members. Aggressive cultures teach aggression; friendlier cultures breed collaboration.

Example of cultural change

Culture can change, but it usually takes a major shock to the system for things to change. Continuing with the research among non-human primates, many of the examples of significant culture change are caused by either a calamity that affects the group, or external intervention (in the cases of research, intervention by the researchers).

The first case, of a calamity that afflicts the group, was demonstrated in Sapolsky's (2006) research of baboons. An aggressive troop of baboons started to exploit a garbage dump at a nearby tourist camp for food. The most aggressive baboons would band together in early morning raids on the garbage dump. Then an outbreak of disease, linked to contaminated meat in the garbage dump, killed half of the troop. Half of the males, 50 per cent of the most aggressive males, died within a short period of time. This change caused an immediate and long-lasting change in the culture of the group. The aggressive culture quickly died out with the loss of aggressive individuals. Even after the troop's numbers recovered, the affiliative and cooperative culture persisted.

Another example of significant culture change comes with combining groups with different cultures (while the previous example is relevant to layoffs, think of this next example in terms of mergers and acquisitions).

What happens when you combine two groups with distinctly different cultures? De Wall and Johanowicz (1993) asked the very same question, and tried it with macaques. The results may seem surprising. They combined two different species of young macaques who are very similar but tend to have very distinct cultures: Rhesus macaques which are aggressive with 'despotic dominance hierarchies' displayed by both males and females; and stump-tailed macaques which have 'egalitarian' hierarchies that minimize aggression and tend to make up after fighting. It is also interesting to note that different cultures of monkeys within the same species often have different cultural behaviours for making up after conflict. For stump-tailed macaques 'the most characteristic conciliatory behaviour is the hold-bottom ritual, in which one individual (usually the subordinate) presents its hindquarters, and the other (usually the dominant) clasps the other's haunches' (de Wall and Ren, 1988). It should also be noted that while this is prosocial behaviour in macaques this is not acceptable workplace behaviour for humans, and will get you into serious trouble.

In this study, where both groups were combined, the authors found that the collaborative style emerged. They explained that a more relaxed, less competitive and combative environment was more conducive and a more successful strategy for the group than an aggressive and counterproductive culture.

This second finding cannot always be generalized to a workplace culture and combining groups with different cultures. Take the example from perhaps one of the most disastrous unions of all time (apart from a marriage to Henry

VIII or Elizabeth Taylor): the merger between Daimler-Benz AG and Chrysler Corporation to create DaimlerChrysler (Vlasic and Stertz 2000). At the time, it was the largest-ever merger, and it was that it would create a company with over $130 billion in sales and market value of over $90 billion. In theory, it looked like a good idea. Daimler had iconic German luxury brands like Mercedes. Chrysler produced cheap and cheerful American cars. At the time, the economy was booming and profits were high on both sides of the deal. It seemed like a perfect opportunity to combine Daimler-Benz's international reach and expertise with Chrysler's inexpensive, mass market vehicles.

But what happens when you combine that German luxury and efficiency with American agility at an attractive price point? Apparently, billions of dollars in losses. It was a culture clash between national cultures as well as corporate cultures, and the merger just never worked. Daimler's corporate culture was described as 'conservative efficient and safe' while Chrysler's was described as 'daring, diverse and creating' (Applebaum et al., 2009). The cultures and the personalities leading each culture never worked successfully together, and they eventually split up nine years later, with Daimler essentially paying US$650 million to get rid of the company that initially cost them US$36 billion.

The lesson is that culture exists in any team or group, whether in the workplace or in other species of animals. The fact that culture exists and is important is impossible to argue – but how it works and the matter of culture change is a more difficult issue (read MacRae and Furnham, 2017a for a more detailed analysis of this).

Social values and work

Values come mostly from social and cultural demands, whether those demands are obvious or subtle. Value systems are organized summaries of experience that capture the key, abstract qualities of past experience, specific 'right' and 'wrong' and function as a framework for evaluating present experience. Values may not always be conscious or deliberately constructed, but they are what make situations 'feel' right or wrong. People who value honesty dislike being lied to and would feel guilty or uncomfortable about telling an untruth. People who value traditions face familiar situations when they 'feel' right and automatically oppose the novel or unfamiliar.

A value is an enduring belief that a specific conduct and/or result is preferable. Once a value is internalized, it consciously or unconsciously becomes a standard criterion for guiding action: for developing and maintaining attitudes towards relevant objects and situations, for justifying one's own and others' actions and attitudes, for morally judging self and others, and for comparing oneself with others.

Value systems are systematically linked to culture of origin, religion, chosen university discipline, political persuasion, generations within a family, age, sex, personality and educational background (Feather, 1975). These values in time may determine vocational choice and occupational behaviour. There are many studies which show that these values (rank ordered) are related to occupational choice and success.

In Malcolm Gladwell's 2010 book *Outliers*, he describes how values and upbringing can influence career choice over generations. He charts the family tree of a tanner who emigrated from the United States to Poland late in the nineteenth century. There are many, similar family trees of Eastern European Jewish migrants whose show similar patterns of parents passing on values such as autonomy, and work ethic, and valuing a certain socioeconomic status (see Figure 11.1 for example).

There are many ways to sort and classify values, but people are often more able to identify and describe their own values than many other psychological constructs. And because values are social, not biological, there is far more room for re-ordering, varying classification systems and for structures and types of values to change over time and vary between cultures.

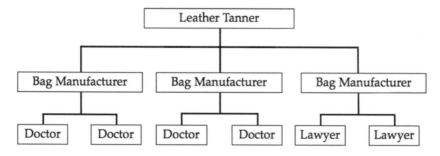

FIGURE 11.1 *Example of a family tree of professions*

The following list shows the terminal values from the famous Rokeach model. He argued that there were two types of values: instrumental and terminal. The former were ways of achieving the latter. There is an extensive literature going back sixty years on this model. It is to be expected that those who have been identified with talent and high potential differ in both their terminal and instrumental values. Little or no research seems currently available to substantiate this hypothesis though.

- A comfortable life (a prosperous life);

- An exciting life (a stimulating, active life);

- A sense of accomplishment (lasting contribution);

- A world at peace (free of war and conflict);

- A world of beauty (beauty of nature and the arts);

- Equality (equal opportunity for all);

- Family security (taking care of loved ones);

- Freedom (independence, free choice);

- Happiness (contentedness);

- Inner harmony (freedom from inner conflict);

- Mature love (sexual and spiritual intimacy);

- National security (protection from attack);

- Pleasure (an enjoyable, leisurely life);

- Salvation (saved, eternal life);

- Self-respect (self-esteem);

- Social recognition (respect, admiration);

- True friendship (close companionship); and

- Wisdom (a mature understanding of life).

Hogan has argued that a person's values are indicators of their motivations. This description has relied heavily on the work of Holland (1973).

What are the values of high flyers? The answer is twofold. First, it depends on the industry or sector the high flyer is working in. Second, it depends on the type of job the high flyer has: it is technical, managerial or strategic. One

TABLE 11.1 *Hogan's taxonomy of values*

Recognition	Desire to be known, seen, visible and famous, dreams of fame, high achievement.
Power	Desire to succeed, make things happen, outperform the competition.
Hedonistic	Pursuit of fun, excitement, pleasure and eating, drinking and entertainment.
Altruistic	Desire to help others, a concern for the welfare of less fortunate, public service.
Affiliation	Needing and enjoying frequent and varied social contact and a social lifestyle.
Tradition	A belief in and dedication to old-fashioned virtues: family, church, thrift, hard work.
Security	A need for predictability, structure and efforts to avoid risk and uncertainty and a lifestyle-minimizing errors and mistakes.
Commerce	Interest in earning money, realizing profits, finding new business opportunities, investments and financial planning.
Aesthetics	Need for self-expression, a dedication to quality and excellence, an interest in how things look, feel and sound.
Science	Being interested in science, comfortable with technology, preferring data based – as opposed to intuitive decisions, and spending time learning how things work.

recent study suggested that for most people in business the high flyer is low on recognition and hedonism, and high on power and affiliation. Few people become successful high flyers through pursuit of their own pleasure (although some make a go of it). Many value the position, the influence and the good work they can do in and for the company.

Clearly knowing the values of high flyers helps gives an insight into their motivation. It also can alert people to the possibility of value clashes between themselves, their colleagues and the organization as a whole. Our research shows, unsurprisingly, that high potentials value interest and engagement at work more than compensation, although the next chapter goes deeper into an interesting discussion of pay, finances and what can happen with a great deal of money and no financial transparency.

12

Motivators and attitudes

The most general survey shows us that the two foes of human happiness are pain and boredom.
– ARTHUR SCHOPENHAUER

It is too difficult to think nobly when one only thinks to get a living
– JEAN JACQUES ROUSSEAU, *LES CONFESSIONS*

Important components of high potential

There many hundreds of psychological tests and concepts that can be assessed. Some are obviously more relevant than others to understanding of the high flyer. We have summarized the most important.

Perceived control

Perceived control is one of the factors that links intention and behaviour. Those who believe they are in control of their own actions, and the results of those actions tend to be more proactive, seek more control and put in more effort to succeed. Perceived control describes whether they feel they are in control of their own actions and outcomes (internal locus of control) or outside forces control their outcomes and action (external locus of control). It assumes that individuals develop a general expectancy regarding their ability to control their lives.

People who believe that events result from their own behaviour and/ or ability, personality and effort are said to have the expectancy of internal control. Those with expectancies of external control believe events in their lives are caused by luck, chance, fate, God(s), powerful others or powers beyond their control, comprehension or manipulation are said to have an expectancy of external control. Managers with internal locus of control tend to see threatening events at work as less stressful and they cope with it better than managers with external locus of control.

Studies since the mid-1960s have found refreshingly consistent and convincing results which support the fact that internal locus of control (instrumentalism) is a cause and consequence of success, while external locus of control (fatalism) is a cause and consequence of failure. Results show the following:

- *Motivation:* Instrumentalists are more likely to believe good performance is a result of personal effort, and they have stronger beliefs in their own competence and abilities;

- *Job performance:* Instrumentalists perform better because of their greater effort, information seeking in complex task situations, and exhibit greater personal career effectiveness;

- *Job satisfaction:* Instrumentalists are more satisfied with their own performance and work than fatalists at work, partly because of their success, and partly because they believe their own actions are the main reason for their success;

- *Leadership:* Instrumentalists prefer participative approaches from their supervisors, rely more on personal persuasion with their colleagues and seem more task-orientated and less socially orientated;

- *Job perception:* Instrumentalists feel more control over their environment, request more feedback on the job and perceive less role strain;

- *Turnover:* Instrumentalists with high job satisfaction have the same rate of turnover (presumably low) as fatalists. But at low levels of job satisfaction, instrumentalists are much more likely to leave the job than fatalists. Instrumentalists believe they can do something about their unhappiness, and do; fatalists are more likely to continue along their current path, believing nothing they do will have an effect on outcomes.

There is considerable evidence to suggest that personality traits and cognitive abilities are significantly and logically related to general as well as work-specific locus of control beliefs. For example, those with higher conscientiousness tend to feel more internal locus of control. Thus, these beliefs may moderate or mediate the relationship between traits, abilities and work-related outcomes. Those with high conscientiousness tend to have more confidence in their ability to control situations so they in turn are more likely to plan, act and succeed.

The Protestant work ethic (PWE)

The concept of the PWE was devised by the German sociologist Max Weber (1905), who saw it as a part of the explanation for the origin of capitalism. People who believe in the PWE tend to be achievement- and success-orientated, stress the need for efficacy and practicality, tend to be more dismissive of leisure pursuits, and are conservative and conscious of wasting time, energy and money.

Despite all the argument and research on the PWE, there are relatively few clear statements on the actual constituents of the PWE. The PWE can be summarized as follows:

A universal taboo is placed on idleness, while industriousness is considered a religious ideal; waste is a vice, and frugality a virtue; complacency and failure are outlawed, and ambition and success are taken as sure signs of God's favour; the universal sign of sin is poverty which is perceived a indicating sloth, and the crowning sign of God's favour is wealth.

Cherrington (1980) listed eight attributes of the PWE. The broader meaning of the work ethic typically refers to one or more of the following beliefs:

- People have a normal and religious obligation to fill their lives with heavy physical toil. For some, this means that hard work, effort and drudgery are to be valued for their own sake; physical pleasures and enjoyments are to be shunned; and an ascetic existence of methodological rigour is the only acceptable way to live;

- Men and women are expected to spend long hours at work, with little or no time for personal recreation and leisure;

- A worker should have a dependable attendance record, with low absenteeism, and tardiness;

- Workers should be highly productive, and produce a large quantity of goods or service;

- Workers should take pride in their work and do their jobs well;

- Employees should have feelings of commitment and loyalty to their profession, their company, and their work group;

- Workers should be achievement-orientated and should constantly strive for promotion and advancement. High-status jobs with prestige and the respect of others are important indicators of a 'good' person; and

- People should acquire wealth through honest labour and retain it through thrift and wise investments. Frugality is desirable; extravagance and waste should be avoided.

At the centre of the concept of the PWE is the idea that the values and beliefs underlying the PWE (morality, control, postponement of gratification, asceticism, hard work) actually lead to economic success on both an individual and a national level. In this sense the PWE can be conceived as a personally held belief system that is predictive of economic success. The latest measure of the PWE assesses seven beliefs:

- *The centrality of work:* The belief in work for its own sake; the central part of one's life;

- *Self-Reliance:* The value of striving for independence and success at work;

- *Hard Work:* Belief in the virtue of hard work – long hours, intense concentration;

- *Leisure:* A belief in productive leisure;

- *Morality and Ethics:* A strong sense of justice at work;

- *Delay of Gratification:* An orientation to the future and an ability to postpone rewards; and

- *Wasted time:* A stress on the productive use of time.

Work passion

Over a twenty-year period Vallerand and colleagues worked on the psychology of passion. Vallerand and colleagues (2008) defined passion as a 'strong inclination toward an activity that people like, find important and in which they invest their time and energy' (p. 1). Over time people discover that some activities rather than others seem to satisfy their needs for competence, autonomy and relatedness. They thus become a passionate, self-defining, identity-determining activity into which people put their time and energy. Passion has powerful emotional outcomes and relates strongly to the persistence in many activities.

He distinguished between healthy harmonious (HP) and unhealthy obsessive passion (OP). He suggests HP is the personal acceptance and internalization of an activity into a person's identity when they freely accept the activity as important for them. It is done voluntarily, and is not forced. HP for an activity is an important, but not overpowering, part of identity and is in harmony with other aspects of a person's life. People who are passionate about their work will say things like, 'I am a skier', instead of, 'I like to ski'. On the other hand, the drivers of OP are essentially specific factors like self-esteem, excitement or self-acceptance. OP clearly has an addictive quality about it because it is perhaps the only source of important psychological rewards such as personal satisfaction and feelings of self-worth. In this sense workaholism is a sign of OP, not HP.

The theory suggests that HP leads to more flexibility, which leads to more engagement through the process of absorption, concentration, flow and positive feelings – otherwise known as work engagement, because it is so important to retention. OP, on the other hand, leads to more rigid and conflicted task performance which reduces engagement. HP controls the activity; OP is controlled by it. The former promotes healthy adaptation while the latter thwarts it.

The question is how organizations can encourage HP, rather than OP. The answer is to 'provide employees with a healthy, flexible, and secure working environment, one where their opinion is valued, will create conditions that facilitate the development of harmonious passion ... organizational support seems to foster an autonomous-supportive context that allows individuals to internalize the activity in their identity in an autonomous fashion' (p. 193). We will discuss the related topics of engagement and flow in Chapter 22, Retention, along with how to improve work engagement.

Happiness at work

The word 'happiness' means several different things (joy, satisfaction) and therefore many psychologists prefer the term 'subjective well-being' (SWB), which is an umbrella term that includes the various types of evaluation of one's own life and feelings about it. It can include self-esteem, joy, feelings of fulfilment. The essence is that the person him-/herself is making the evaluation of their own life. Thus the person is the expert here: is my life going well, according to the standards that I choose to use?

It has also been suggested that there are three primary components of SWB: general satisfaction, the presence of pleasant affect and the absence of negative emotions including anger, anxiety, guilt, sadness and shame. More importantly, SWB covers a wide scale, from ecstasy to agony: from extreme happiness to great gloom and despondency. It relates to long-term states, not just momentary moods. It is not sufficient but probably a necessary criterion for mental or psychological health.

Many researchers have listed a number of myths about the nature and cause of happiness. The first books on the psychology of happiness started appearing in the 1980s. Then a few specialist academic journals appeared but it was not until the turn of the millennium that the positive psychology movement was galvanized into action by significant grant money and research focus of many famous psychologists.

The relatively recent advent of studies on happiness, sometimes called SWB, has led to a science of wellbeing (Huppert et al., 2005). Argyle (2001) noted that different researchers had identified different components of happiness like life satisfaction, positive affect, self-acceptance, positive relations with others, autonomy and environmental mastery. It constitutes joy, satisfaction and other related positive emotions.

Myers (1992) noted the stable and unstable characteristics of happy people. They tend to be creative energetic, decisive, flexible and sociable. They also tend to be more forgiving, loving, trusting and responsible. They tolerate frustration better and are more willing to help those in need. In short they feel good, so do good. Diener (2000) has defined SWB as how people cognitively and emotionally evaluate their lives. It has an evaluative (good-bad) as well as a hedonic (pleasant-unpleasant) dimension.

Need for cognition

One variable that has been shown to relate to both intelligence and personality traits is the need for cognition (NFC). This was introduced by Cacioppo and Petty (1982) as a stable personality trait relating to the tendency to engage in and enjoy effortful cognitive activity. It is similar to the HPTI trait curiosity (see Chapter 6). Individuals high in NFC tend to seek out information when faced with a problem.

They also think about and reflect on issues, use more rational arguments and are more open to new ideas. Individuals who are low in NFC, by contrast, tend to use cognitive heuristics, relying on others for information or opinion. NFC is not an ability to think, but an intrinsic motivation to think, and indeed correlates strongly with various measures of intrinsic motivation. Tanaka et al. (1988), for example, identified three factors which they labelled cognitive persistence (enjoyment of engaging in cognitive tasks), cognitive confidence (confidence about engaging in cognitive activities) and cognitive complexity (preference for complex or simple information processing demands).

Typical intellectual engagement

Goff and Ackerman (1992) developed the Typical Intellectual Engagement (TIE) scale as a measure of an individual's typical level of intelligence and developed a self-report scale to assess this instead of a measure of an individual's level of intelligence. Higher scores mean stronger inclination to engage in intellectual activities. Sample items of the TIE scale are 'You enjoy thinking out complicated problems', 'The notion of thinking abstractly is not appealing to me (reverse scored)' and 'I read a great deal'.

The conceptual importance of TIE is advocated on the basis of possible differences in individuals' level of intellectual investment. Two individuals with the same IQ score or top performance may differ in their level of intellectual investment or typical performance. The theory of TIE posits that an individual's level of intellectual investment will have positive developmental effects on the acquisition of adult skills and knowledge. This theory implies that typical performance may be as important in determining future intellectual competence as is maximal performance; in simple terms, a personality may explain differences in adult intellectual competence where ability may not. TIE may refer to aspects of typical performance not encompassed by other, established personality traits and is therefore of potential value for expanding our understanding of individual differences, in particular with regard to the dispositional or trait determinants of educational achievement.

Entrepreneurial spirit

Many, but not all, high flyers tend to have an entrepreneurial spirit. There are various components to this including ideas as need for achievement. Those who have high need for achievement tend to:

- Exercise some control over the means of production and produce more than they consume;

- Set moderately difficult goals for themselves;

- Try to maximize likelihood of achievement satisfaction;

- Want concrete and regular feedback on how well they are doing;

- Like assuming personal responsibility for problems;

- Show high initiative and exploratory behaviour in their environment;

- Continually research the environment for opportunities of all sorts;

- Regard growth and expansion as the most direct signs of success; and

- Continually strive to improve (the Japanese concept of kaizen).

Entrepreneurs show a number of clear behaviour patterns. They tend to be proactive and opportunistic. They are always after efficiency and high-quality work. They can be very driven and competitive. They show deep commitment to others and their business relationships.

Motivation

Motivation is an 'energizing force that induces action' (Parks and Guay, 2009). Over sixty years ago a group of psychologists led by Herzberg developed the most important theory of motivation, which is still relevant today. Hertzberg et al.'s (1959) *Two-factor theory* explains how there are two main factors that motivate or demotivate people at work. One factor is directly responsible for *job satisfaction*, while the other main factor is responsible for *dissatisfaction.*

Certain job characteristics related to what a person *does* at work such as achievement, independence and a sense of pride in work lead to a sense of satisfaction. However, dissatisfaction came from a quite specific but very different set of factors at work. Problems with job factors like company policy, poor management, disappointing pay packets or insufficient compensation were more directly linked with dissatisfaction.

The two-factor theory makes a clear distinction between:

- **Motivating Factors** such as challenging work, recognition for one's achievement, being given responsibility, opportunity to do something meaningful, involvement in decision-making, sense of importance to an organization. These together give positive satisfaction, arising from intrinsic conditions of the job itself, such as recognition, achievement or personal growth. These factors are now more commonly referred to as *intrinsic motivation.*

- **Hygiene Factors** such as job security, salary, fringe benefits, work conditions, good pay, paid insurance and vacations paradoxically do not give positive satisfaction or motivation, though dissatisfaction results from their absence. The term 'hygiene' is used in the sense that these are maintenance factors. These are extrinsic to the work itself, and include aspects such as company policies, supervisory practices or wages/salary. These factors are now more commonly referred to as *extrinsic motivation.*

Factors and facets of motivation

The most enduring model of motivation is based on two factors. While there have been minor modifications to these two factors over decades of research, the original two factor model holds up surprisingly well.

Although this has been tested, tweaked and honed over the past decades, it is remarkably similar to its initial conception. Findings consistently demonstrate two main motivational factors. Like all good science, the theory has endured because research findings consistently demonstrate the two-factor model works.

Thus, in the most basic sense, there are two different types of motivation.

- **Intrinsic Factors** that are internal to the person such as challenging work, recognition for one's achievement, being given responsibility, opportunity to do something meaningful, involvement in decision-making, sense of importance to an organization.

- **Extrinsic Factors** that are external to the person such as job security, salary, fringe benefits, work conditions, good pay, paid insurance, vacations.

The science has been refined further and MacRae and Furnham (2017a) explain the facets of intrinsic and extrinsic motivation in the workplace.

The three facets of intrinsic motivation are:

- **Autonomy** which means a focus on engagement, active participation and stimulation and personal development. Those which are motivated by autonomy want a job that is consistent with their own passions, career development or self-expression.

- **Accomplishment** means being motivated by achievement, advancement and visible success. It often is related to a desire for promotion, power, status and recognition. People who highly value this want to be known either publicly, within the company or within their team for their accomplishments at work.

- **Affiliation.** Social responsibility, passing on knowledge, teaching and instruction and working with others. Those who value affiliation prefer to work with others, like to pass on their knowledge and experience, and value the social aspects of work.

- The three extrinsic facets are:

  - **Security** involves job security, personal safety as well as consistency and regularity. This could mean a job in a company or profession with a long-established history, consistent reputation or clear organizational culture. Valuing security is a focus on stability, consistency and reliability.

  - **Compensation** includes material rewards such as pay, insurance, bonuses and job perks that are easily measurable, counted and defined. It may also include other perks or advantages that make work life a bit easier: a convenient location, a nicer office or a more desirable working schedule.

- ○ **Conditions** include elements of safety and security and personal convenience. Conditions require that a job fit within the person's lifestyle and provide an environment conducive to their needs and comfort.

So one interesting and persistent question that always comes up at work is the relative importance of pay. What is the role of money in work? Of course, it is an essential part of work, and most people would not show up to work every day if they were not being paid (although some still would). For a detailed discussion about how extrinsic and intrinsic factors motivate people at work, see MacRae and Furnham's (2017a) book *Motivation and performance: A guide to motivating a diverse workforce*. Another interesting issue, though, is about pay and confidentiality.

Should pay be kept confidential?

Most companies and countries maintain a level of confidentiality and privacy. In the UK one's personal tax returns are between that person and Her Majesty's Revenue and Customs. Similar privacy arrangements exist in most countries – except for some notable exceptions like Norway, Finland, Sweden and Pakistan.

The issue of pay and confidentiality is an interesting but complex one, with no clear-cut answer. Do people have the right to privacy or confidentiality? Or a responsibility to publicly report their income and assets? On the surface it seems that other people reporting their incomes might be a good thing, but would you be comfortable disclosing your own income or assets? A YouGov poll suggested that 52 per cent of people surveyed said they would be comfortable disclosing their income while 30 per cent of people were opposed (Lilico, 2016).

Pay is a thorny issue and there are strong arguments both for and against it, and it is worth considering transparency and privacy at individual and corporate levels.

Why people want pay to be kept confidential

There are strong arguments for keeping personal income private and confidential. If your income levels are published and publicly available, it becomes remarkably easy for criminals and marketers alike to target people based on their income. It also makes it easier for those same people to target individuals based on their source of income or specific assets.

Publicly available statements of personal income could also lead to challenges in the labour market. Imagine someone looking for a new job with higher salary. It could become far more difficult if the employer could see the person's previous (or current) income level. Or what if an employer could easily see that someone had a lucrative hobby or recently had a windfall from inheritance or some other source, is that really a piece of information one would be happy to share with the world without any choice in the matter?

The other uncomfortable fact about publicly available income records is that it allows co-workers, friends, family and neighbours to see how much everyone else earns. Envy or resentment can be an uncomfortable by-product from perceived inequality.

The argument against: Transparency prevents corruption

The argument for transparency in personal income is equally straightforward: transparency prevents corruption. There is precedent for this in some countries. In Norway, tax returns have been a matter of public record since the early nineteenth century (Collinson, 2016). Interestingly three countries that publish tax returns are some of the least corrupt in the world. Finland scored as having the second-lowest corruption by Transparency International (2015), with Sweden the third and Norway coming fifth. The fourth country publishing tax returns, Pakistan, was rated as highly corrupt (117 out of 168 countries).

The Norwegians introduced a new limitation to prevent nosy neighbours and envious rivalries. Records are still public, but when someone looks at your tax records you will be notified. Your neighbour may still be snooping around your financial information, but at least you will know what they are doing. Indeed, after this new rule was introduced in 2014 the number of requests for tax information fell substantially (Collinson, 2016).

It's also difficult to compare countries like Norway and Sweden to countries like the USA and UK because of the substantially different levels of income inequality. Norway has one of the lowest levels of income inequality in the OECD developed nations (OECD, 2015), with Sweden and Finland also being relatively low. The USA and UK were ranked in the top 6 for income inequality in the OECD developed countries. It may be that countries with higher levels of income equality are more reticent about publishing individual income levels.

Another consideration is that transparency does not automatically lead to change. Slemrod (2005) suggested that even when there is public stigma towards tax avoidance or evasion it does not always discourage the behaviour. Companies or individuals may actually use public records to disclose or demonstrate their 'tax efficiency' or lower payments in comparison to competitors. Disclosure alone does not always achieve the desired behaviour.

Example of closed records and corruption

To turn to an example of completely secret and impenetrable records let's turn to the example of the 'Vatican Bank' (Instituto per le Opere di Religione, or Institute for the Works of Religion in English) and its complex international financial arrangements and strange interdependencies with the notoriously volatile Italian banking system. The following example may seem like an excessively convoluted way of demonstrating the point – but keep in mind these are the types of corrupt arrangements that emerge without transparency.

Gerald Posner (2015) provides a fascinating account of the interesting, convoluted and often corrupt workings of a bank that somehow found itself in a unique state with special exemptions and an impenetrable veil of secrecy. It developed into a sprawling network of offshore holding companies. One of its many scandals revolves around three interesting characters with intricate and inscrutable finances.

Within a dizzying sphere of complex networks, one interesting character in the story is Michele Sindona, close friend and special advisor to Pope Paul VI who was one of Italy's most renowned tax attorneys in the 1950s and 1960s. He partnered with the Vatican Bank starting in 1960 as both started up buying large stakes in Italian banks, property development companies among other investments. Sindona severed on dozens of company boards alongside other Vatican Bank representative. As Sindona's wealth and influence rapidly increase he founded an international currency clearing house (partnering with the Vatican Bank, among others) which was eventually trading about $200 billion annually.

Sindona met with our second interesting character, Archbishop Paul Marcinkus in the late 1960s. Marcinkus was also a close friend and advisor of Pope Paul VI, and Marcinkus climbed to a controlling position in the Vatican Bank, and then became its president in 1971. Marcinkus, an American archbishop, was an extremely influential figure in the pope's dealings with the English-speaking world, as well as the business dealings of the Vatican Bank around the world.

The third character relevant to this story is Roberto Calvi, a prominent Italian banker who had risen quickly through the ranks of Banco Ambrosiano to become chairman of the bank in 1963 and then the general manager of Ambrosiano in 1971. Calvi was initially very successful in finding novel and innovative ways to invest in foreign markets (far ahead of other Italian banks). Calvi met Sindona in 1969 to devise a plan to free up much of Ambrosiano's capital for more risky and speculative overseas investments. To convince the bank's conservative board, Calvi and Sindona got the backing of Marcinkus and the Vatican Bank for overseas investment.

Much of this coincided with civil unrest in Italy during the 1960s, various new government taxes that would hit the Vatican Bank's process, and work around the tax-free status it had enjoyed on investments and earnings. Towards the end of the 1960s, and by the early 1970s the Vatican Bank had sold controlling stakes in all of its Italian holdings and began moving the money overseas. This included a dizzying array of new shell companies around the world from Luxembourg to the Bahamas, Costa Rica and Panama, some of the countries which most prided themselves on strict client secrecy. For example, Calvi used a Luxembourg holding company to create the 'Cisalpine Overseas Bank in Nassau'. Shortly after, Archbishop Marcinkus joined the board of Cisalpine in the Bahamas.

If this all sounds complicated, it is just scratching the surface – and that's without going into allegations that Sindona was using these complex financial systems to launder drug money, or (unproven) American allegations that the Vatican Bank was laundering fake US Treasury Bills. Sindona was, however, arrested by the FBI and charged with sixty-five counts including fraud, perjury and misappropriation of bank funds. He died in prison in 1984 when too much cyanide found its way into his coffee.

Roberto Calvi also came to an unfortunate end, after years of scandal through the late 1970s and early 1980s. While Calvi was implicated in widespread fraud, the Vatican bank's direct knowledge of these actions could never be legally proved, so the Holy See seems to have been absolved (although they did pay $224 million to Ambrosiano creditors after the bank collapsed). Calvi went missing in Rome in 1982, and under mysterious circumstances was discovered dead, hanging from Blackfriars Bridge in London.

The point of this story is to illustrate some of the fantastically corrupt and dishonest behaviour that can result and spread from lack of financial accountability, transparency and oversight. With complete secrecy, companies and organizations can get up to all sorts of naughtiness and misbehaviour. The example above is only a small, but convoluted and fascinating, example of what can go wrong.

Contrast this with individual cases of pay, where there should be proper oversight within the companies, perhaps by shareholders, and ultimately through Her Majesty's Revenue and Customers or other national tax authorities. Completely opaque finances can lend themselves to creative accounting and misbehaviour, but a certain degree of individual privacy is less problematic.

Conclusion

Understanding the role of motivation and attitudes at work is important to understanding why people do what they do (or do not do). We discuss in detail the example of money, because money can be a taboo topic in many cultures and often leads to a desire for privacy. But it's also important to consider the level of accountability at individual, companywide or nationwide levels to manage performance and ensure ethical conduct takes place. The same is true of understanding all factors of motivating people at work, and understanding motives and attitudes.

13

The dark side and derailment

Bad appointments to office are a threefold inconvenience: they are an injury to public business; they dishonor the prince; and they are a kind of robbery of those who deserve advancement.

– FREDERICK THE GREAT

One must do violence to the object of one's desire; when it surrenders, the pleasure is greater.

– MARQUIS DU SADE

Introduction

It is an interesting time to study what makes people derail and fail. There has been a growing interest in the dark side of personality at work, and that interest is only getting stronger. Dark side personality traits can help to explain why people who are overly confident beyond their abilities often overextend themselves. It helps to explain why people who are narcissistic, self-obsessed braggarts eventually alienate the people around them. Often the darker side of people's personalities can help them succeed in the workplace. Yet traits and behaviours that sometimes bring short-term success like narcissism, bullying, manipulativeness, chronic lying and demanding flattery can also lead to a person's ultimate downfall at work.

Interest in leadership failure, sometimes called derailment, is not new, but it is growing rapidly. Its importance continues to generate greater and greater interest. Publications about leadership failure have been steadily increasing for the past decade. Typically much more is written about leadership *success* than leadership *failure*. The chart below shows the rise of books published on leadership success and failure. The Google n-gram (in Figure 13.1) shows how frequently these terms appear in Google's library.

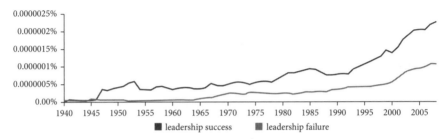

FIGURE 13.1 *Google n-gram showing frequency of the terms 'leadership success' and 'leadership failure'.*

The previous chapters have primarily focused on positive traits and desirable outcomes at work. The focus has mainly been on high potential to *succeed*, not high potential to *fail*. Desirable traits are important to predicting high potential, but sometimes individuals with many desirable characteristics can also have a dark side, or destructive potential.

Leaders sometimes fail because they are incompetent or inexperienced, or sometimes they seem to have potential because of their experience or past performance but then fail because they do not have enough of a desired characteristic, like intelligence, conscientiousness or adjustment. They also fail and derail through the extremes of traits like risk taking which can turn into thrill seeking, or self-esteem which may balloon into narcissism.

One common reason that potential derailment is missed is because people who are viewed as high potential are selected based on 'selecting in' factors but potential 'selecting out' factors go unnoticed or ignored. In other words selectors look for the good, but completely forget about the dark or derailment factors that could lead employees astray. 'Selecting out' implies looking for evidence of the traits that could potentially cause problems and lead to derailment. There are any number of potential derailment factors like arrogance, paranoia and being overly emotional. These, along with other characteristics, can be used to identify potential derailment. They are often ignored because they don't appear on the competency checklist, and job descriptions rarely include *undesirable criteria*. But ignore these characteristics at your peril. As Lloyd Craig put it (interviewed in Chapter 6), 'check references, do thorough background checks, don't hire assholes'.

Undesirable, 'dark side' traits can inhibit leadership potential and can lead to situations and behaviours that can derail whole careers and organizations. But keep in mind that desirable and undesirable characteristics are not always mutually exclusive. People who are clever can also be cruel; people who are open to new experiences can get themselves into trouble in many new and creative ways; the greatest charmers can convince people to do unpleasant things; the motivated and dedicated can become committed to the wrong causes and prop up toxic leaders.

Derailment potential is another facet of the question, *potential to do what?* It is perilous to ignore. In derailment potential, the question can be framed as *potential to do what damage?* Derailment can be limited to an individual career, but can easily and quickly spill over to derail entire teams, departments or organizations. Estimates suggest that somewhere between one half and three quarters of managers will 'derail' (Dalal and Nolan, 2009). The effects of derailment vary significantly depending on the individual's position and power in the organization. It should not be surprising that derailment is very common, and is exacerbated by the fact that most people do not recognize or look for the signs of derailment. The problem of derailment potential is something that many leaders fail to spot, or even when they do notice the warning signs they do not deal with the problem swiftly enough.

Bad, Sad or Mad?

Not all derailment is the same, nor does it happen for the same reason. Sometimes people find themselves in difficult situations at work they are just not equipped or experienced enough to deal with. Other times people have traits that make them prone to aggressive or self-destructive behaviour. Other times, difficult circumstances bring out the worst in people that no one noticed previously. In the most basic sense, derailment can be sorted into three different categories (Furnham, 2010).

Bad

Looking at the dark side of personality at work, 'bad' means the person has dysfunctional, underlying personality traits that lead them towards purposely and consciously destructive, mischievous, immoral or autocratic behaviours. This means that people are explicitly or deceitfully ignoring the interests of colleagues, the purpose of the organization, the shareholders or basic decency and morality. They have destructive tendencies that they spread around them, causing difficulty and destruction. Of course morality and group interests have a subjective element. But in the context of 'bad', bad leaders and the bad sort of derailment are primarily about self-interest trumping all other priorities and overriding the interests of others. They often make poor leaders because they use their power in an entirely self-serving way and actually enjoy seeing the damage they cause to others.

- *Bad derailment of high potential:* These are the people who deliberately set about to personally benefit from power, cause mayhem or enjoy hurting others. They may overtly show aggressive or bullying behaviours but are often the best at appearing to be high potential, even when they are not. They may present different images to different people, charming their boss, flattering clients and bullying subordinates. Their ambition tends to expand even as their abilities plateau. They are usually driven by greed and excitement and have no problem if they fail to obey legal and moral obligations in their role. They will quickly drive a team or company into the ground either because they do not care about the consequences or because they enjoy the carnage.

Mad

Mad leaders have some sort of subclinical disorder. Instead of deliberate destructiveness, mad suggests psychological illness or instability. These tendencies may be a driver of initial success as well as ultimate failure. Or, it can be illness or mental instability that develops, sometimes because of the demands, pressures and rewards of the position. In *The Hubris Syndrome* David Owen (2012) describes how the benefits of power can become intoxicating and distort behaviours and values while a leader is in power. What Owen calls the Hubris Syndrome is a description of how prolonged exposure to unchecked power can turn attitudes and behaviour toxic. Owen uses the case of Tony Blair, which will be discussed later in this chapter. They often make poor leaders because they have underlying instabilities that emerge when under the strain and pressure imposed by power.

- *Mad derailment of high potential:* The person appears to have all of the right characteristics, all the desirable attributes that make a good leader, but their 'dark side' attributes are minimal, dormant or concealed. The person may not even realize their own tendencies towards instability,

and they likely do not set out with malicious intent. They may initially
be highly confident and self-assured and good at self-promotion, which
helps their progression. As they are promoted into more senior positions,
with more responsibility, the job demands begin to take their toll.
What was once cheerful self-promotion becomes self-aggrandisement.
Confidence gives way to frenetically protecting their feelings of self-worth
and competence, all at the expense of productivity. This is not to say this
will happen to most people, but overwhelming situations can bring out
the worst (or the best) in people.

Sad

Sad leaders' derailment is unassuming and not intentionally mischievous.
This is the case of the optimist who has performed very well, but does not
realize that he would be entirely deficient in more demanding or complex
roles. This is the most common derailment that comes from simple optimism,
overestimation or lack of self-awareness. They misread the signs of high
potential, or their manager does not realize they are not competent for the
newer, more demanding role. It is usually cased, essentially, by misreading the
signs of high potential. It is what's known as a false positive: seeing something
(in oneself, or someone else) where it doesn't exist. They often make poor
leaders because they are ultimately not competent for the leadership role.

- *Sad derailment of high potential*: The person is assessed poorly;
  intelligence, experience and other traits are overestimated either because
  of poor tools or inexperienced assessors. The person is promoted
  beyond their abilities, struggles through positions they cannot handle
  and eventually they leave or are removed. They may just think the 'game
  is not worth the candle' and give up, opting for a quieter life with less
  demanding work requirements.

TABLE 13.1 *Career markers of bad, mad and sad derailers*

	Bad	Mad	Sad
Reasons for Selection	Manipulative, misleading, deception	Failure to screen for negative traits	Poor assessment, excessive optimism
Reasons for Advancement	Deceptive, manipulative, convince people of their potential whether it is real or not	Problematic traits mistaken for positive (aggression as courage, narcissism as confidence, psychopathy as charm)	Need position filled, lack of qualified individuals, misguided selection criteria
Reasons for Derailment	Hit-and-run approach, trail of destruction eventually catches up	Hubris, dark side traits dominate under stressful situations	Doesn't meet expectations, not competent, insufficient leadership or skill

Table 13.1 summarizes the three general categories of derailment, and why people are selected, promoted and reasons they can derail.

Bad apples or bad barrels?

Derailment is not just about internal factors, and particularly in the case of 'sad' derailment, a person may just be caught up in events and forces around them. It is necessary, when thinking about derailment, to consider what derailment potential is internal to the person (inability, illness, immorality) and which forces are external and that arise from the situation, such as lack of oversight, rewards for misbehaviour, workplace cultures that allow or endorse unethical behaviour, or poor role models. Many people have the experience, especially early in their careers, of being part of an organization or group where situational or social pressures can drastically change their behaviour;

new job demands, new environments and expectations all impact behaviour. New organizations, groups or peers can all influence a person's behaviour, especially when that person doesn't know how to behave in a new situation.

There is an ongoing argument in psychology about whether derailment comes from within people, and can be attributed to their personality and other individual traits. Whereas social psychologists put more emphasis on the social situations, and external factors that influence a person to act in certain ways. The debate is far from settled, but we can firmly say that both are important. People behave in certain ways based on their own individual attributes, but external forces also influence how people behave.

Phillip Zimbardo describes how quickly and strongly situational forces (bad barrels) can create bad apples. Zimbardo was responsible for the landmark Stanford Prison Experiment. He conducted a study with twenty-four young, middle class college students. In only five days the study turned these healthy and psychologically stable young men into terrifyingly real captives and prison guards. The students were assigned, randomly, to be either prison guards or prisoners. The prisoners were taken from their homes in a mock arrest, and placed in a makeshift prison in Stanford. The guards were given matching uniforms and equipment, and assigned the task of arresting, managing and disciplining the 'prisoners'. Within days, the prison became what Zimbardo (2008) describes as a 'descent into Hell' (p. 39).

The prison guards became cruel and abusive captors, finding elaborate and appalling techniques to make the prisoners behave. Figure 13.3 shows some of the key differences in behaviours between prisoners and guards. Guards became more aggressive, threatening and abusive, although there was nothing in their personality or particular psychological makeup that would predispose them to such behaviour any more than the prisoner.

Zimbardo himself stresses his own complicity in allowing unethical behaviour to flourish because of improper oversight and commitment to the continuation of the experiment, despite moral issues. Zimbardo said that in his

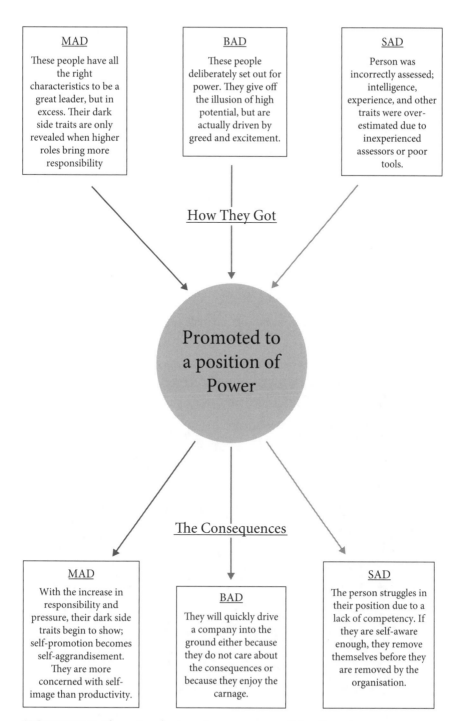

FIGURE 13.2 *The antecedents and consequences of derailment*

dual role, as researcher and prison warden, he too got caught up in the details of the experiment, he protected and continued the experiment because of his own investiture its continuation. However, he acknowledges in hindsight it should have been shut down much earlier.

This is an example of how a 'bad barrel', in this case a simulated prison, can create 'bad apples', the guards and even a 'bad' experimenter/warden. Yet after terminating the experiment, Zimbardo became one of the strongest advocates for ethical oversight and control in psychological research. People derail, and can turn toxic in the wrong environment, but can recover and learn from errors. *The Lucifer Effect* (2008) describes the Stanford Prison experiment as well as the more wide-ranging moral and social implications is well worth a read.

Zimbardo in later years thoroughly investigated causes of unethical behaviour, and the transformation of 'normal' and 'healthy' people into bad

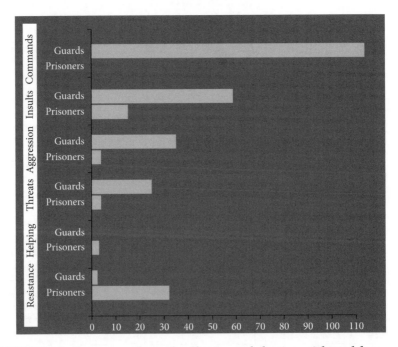

FIGURE 13.3 *Frequency of guard and prisoner behaviour. Adapted from Zimbardo (2008).*

apples. He investigated and testified on behalf of members of the US Armed Forces, who had been involved in torture and sadistic behaviour at Abu Ghraib prison in Iraq. He testified that lack of oversight and unhealthy organizational culture creates an environment when most normal, healthy, promising and possible high-potential people seriously misbehave. In the case of Abu Ghraib, where a group of soldiers humiliated and tortured Iraqi prisoners, there is obviously no excuse, no escaping the personal accountability of bad behaviour.

The lesson to be learned is what can be done to stop bad behaviour from developing: in other words, reducing people's derailment potential. It must be shut down from the top. In Abu Ghraib, military prison guards had no training as prison guards; they worked twelve-hour shifts with few or no breaks, seven days a week. Prison guards who were normally physically athletic had no time to exercise and did not take regular meals. Guards reported constant fear of prisoners, of Iraqi guards, and constant fear of external attack that created mounting exhaustion with little supervision, training or oversight. The message is not that people are not responsible for their own behaviour, but there are systematic factors, neglect from leaders, lack of oversight and threatening environments that can drastically alter behaviour and lead people into very bad behaviours.

Bad apples are sometimes born rotten, but they can be and are created by situation and circumstance.

David Owen describes how power, combined with the right conditions, can create a 'bad barrel' by what he describes as *The Hubris Syndrome*. Owen uses political leaders as an example, focusing particularly on the recent example of Tony Blair and George Bush's handling of international affairs after 11 September 2001. He describes Tony Blair launching himself onto the world stage as a forceful personality, personally dedicated to forming an international coalition for the invasion of Iraq. He was charming; he seemed to have boundless energy, combined with enthusiasm for the big picture but a poor grasp of the details. Limited planning, with nearly delusional optimism, led George Bush to stand under a banner proclaiming 'Mission Accomplished' in Iraq on an aircraft carrier off the coast of California in 2003, eight years before American troops withdrew from Iraq.

Owen's book details the failures of planning, combined with the hubris of both Bush and Blair, working together on a vision while ignoring the details and much of the evidence that was available at the time. Zimbardo's Stanford Prison Experiment, the abuse of prisoners at Abu Ghraib prison in Iraq and the way Blair and Bush presented the evidence for invading Iraq all had three key elements in common that led to derailment and abuses of the system: this is typically referred to as the *toxic triangle* which the next chapter delves into in more detail.

14

The toxic triangle and derailment prevention

Successful and fortunate crime is called virtue
– SENECA, *HERCULES FURENS*

Fortunately the Italian people is not yet accustomed to eating several times per day.
– BENITO MUSOLINI

The people never give up their liberties but under some delusion.
– EDMUND BURKE

Introduction

Leaders usually get the lion's share of the credit for success, and the blame for failure. When Steve Jobs died, his *Telegraph* obituary gave him complete credit for Apple's success: 'it was because of him that Apple products, even when they do largely what other products do, are perceived to be different and infinitely more cool'. Derailment cannot happen alone. Leaders cannot be successful without the right situations, times and colluders.

Toxic leaders are infamous: it's easy to think of examples of people who have run countries, businesses or their own lives into the ground. There are dictators like Japan's Hirohito, North Korea's trinity of Kims or Gaddafi, the Arab League's answer to Little Richard, who had led their countries into ruin. In business, CEOs also get blamed for the success or failure of their company.

An excellent example is in Enron's spectacular rise, and equally spectacular fall. In April, 1999, a *New York Times* lauded Enron and credited President Jeff Skilling for its culture in an article titled 'Firing Up an Idea Machine; Enron Is Encouraging the Entrepreneurs Within' (Salpukas, 1999). By 2001, *The New York Times* was describing Skilling in less complimentary terms, 'The Securities and Exchange Commission has launched its own formal investigation. Mr. Fastow was forced to resign, following Jeffrey Skilling, the man credited with driving Enron into new cutting-edge businesses, out the door' (NY Times, 2001). Leaders get the praise, but also have to take the blame. We discuss the lessons learned from Enron's failure later in this chapter, but first look at the structures that encourage derailment, before looking at systems to prevent derailment.

The toxic triangle

There are three fundamental aspects of leadership derailment. Adrian Furnham describes the toxic leadership triangle in his book *The Elephant in the Boardroom*. The toxic triangle is three corners which collude with derailment potential.

Toxic leaders

Toxic leaders can create, be born from and go into toxic environments. They are not simply incompetent; they deliberately manipulate positions of influence or power for their own interests. They are the *bad;* they are malicious, destructive,

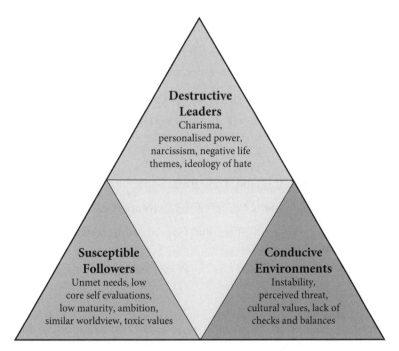

FIGURE 14.1 *The toxic triangle.*

malevolent, vindictive or pernicious. They are not just passive victims who let bad things happen through apathy or neglect; they enjoy being destructive or aggressive. They know what they are doing, and they can create an entire culture around them that supports their own vision or objectives. Toxic leaders can be charming, energetic, and will oversell their own achievements.

Toxic leaders are often excellent manipulators and convince others that they are well suited to commanding a leadership. They may spread their own confidence amongst others, but are only interested in bettering themselves. However, they may find it simple to find followers, because they have no compunctions about misleading, lying or selling simplistic answers.

They will tell employees what they want to hear, and manipulate people to achieve their own ends. For a toxic leader, they are not leading the company or country; they *are* the company or country. Louis XIV supposedly said in response to the President of Parliament speaking in the interest of the state,

L'État, c'est moi (I am the state). This quote was actually invented by Voltaire (Bent, 1887), but it exemplifies what toxic leaders can become. Toxic leaders contribute to, and encourage, failure because they pursue their own agenda, irrespective of others around them. They will eventually lead the fate of a nation or company, and, unchecked, will eventually lead down a dark, dangerous or destructive path.

I am not going to leave this land. I will die as a martyr at the end. I shall remain, defiant. Muammar is Leader of the Revolution until the end of time.

– Muammar Gaddafi, addressing the nation, 2011

Colluding followers

Toxic leaders will not get far without strong and active supporters. Because leaders can influence hiring decisions, toxic leaders can build up a talent pool – a talent swamp perhaps – of loyal followers and colluders. Thus, a leader can use their position to transform the entire organization and its culture to conform to the toxic leader's own particular vision; they need supportive people who carry out orders without question. And the toxic leader will have no compunctions about disposing of their colluding followers if and when it suits the toxic leader's self-interest.

There are many reasons followers support leaders who are either blatantly or subtly malicious. Ambitious people may be tempted to support toxic leaders to secure their own positions, and toxic leaders are happy to capitalize on others' ambitions, although they may not deliver the rewards they promise. Many followers will truly believe in the leaders; an impassioned speech from a toxic leader who knows *exactly* how to get what he or she wants can be extraordinarily convincing. Many times a toxic leader will appeal to followers' sense of self-interest, and will promise whatever it takes to get people to follow.

Followers collude with toxic leaders because of either blind loyalty or self-interest. Some followers will actively work with leaders, knowing their behaviour is bad; others work hard because they are convinced the leader's vision is right.

Threatening environment

Certain situations, organizations and times make it much easier for toxic leaders to thrive. It can be difficult, but not impossible, for toxic leaders to gain influence when circumstances are good. However, when times are bad the toxic leaders really have a chance to thrive. Economic or social dislocation or perceptions of external threat make people more eager to accept extreme solutions. Toxic leaders often capitalize on real or imagined external threats to create a sense of 'us' and 'them'. Being part of the in-group can be extremely attractive for people who feel alienated. A threatening environment often gives an opportunity for a toxic leader and their followers to assign external blame. For example: 'Everything bad that is happening is someone else's fault, and we're going to make them pay for it'. Once a toxic leader gains power, they continue to promote the feeling of external threat to promote internal unity and dedication to the leader's cause.

Toxic leaders will offer clear and simple solutions that sound appealing. A toxic leader has no compunctions about offering dishonest or misleading solutions particularly when the truth is unappealing. They will use any means necessary to gain power, and, when large numbers of people are uncertain or feel threatened, unscrupulous leaders can swoop in and take control.

Threatening or uncertain circumstances encourage followers to look for simple solutions. Toxic leaders will make external threats seem much worse than they really are, and offer solutions that seem simple. They smooth over complexities, difficulties and offer their own ideology, their own power as a simple solution to all problems.

Toxic leaders have trouble succeeding when there is oversight, regulation and enforcement. Toxic leaders need to find conditions where the position of power is not monitored or controlled. Furthermore, toxic leaders often seek to undermine traditional regulatory structures, avoid oversight and hijack enforcement structures for their own purposes. They often try to undermine the credibility of people and structures around them to present themselves as a more credible alternative.

This leads us nicely into discussing an important topic: what can we do to prevent high-potential people from derailment? There are two key areas: the first is at the individual level, of identifying individual derailment potential and being wary of dark side traits. The two key issues at the individual level can really be divided into potential for hamartia (fatal errors) and potential for hubris (fatal flaws). Finally, there are systematic checks and balances that can be put in place.

Methods to prevent derailment

There are four key ways to prevent derailment. Of course none of these is a guarantee, but organizations can combine these methods to develop resilience in the organization, making it less likely for toxic leaders to get into power, and checking their more destructive tendencies if they do get into power, and removing toxic leaders who do gain power and let their destructive impulses control their behaviour.

Proper oversight

Good corporate governance is essential: striking the balance between giving the leader enough flexibility to do their job, while making sure the leader is not overstepping his or her bounds and taking their power too far, and to the wrong places. Good governance cannot eliminate the derailment of high-potential leaders, but can reduce the occurrence and the damage. Leaders need enough freedom to manoeuvre but not unlimited power. In the case of managing CEOs, the board needs to be connected enough, involved enough and aware enough to spot the warning signs; they also need the power and courage to step in *if need be.*

Sophisticated selection

Some people with very high derailment potential can be spotted, and screened out right in the selection process. Assessors must have an understanding both of assessments, and what to look out for. There is now much more interest in this issue and excellent psychometrically validated tests to evaluate the dark side of personality. These can indicate possible areas of concern about leaders' behaviour when put under pressure, which they inevitably are. Often good reference checks are sufficient to select out many people with a long history of derailing behaviours.

Personal support

Friends, spouses, trusted coaches or mentors can mitigate or halt derailment. Those who are not able to proceed with the job or whose environment is turning their behaviour toxic need people they trust and can rely on. Unfortunately, those who need the honest opinion of a friend or colleague can be most resistant, least willing to listen, or have lost friends to bad behaviour. It takes a highly skilled and courageous coach, colleague or board member to confront a very senior manager/leader and help him/her to avoid derailment.

Self-awareness

Not all derailment is inevitable, or is a result of immutable personal attributes. Leaders can become corrupted by systems and situations. Almost anyone can be corrupted by getting caught up in the toxic triangle (Zimbardo's *Lucifer Effect*).

Understanding how strongly situations can affect individual perceptions, valuing independence, admitting one's errors and noticing situational clues all help to avoid or stave off derailment. Experience of past failure can be a powerful buffer.

Hamartia, and mitigating the 'sad'

Derailment is not always the result of deliberate mischief, wickedness or dysfunction. Ancient Greek myth abounds with examples of major judgement errors, *hamartia*. These are not fundamental character flaws that make someone deserve a dire fate; they are errors that consequentially lead to a downfall. Aristotle thought that hamartia was the only way to bring down an epic hero: it's an explanation for failure, without the *person* being a failure.

It can just as easily be poor placement, and the result of innocent mistakes. Someone is put into a position where they are not competent, is not ready or don't receive sufficient instruction to do the job well. Sometimes they might crash and burn and bring other people down with them, or they resign in frustration, leave for another position or are asked to leave because they are not competent.

It's easy to spot when people are not performing their job as they need to be, but it's not always easy to spot why or to make a change. Frequently these people leave (whether or not of their own accord). While the 'mad' and the 'bad' can rise many positions above their real potential for success, the 'sad' find themselves in a position beyond their ability, and start to peddle backwards. Some, with self-awareness and courage, are able to admit to themselves and others that the new position is just not for them.

It is common for people to want to succeed, to earn more money, earn greater benefits and be recognized for achievement. It is also common for people's ambitions and appetites to exceed their talents, particularly early in their career. Many people are self-confident, and a moderate degree of self-confidence is healthy. But levels of ambition do not always match up with talent and potential. Successful and accurate identification of potential means mitigating the causes of 'sad' derailment. Good selection techniques should pick up what self-awareness does not (which is why, as will be discussed in the next part, not every method of getting information about people is equal).

It is not uncommon in work relationships for ambitious colleagues or complicit managers to form a minor folie à deux relationship. Each overestimates each other, and what they can accomplish together. It is easy to believe in potential, or at least create the illusion of potential where none actually exists, especially over a good dinner or a few glasses of wine. This is not necessarily done maliciously or manipulatively, but when people have strong, positive relationships it is easy to trust the other person's judgement more than one should in a work situation. The complimentary manger can provide more praise, and boost employees' confidence; the overconfident employee can oversell their own ability.

Even after both have overstepped, the relationship and mutual confidence can lead to derailing situations. It can be a mutually deceptive. Neither wants to admit (nor believes) they are wrong. That is certainly not to discourage trust in working relationships, but simply to say that when selection and development decisions are to be made, rely on objective evidence. Ironically, the better you think you know someone, the more challenging it can be to make truly objective decisions. In this case, external advice and oversight in hiring and promotion decisions are always a good idea. Always remember the lessons of experience from Chapter 5: a good friend or a good volunteer does not necessarily make a good employee.

A management culture that focuses solely on accentuating the positive and celebrating success can turn toxic. A philosophy that *there are no bad people, just bad attitudes* can eventually lead to very bad results indeed. Balance is important, appreciating the positive combined with a healthy wariness of the negative. Understanding and screening for potentially negative traits will improve the overall selection process.

Mitigating the 'sad' derailment misses many of the spectacular and explosive types of derailment, but it's the garden variety that springs up again and again – it's not sordid, nefarious or malicious; it's just good intentions, optimism and ambition gone astray. Most people at some time in their life realize they have made a poor decision, have taken the wrong path or are in the wrong career. That's minor derailment, and, when caught early, has minor consequences. But the key is that *the person realizes.* When the person isn't aware enough to see they are headed for self-immolation, or cannot see the trail of destruction they are leaving behind (or, consciously hide both), it indicates the more serious, *mad* or *bad* derailment.

Hubris, identifying and deselecting the 'Mad' and 'Bad'

Where sad derailment can be as simple as over-optimism and poor selection criteria, the mad and the bad are completely different; these are more poetic and compelling, because the characteristics that assist the climb precipitate the fall. Where hamartia was about an error of judgement, hubris implies something more fundamental to character. Aristotle thought that: 'as for the pleasure in hubris, its cause is this: men think that by ill-treating others they make their own superiority the greater'.

Hubris is not necessarily consciously planned wickedness; it may not be deliberate but it is still destructive. The major and important difference is that this is not just a competence failure. It is not passive, nor is it accidental. These are active traits that dominate not just personality, but performance and potential. A serious challenge for identifying potential is that dark side traits can pass for desirable characteristics. Narcissism can masquerade as confidence. The paranoid micromanagers may appear to be very conscientious. People who are manipulative learn exactly what to say and how to say it, and they learn what people are looking for and how to present themselves.

Nearly all the spectacular derailers were originally judged by their organization to have great potential. These are people with clear personalities that are apparent relatively early in their career. It is important for anyone interested in managing potential to be aware of them. The same traits that can be assets at some points in a career, like superficial charm, can eventually lead to that person's downfall.

There are serious observable and hidden costs to dark side traits and management derailment. Once derailment occurs in large companies, share prices tumble or decline. Mistakes compound, are missed or neglected and can eventually become spectacles of public (or internal ridicule). There are all sorts of disasters that can be created or exacerbated by management derailment. The characteristics that lead to derailment are also the characteristics that are more likely to compound problems instead of resolving them. Those who care more about their own image than their organization, or feel unable to admit their own mistakes, will cover up their own errors instead of taking responsibility and resolving problems.

It is the hidden costs that are most severe. Derailment is actually a long process that has consequences far before the large-scale failures are publicized. Staff and colleagues can become demoralized, disengaged and less productive, or, worse, become colluders. When problems are not resolved, they fester. The leader with dark side traits is more focused on self-interest than corporate improvement. Some people leave the organization whereas others become disengaged or unable to work properly when large problems remain unsolved. When people leave, the loss of intellectual and social capital decreases the capacity of the organization, higher turnover increases training and development costs and lead to a toxic culture and environment within the organization.

The lesson to be learned from dark side attributes and derailment is to be mindful that 'deselection' is equally important as selection. It is just as important to have a list of undesirable traits during the selection process. Otherwise, it is easy to overlook dark side traits, or to see every trait as a strength instead of acknowledging weakness. This is not to say all these traits should be automatically and wholly avoided. They should just be considered, and when comparing candidates for suitability, if two candidates are equally qualified, weaknesses may be a good way of distinguishing between people.

Some of these are traits that may be difficult or impossible to change when they are symptomatic of personality traits. Perfectionism is highly related to conscientiousness. Other attributes, like excessive caution, may be present for good reasons early in a job, but may be overcome through experience. But, it is something to remember if someone tends to be excessively cautious early in a role – they are probably not the right candidate to parachute into a demanding role that requires immediate action.

Lessons from Enron's collapse

Enron is a perfect example of a spectacular corporate rise and fall, with the very same characteristics that led to its initial success triggering its downfall: corporate greed, toxic leadership, unethical and illegal practices which turned a $100 billion company into a bankrupt company almost overnight.

Motivation and Performance: A Guide to Motivating a Diverse Workforce (MacRae and Furnham, 2017a) describes in detail the story of Enron's rise and fall, along with the details of its toxic leadership. For the even more detailed story about Enron, McLean and Elkind's (2004) book *The Smartest Guys in the Room* is highly recommended. For the purposes of this chapter, there are six useful points about improving corporate governance and preventing derailment initially suggested by da Silveira (2013) and discussed further in MacRae and Furnham (2017a).

1 **Gap between stated policies on paper and actual practice.** Enron, like many organizations, had official, published governance structure, conduct procedures and auditing practices. Although they were official and well documented, they were completely ignored. A gap between official and informal practice can be a problem, especially when actual practice falls foul of ethical guidelines.

2 **Illusion of success.** Like in the case of Enron, many toxic leaders are skilled at obtaining positive and widespread coverage of themselves or their organization. They often use this to create an image of success, even if the reality of the situation is different or they have no real evidence to back up their claims. Creating an illusion of success when it cannot be backed up is a recipe for disaster. It spreads misinformation which does not allow people to make informed decisions based on reality.

3 **Incentivizing counterproductive behaviour.** Rewarding short-term unethical behaviour over long-term priorities almost always leads to problems in the long run. In Enron, the executives were under such severe pressure to post profits that they did so at the expense of the truth. Employees and leaders should be incentivized to perform in the company's best interest.

4 **Relying on reputation instead of substance.** Enron relied on big business names, fame and a hyped-up reputation instead of actual business success. They dropped the biggest names and tried to align themselves with the most respected institutions like Harvard Business School to prop up their representation. They were also very skilled at obtaining widespread and positive media coverage. But without substance, a company or leader is doomed to fail.

5 **Blind trust and greed.** Get-rich schemes, pyramid schemes and the like are doomed to collapse, but many people usually get caught up in blind trust and greed. Enron stocks, for example, quickly became a

get-rich-quick scheme, and investors played their own part in creating a bubble that was doomed to burst. Scrutiny should be paid, especially when growth or profits seem unbelievable.

6 **System susceptible to fraud.** Lack of oversight along with deregulation allowed Enron to get away with far more than they should have, as is common for companies and individuals who operate within a system that allows them to make colossal profits without any oversight or scrutiny. As mentioned previously, proper and effective oversight systems are an essential part of preventing derailment.

Conclusion

There are consistent patterns we can see in systems that lead to and can even encourage derailment and destructive behaviours. The toxic triangle is a system that is present in derailment from small businesses, multinational corporations or governments. It is essential to have good governance structures and oversight, along with systems in place to detect individual derailment potential as well as being vigilant to ensure systems and structures are not corrupted. Unethical and destructive behaviours often seem attractive in the short term when the rewards are great – but the costs are always much more severe in the long term.

15

The dark side traits and characteristics

Evil is easy, and has infinite forms.
– BLAISE PASCAL, *PENSÉES*

A man's virtue is his monument, but forgotten is the man of evil repute.
– EGYPTIAN TOMBSTONE INSCRIPTION (C. 2100 B.C.)

Dark traits and tendencies

A general list of characteristics to look for is as follows; these are by no means exhaustive, but a good place to start:

- *Arrogance:* they believe they are always right, their way is always the best and they are the most important. They can't acknowledge their own failure, but are quick to take credit for anything, even if their contribution was modest or non-existent;

- *Melodrama:* they need to be the centre of attention whether it is good or bad. Their thoughts, feelings and emotions are regularly a matter of public discussion far too often. They are always asking (loudly) why they seem to attract all of the world's troubles. They tend to have low self-awareness, believe that other people's troubles follow them around, not realizing that they create most of their own trouble and can be a constant source of conflict for those around them;

- *Volatility:* they can be moody, or take pleasure in business risk taking for the thrill of it. They might give instructions and inexplicably change their mind shortly after. They have completely new ideas the night before an important event. They might be pleasant one minute and angry the next. Or, they make decisions that regularly put the business at risk, without good reason;

- *Excessive caution:* they are paralysed by indecision and uncertainty. For them, growing pressure crushes their ability to make decisions. Caution can be good in certain circumstances, but people who are excessively cautious are unable to make decisions, especially when the decisions are vital. They ask other people their opinion; then they ask the same people the same question, to reaffirm their decision. When possible, they postpone important deadlines and decisions. Many windows of opportunity close because of their difficulty committing to important plans or decisions;

- *Habitual distrust:* they automatically assume the worst in situations and others. They tend to believe others' mistakes are a subtle attempt at sabotage. They might see others' success as a direct threat to their own performance. Whatever happens, they assume the very worst;

- *Aloofness:* they disengage and disconnect from colleagues. They avoid interaction with colleagues as much as possible, and try their best to seal themselves off or they deliberately put themselves in situations to make a point of ignoring others. It is noticeable, sometimes hysterical self-imposed isolation;

- *Eccentricity:* they like to feel different and unique, and want other people to know it. They will play up little differences, and delight in other people noticing their peculiarities. This can be excessive attention seeking, and drawing focus to things completely unrelated to their work;

- *Passive resistance:* they oppose decisions, but do not voice their disagreement. They stay quiet, withdraw or sulk. But for their own personal reasons they will not argue. Their silence is easily misinterpreted as agreement. They complain and sulk but avoid direct confrontation;

- *Perfectionism:* they feel an obsessive need for everything to be the best, but become preoccupied with minor details. They seem to get the little things right even if the big things go wrong. They obsess about the alignment of page margins before even beginning to write the report. They would be 40 minutes late instead of leaving the house with a hair out of place. In their own work, they cannot get things done on time because their work is never finished. They constantly make changes, and create more errors that need to be fixed, and focus on details that are not important;

- *Eagerness to please:* they want to be liked and want to be popular. The results of their work are more focused on making friends than getting the job done. They feel they have the best intentions: they want to make friends and preserve relationships at all costs. They can be lovely to work with, but difficult when decisions need to be made.

All of these traits are relatively minor manifestations of dark side personality traits. Most of the above characteristics can be relatively benign. In certain jobs they may even be advantageous. However, they are characteristics that can become more problematic at higher levels of a career or when job demands become more taxing. Eagerness to please in small doses can be endearing. At higher levels it can lead to sacrificing business performance for the sake of avoiding conflict.

Researchers in the area of 'bad' derailment suggest there is a Dark Triad of *subclinical psychopathy*. 'People of the Dark Triad' have high self-interest but low empathy. They are therefore not interested in, well suited for or good at long-term relationships where a degree of reciprocity is called for, such as leading people, leading an organization, or leading a nation. A successful career and strong leadership requires a degree of reciprocity.

Leadership, especially at higher levels, requires suspending personal desires for the success and interests of the company. People with dark side traits do not have the capacity or desire to suspend self-interest, so that disparity can be a key factor in derailment. These individuals can be classified as psychopathic, Machiavellian, or narcissistic. Really, there are many similarities between these three traits that involve lack of empathy, manipulativeness and what most people would describe as immorality. The Dark Triad traits lead to the exploitation of others and pursuance of self-centred objectives. Each of these traits involves wilful exploitation of others for pleasure, power or persona.

For the narcissist there is no higher goal than improving one's own image. Narcissists are not just concerned with power, but power and influence for the sake of praise. The narcissistic leader will value success of the organization most when they are the name and face of the company. The narcissist then uses power and influence as a tool for their own self-promotion; their leadership position is only valuable as a method of feeling good about themselves. This may lead to temporary successes, because the narcissistic trait creates a strong drive to achieve at any cost. However, the drive to protect their own reputation and image can lead to hiding mistakes instead of resolving them or focusing on self-preservation at the expense of company priorities.

Machiavellians can be exploitative charmers. They are interested in the pursuit of power, and may view morality as unnecessary except as a useful

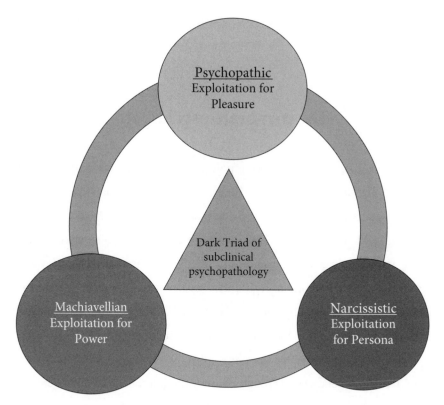

FIGURE 15.1 *The dark triad of subclinical psychopathology*

artifice. Like narcissists, Machiavellians are focused on success, but do not necessarily need praise. They derive satisfaction from power and influence, whether others notice their power or not. The narcissist would trade influence for image; the Machiavellian would happily make that trade with the narcissist.

Psychopaths are exploiters. They seek thrills, enjoy manipulating others and take risks for the sake of it. Whereas Machiavellians and narcissists use their talents instrumentally for selfishness, psychopaths may use their talents to deliberately torment others. They enjoy other people's misfortune and delight in being abnormal. Not just being 'quirky' or getting an unconventional haircut, psychopaths enjoy transgressing on social and cultural norms for the sake of shocking and disturbing other people. Psychopaths may be extraordinarily successful because they have no trouble using any social tools at their disposal to get what they want.

The corporate psychopath

Psychopaths like power and having power over people, so they are naturally drawn to positions of leadership. There are two dimensions of psychopathy. The first is socio-emotional where the psychopath is superficial and lacking in empathy, guilt or remorse. They are also deceitful and manipulative while being prone to egocentricity and grandiosity. The second is their social deviance associated with boredom susceptibility, impulsivity and lack of self-control. In children they show evidence of behaviour problems and in adulthood antisocial behaviour. This has led to the development of a checklist.

Hare (1999), in a chapter on white-collar psychopaths, noted how many were 'trust-mongers' who, through charm and gall, obtained and then very callously betrayed the trust of others. He notes how they make excellent imposters and how they frequently target the vulnerable. He calls them sub-criminal psychopaths, and they can thrive as academics, cult leaders, doctors, police officers or writers. They exploit their positions; violate rules, conventions and ethical standards; and cross legal boundaries. He also gives a rich case study description of what he calls a corporate psychopath. He notes that there is certainly no shortage of opportunities for psychopaths who think big. It's lucrative. 'They are fast talking, charming, self-assured, at ease in social situations, cool under pressure, unfazed by the possibility of being found out, and totally ruthless' (p. 121).

Babiak and Hare (2006) believe most of us will interact with a psychopath every day. But their skills and abilities make them difficult to spot. Often they are charming, emotionally literate and socially skilled. Next they are often highly articulate. They are brilliant at managing and adapting their own image.

The non-institutionalized psychopaths are described as carefree, aggressive, charming and impulsively irresponsible. They have the essential characteristics of the psychopath but seem to refrain from serious antisocial behaviour.

Researchers have identified many politicians and business leaders as non-criminal psychopaths. They are duplicitous, but not illegally so. They show many patterns of misconduct but seem not to get caught. They seem brilliant at tactical impression management and are drawn to unstable, chaotic, rapidly changing situations where they can more easily operate. Successful, non-incarcerated psychopaths seem to have compensatory factors that buffer them against criminal behaviour like higher social class and intelligence. They can talk, buy, threaten, coerce or convince their way out of most consequences. In this sense the successful psychopath has a wider set of coping mechanisms than less privileged and able psychopaths who soon get caught.

Self-report measures of the psychopathic personality give a clear indication of the sort of behaviours that are relevant (Benning et al., 2003).

These seem to factor into two dimensions: one related to high negative emotionality and the other low behavioural constraint. Further research by Benning et al. (2005) led these authors to think about two distinct facets of the psychopath: *fearless dominance* (glib, grandiose, deceitful, low stress) and

TABLE 15.1 *Behaviours of the psychopath*

Psychopathic manifestations	Relevant behaviours
Impulsive nonconformity	Reckless, rebellious, unconventional.
Blame externalization	Blames others, rationalizes own transgressions.
Machiavellian egocentricity	Interpersonally aggressive and self-centred.
Carefree non-planfulness	Excessive present orientation with lack of forethought or planning.
Stress immunity	Experiencing minimal anxiety.
Fearlessness	Willing to take risks, having little concern with potentially harmful consequences.
General cold-heartedness	Unsentimental, unreactive to others' distress, lacking in imagination.

impulsive antisociality (aggressive, antisocial, low control). This suggests that within the psychopath population one may be able to distinguish between these two groups.

Antisocial (psychopathic) managers show a blatant and consistent disregard for, and violation of, the rights of others. They often have a history of being difficult, delinquent or dangerous. They show a failure to conform to most social norms and frequently, if not bright or privileged, get into trouble with the law for lying, stealing and cheating. They are always deceitful, as indicated by repeated use of aliases and 'conning others' for personal profit or pleasure. They can be, in short, nasty, aggressive, con artists – the sort who often get profiled on business crime programmes.

Psychopaths are also massively impulsive and fail to plan ahead. They live only in, and for, the present. They show irritability and aggressiveness, as indicated by repeated physical fights or assaults. They manifest a surprising reckless disregard for the physical and psychological safety of self and others – or the business in general. In an environment that values risk taking they are clearly in their element. They are famous for being consistently irresponsible. Repeated failure to sustain consistent work behaviour or to honour financial obligations is their hallmark. Most frustrating of all, they show lack of remorse. They are indifferent to or cleverly rationalize having hurt, mistreated or stolen from another. They never learn from their mistakes. It can seem as if labelling them as antisocial is a serious understatement.

It is an interesting question to try to understand in what sorts of jobs psychopathic traits might be, at least for a time, advantageous. This may refer both to the type of job and a particular situation such as when an organization is changing rapidly, is in decline or is under investigation. They like outwitting the system – opportunistically exploiting who and what they can. They usually hate routine and administration, which are seen as drudgery. No wonder people who work for them feel so demoralized.

They make bad bosses and bad partners because they are egocentric and only continue on in a relationship as long as it is good for them. They rarely have long-lasting, meaningful relationships. They have two missing human ingredients which are pretty crucial to a fully functioning person: conscience and compassion. They score very low on agreeableness and conscientiousness. Hence they can be cruel, destructive, malicious and criminal. They are unscrupulous, and are exploitatively self-interested with little capacity for remorse. They act before they think and are famous for their extreme impulsivity.

Dotlick and Cairo (2003) notes that the mischievous psychopath knows that the rules are really 'only suggestions'. They are rebels without a cause, rule breakers who believe rules, laws and other restrictions are tedious and unnecessary. They clearly have destructive impulses and preferences for making impulsive decisions without considering any consequences. They can, and do, speak their mind, use their charms and creativity but for no clear business goal.

How to deal with the psychopath? Dotlick and Cairo (2003) offer four pieces of advice for what is no doubt a successful psychopath.

- *First:* encourage them to take ownership for their action and interrogate their rule-breaking, consequence-ignoring behaviours;

- *Second:* encourage them to think clearly about which rules they will really follow as opposed to break;

- *Third:* they may benefit from being on the receiving end of the sort of mischief they dish out; and

- *Fourth:* they might benefit from confiding in a coach. We would suggest sophisticated selection techniques to weed them out, or keep them away from positions of power.

Hogan and Hogan (2001) call the antisocial person 'Mischievous'. They note that these types expect that others will like them and find them charming and they expect to be able to extract favours, promises, money and other resources from other people with relative ease. However, they see others as merely to be exploited, and therefore have problems maintaining commitments and are unconcerned about social, moral and economic expectations. They are self-confident to the point of feeling invulnerable, and have an air of daring and sangfroid that others can find attractive and even irresistible. In industries where bold risk taking is expected they can seem a very desirable person for senior management position.

Babiak and Hare (2006) believe that psychopaths are indeed attracted to business. They devised a questionnaire to help people at work spot them. There are, according to the authors, ten markers of the problem. The successful, industrial psychopath is characterized by the following. He or she:

- Comes across as smooth, polished and charming;

- Turns most conversations around to a discussion of him or herself;

- Discredits and puts down others in order to build up own image and reputation;

- Lies to co-workers, customers or business associates with a straight face;

- Considers people he or she has outsmarted or manipulated as dumb or stupid;

- Opportunistic; hates to lose, plays ruthlessly to win;

- Comes across as cold and calculating;

- Acts in an unethical or dishonest manner;

- Has created a power network in the organization and uses it for personal gain; and

- Shows no regret for making decisions that negatively affect the company, shareholders or employees.

Psychopaths can easily look like ideal leaders: smooth, polished, charming. They can quite easily mesh their dark side – bullying, amoral and manipulative. In the past it may be politics, policing, law, media and religion that attracted psychopaths, but more and more it is the fast-paced, exciting, supposedly glamorous world of business.

A final note on derailment

It's important to remember that not all derailment happens because of dark side personality traits or deliberate malfeasance. Leaders and experts can, like anyone else, become victims of circumstance. Leadership roles particularly involve not just power, influence and prestige but can also become straw man positions of blame. It's one of the risks of leadership. When a company or organization has a general humiliation, the top-level leader is the automatic target for blame. The leader must take ultimate responsibility and bear the consequences. As we now know, the best leaders are not autocrats with eyes and ears everywhere in the organization. Good leaders cannot be omniscient and should not seek to be omnipotent. So, things can go wrong, external factors can take over and internal issues can be missed.

Leaders have the unique pleasure of getting most of the praise from success, but will be personally responsible for failure in the organization. This is why it is so important to distinguish between a *good* person and the *right* person. It's easy for a leader to get on the wrong track, either by their own mistakes or by other circumstances. Someone who has much experience, many of the right traits and is very intelligent can miss important signs of impending doom and plunge headlong onto a track that will lead to failure. Or, a leader may see the warning signs but feel they cannot change the circumstances.

Sometimes it is hard to spot the warning signs. So, look for history of failure and *how failure was handled*. How they have handled difficult times in the past and how they have persevered and recovered. Have they learned lessons from the failure, and are they able to apply those lessons in the future? A formal interview is not always the best time to ask people about their past failures because the context demands certain types of presentation (discussed in Chapters 8 and 9). But for internal candidates, it is probably possible to discuss previous failures in a more informal, honest context.

If the person believes they have never failed, or are not willing to acknowledge a failure (won't call a fail a fail), then there may be issues ahead. If there are more serious challenges in the future they might not recognize (or they may not be willing to acknowledge) when they are laying down the tracks to derailment. Whereas others should be able to critically evaluate their past performance, recognize their own success and others' successes, and be able to change course before it is too late. Never underestimate the importance of the capacity to take responsibility, apologize, and commit (honestly) to doing a better job next time.

Finally there are three indicators of problems ahead. The psychiatrists say they underlie all the personality disorders like narcissist, psychopath, obsessive-compulsive and paranoid. They are not difficult to spot if you ask the right questions and collect the right data.

First, *can the person 'do relationships'?* Do they have a history in the workplace and out, in past and in the present of being able to initiate and maintain good healthy relationships? Are they socially skilled, emotionally intelligent and able to understand, enjoy and benefit from friends and acquaintances? Have they built a support group who they support in turn?

Despite their often considerable superficial charm psychopaths can't sustain relationships of any sort. They often leave paths of amazing psychological destruction behind them. They consistently lie, hoodwink and bamboozle. They are particularly dangerous when they are articulate, educated and good-looking. Narcissists don't do relationships because they are so caught up in themselves: so demanding of adulation that they have no time for reciprocation.

It is not difficult to find out about a person's relationship management through references and careful questioning. The issue is not only the forming of relationships through 'networming', but the ability to develop and sustain healthy, reciprocal relationships. You can see it at school and university. The potentially dangerous and derailing leader usually has a history of using people for their own ends. Selfish, manipulative and often psychologically abusive.

Second, *are they self-aware?* Do they have a reasonably accurate image of themselves at least compared to the judgements of others? Are they realistic about their talents? Do they significantly over- or underestimate things like their attractiveness to others or their moral rectitude?

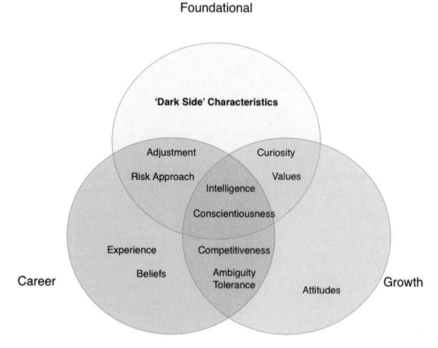

FIGURE 15.2 *Dimensions of potential, revised.*

The use of multi-source feedback, sometimes called 360-degree feedback, helps get at this issue. Most people overestimate their strengths and underestimate their 'developmental opportunities'. That is both normal (in the statistical sense) and may even be psychologically healthy. But the question lies in the size and nature of the disparity between their view and those of others. Or indeed their view versus some behavioural or test measures.

Narcissists, of course, grossly overestimate their abilities, charm and decision-making. Psychopaths believe they are both moral and working in the interests of others. Many a derailing leader has found that their very strong self-esteem helped them climb the greasy pole but pulled them down once they were 'found out'.

Third, *is the issue of adaptation and flexibility?* Success, unlike failure, can be a poor teacher. Individuals, like organizations, with a strong history of success are too often tempted to do what they always did, in the hope that the good results will be repeated. The ability to learn from experience is a crucial sign of success and failure.

PART THREE

ASSESSMENT – TECHNIQUES AND APPLICATIONS

16

Assessment: Methods to learn about other people

The good have no need of an advocate.

– PHOCION

Introduction

The previous part discussed different indicators of high potential and why factors like personality, intelligence and experience lead to potential to succeed or fail at work. Assessment builds on that by testing whether or not people have that characteristic and to what degree. It is a more practical way to ask the questions about who really has high potential and of what type. Assessment helps to answer the questions: How do you attract those with high potential? How can you spot them? What tools can be used to separate the wheat from the chaff? A robust assessment of the right traits can be a valuable resource in spotting high potential

Some would say they can intuitively spot high potential based on their own experience, knowledge, psychological-mindedness or some other trait. But intuition is not always enough and personal opinions are not the best way to identify the host of attributes that make someone high potential at work.

What if there are lots of impressive candidates from top-flight universities with stunning, varied and successful work experience? Is it possible to see those who will really fly very high and very far? What methods are most useful for this task? This chapter provides an overview of assessment and answers these questions; then the subsequent chapter goes into detail about specific types of assessment.

An example of assessment

Imagine you are put in the position of hiring two hopefully high-potential people. You are in the process of launching a small, start-up company. You have investors and the resources to build and grow the business along with a brilliant idea that you're sure is going to be very successful. You have done your research, and you are certain that your business idea will work. You have read Parts One and Two, so you now have a fairly good understanding of potential, the characteristics of potential and how to look for potential in certain positions. You have specific objectives in mind, and enough expertise to know generally what is required of success and the skills required for two key positions. You need one skilled internet technology expert for a technical position, and you need a manager who can manage the vagaries and delicacies of customer service (until your business expands enough to hire a dedicated customer service employee). Let's assume you have a large pool of applications for the job, a host of eager candidates with a wide range of talents and abilities applying for the job. So how would you go about figuring out who are the best candidates to fill the positions? *Assessment.*

Assessment is a process that can be used to find out information about another person (Cohen, 2012). Assessment *refers to an overall approach to finding that information.* Assessments combine all the relevant sources of information to get a clear picture of who is the best fit for the position. It's an art and a science. Different types of tests of different characteristics are combined to create an assessment. A test usually has a very specific purpose whereas an assessment is designed to answer a broader question and can be composed of multiple tests or information sources (MacRae and Furnham, 2017a).

Testing. Using a single independent measure a specific behaviour or attribute.

Assessment. The process of combining multiple sources of information (often tests) to answer broader question(s).

Adapted from MacRae and Furnham (2017a).

An assessment that would be used to find out a person's suitability for a position in senior leadership, for example, would and should include multiple tests, combined to comprehensively assess the person's potential. It might include a test of competences, either a written test of knowledge, or a practical test to demonstrate the person's ability. It may also include an interview, to ask certain questions about the person's values, goals or personal attributes. For some jobs it may be a test of physical health, athletic ability, detecting the presence (or absence) of certain chemicals in the body. It could include background checks, reference checks or other tests to make sure the person is the best candidate for the person. The assessment can build up a full picture of that person's potential.

Unlike assessments, tests are a method of gathering information about a very specific piece of information. For example, a test might ask, 'how well can someone solve mathematical problems?' 'Does this person have optimal personality tests for a leadership position?' Assessment is the process of answering more complex problems such as, 'is this person suitable for a promotion?' Then a variety of tests can be used to build up the fuller picture of that person's potential. Assessment may combine tests of intelligence, personality, values and more. Assessment involves identifying all the factors that will help to answer the question, then combining tests to collect information about all of the relevant factors.

To find out who is the best to fill the two positions in the earlier example, one should use a customized assessment process. The previous chapters have talked about some of the desirable characteristics and how they relate to potential. But assessments would differ in finding suitable candidates for different positions.

A challenge for any company, large or small, is always how to allocate resources. A robust assessment process does cost money, and the business may not choose to allocate resources to a selection or development process. In the example of the start-up, resources may be a limiting factor in the complexity of the assessment process. This is where the specific definition of *potential to do what* becomes even more important. To decide what to include in the assessment, first make a list of key indicators of success for the potential positions. For example:

- Technical Skills (IT)

- Intelligence

- Conscientiousness

- Interpersonal Skills

- Management Skills (Experience)

- Values: Innovation

Different characteristics have varying degrees of importance depending on the vision and objectives of the organization and the current objectives and realities in the specific job opening. It is very useful to clearly identify the relative importance of each characteristic being assessed and should stem from that fundamental question, *potential to do what?*

Then it will be possible to make a chart and rank the relative importance of each attribute for each position. In this case of a small business there may be more overlap between some of the skills and attributes of all employees may have some overlap in their roles and responsibilities. If we're thinking about longer-term development plans (which we will discuss in Chapters 21 and 22), it is helpful to keep in mind more than the entry-level position but also thinking, but *where do we want them to go in companies future.* This is mutually beneficial because it adds longer-term capacity to the business, but clearly identifying long-term opportunities in the company increases employee loyalty and commitment to the company (MacRae and Furnham, 2017a).

The manager may take on a more clearly defined and more strategic leadership role as the business grows and once more people can be hired to take on more specific and less general responsibilities. The chart for this example might look something like Table 16.1, which estimates the importance of each skill/characteristic for the respective positions (1 is the least important, ranging to 5 which is the most important).

Then, after determining the optimal criteria for high potential to succeed in that position, the next step is to find out to what extent each candidate

TABLE 16.1 *Sample chart rating importance of characteristics for different roles*

Characteristic	Technician	Manager/Customer service
Technical skills (IT)*	5	3
Intelligence	5	4
Conscientiousness	5	4
Interpersonal skills	2–3	5
Management skills (Experience)	1–2	5
Values (Innovation)	4–5	3–4

*Note: In this example we assume that the manager will need some technical knowledge and experience, enough to be able to monitor and judge the work of the technician.

possesses each characteristic. A clear framework helps to make sure people are being judged using the correct criteria. Evidence, where possible, should lead and guide the evaluations of each characteristic. Quite simply, the problems arise when one either does not consider the appropriate assessment criteria, or is unsure of how to properly assess particular traits and characteristics. Opening an interview process and selecting the most affable candidate is and can be a quick route to selecting a poor performer.

Good assessment is a process of first determining the *potential to do what,* and then finding a way to measure the characteristics that predict the potential to achieve the defined success criteria. Failures in the assessment process often stem from ignorance or omission of the truly important predictors of potential. Selecting based on the wrong criteria or irrelevant criteria inevitably leads to poor selection, development or retention decisions. This in turn increases the potential of derailment: When the wrong people are selected, they are less likely to succeed, more likely to fail. Hiring someone you get along well with may very well be an indicator of their success in the job – but it is not necessarily the best predictor of who has the greatest potential to succeed in that job. Poor assessment can stem from two fundamental problems:

1   Failure to identify the key predictors/indicators of success. If the characteristics that help to predict success in a role are missed, it is much more challenging to choose the right person for the role.

2   Failure to properly assess/measure the key indicators of success. Even if the predictors of success are correctly identified, it is still possible to test them poorly. If a test does not actually measure the characteristic of interest, it gives poor, inaccurate or misleading information.

The result of a well-planned assessment for the desirable employee would look something like Table 16.2:

TABLE 16.2 *Assessment for particular desirable attributes*

Characteristic	Technician	Assessment method	Score (-/10)
Technical skills (IT)*	5	On-the-job observation	
Intelligence	5	Test	
Conscientiousness	5	Personality test	
Interpersonal skills	2–3	Interview, on-the-job observation	
Management skills (Experience)	1–2	Past experience, interview	
Values (Innovation)	4–5	Test	

*Note: In this example we assume that the manager will need some technical knowledge and experience, enough to be able to monitor and judge the work of the technician.

Quality of different assessment methods

Not all tests are made equal, and in practice, there are a few key criteria for choosing methods of testing and assessment. The reality of limited time, resources and other considerations is always an important consideration for any business. It may not be realistic to use the most expensive and expansive assessment process in all companies, in all roles or at all times. Sometimes the process needs to be a bit less expensive and 'quick and dirty' or 'cheap and cheerful'.

The opinions of human resource professionals provide a nice overview of different assessment methods in practice. Furnham (2008b) examined attitudes amongst over 400 HR professionals, and found that generally attitudes about tests were quite favourable but varied greatly based on the exact method (many of these methods are reviewed in greater detail in the next chapter). References were rated as one of the least valid, just slightly better than 'personal hunch'; however, they were also rated as one of the least costly methods, most practical. Thus, unsurprisingly, they are so widespread because they are cheap and easy even though they are not generally believed to be as valid as other methods.

These methods are rated using Cook's notes (pp. 283–287) on useful criteria for judging selection tests:

1 *Validity* is the most important criterion. Unless a test can predict productivity, there is little point in using it. A valid test needs to measure what it says it measures, and have a link to effectiveness at work. A valid test, even the most elaborate and expensive, is almost always worth using.

2 *Cost* tends to be rated as a very important consideration for selectors. Psychologists would argue that cost should not be and is not an important consideration, as long as the test is valid and is the most effective tool. The business case and financial considerations are important in the workplace though, and cannot be played down.

3 *Practicality* is a negative criterion; it is a reason for not using a test. Tests which involve elaborate equipment (such as a brain scan), take a great deal of time or are difficult to administer are not practical tests.

4 *Generality* simply means how many types of employees the test can be used for.

5 *Acceptability* to candidates is important, especially in times of full employment.

6 *Legality* is another negative criterion, and another reason for not using something. It is often hard to evaluate, as the legal position on many tests is obscure or confused. But if a test is not legal to use or has the potential to create legal difficulties, it is a very significant barrier to using the test.

Furnham's (2008b) results from surveying HR professions about the attitude of HR professions are shown in Table 16.3, and Cook provides a very useful guide to judging each of the criteria for judging tests which is summarized in Table 16.4.

TABLE 16.3 *Human resource professionals' ratings of assessment methods*

	Technique	A. Validity	B. Cost	C. Practicality	D. Legality
			Criteria		
1.	Interview	3.11	2.99	3.83	3.61
2.	Reference	2.23	1.71	3.37	2.95
3.	Peer ratings	3.08	2.39	2.74	2.56
4.	Biodata	2.80	2.58	2.94	2.76
5.	Cognitive ability tests	3.90	3.41	3.20	3.37
6.	Personality tests	3.55	3.56	3.25	3.23
7.	Assessment centres	4.03	4.42	2.71	3.70
8.	Work sample	3.90	3.07	3.00	3.51
9.	Job knowledge	3.65	2.27	3.49	3.47
10.	Educational qualifications	3.13	1.64	3.69	3.43
11.	360-degree appraisal data	3.56	3.46	2.73	3.03
12	Personal hunch	1.83	1.39	3.03	1.53

Choosing which factors are most important in deciding upon whether or not to use the test is a nuanced process. Furthermore, not all criteria are made equal. Some judgements are more important and bear more weight than others. Choosing the cheapest selection method will often lead to further costs in retention problems and poor performance down the line. Choosing the most valid test that falls fowl of employment law will create trouble for the organization and the selectors.

Cook describes how different assessment methods rate on his six criteria for judging tests. This model correctly implies that many organizations have to make a trade-off in the testing process. For example, expense may be sacrificed for validity and practicality may be traded for generality. These issues often come from interrelated pressures. Does the company spend all of the budget testing only a few people? Or does the budget extend to testing everyone in the company? It's also important to note that some testing methods do well in some criteria and poorly at others; very few succeed at all criteria: Assessment centres probably do best when they are comprehensive and use robust tests.

TABLE 16.4 *Summary of twelve selection tests by six criteria*

Selection test	Validity	Cost	Practical	Generality	Acceptability	Legality
Interview	Low	Medium/Low	High	High	High	Uncertain
Structured interview	High	High	Limited	High	Untested	No problems
References	Moderate	Very low	High	High	Medium	Some doubts
Peer rating	High	Very low	Very limited	Very limited	Low	Untested
Biodata	High	High/Low	High	High	Low	Some doubts
Ability	High	Low	High	High	Low	Major problems
Psychomotor test	High	Low	Moderate	Limited	Untested	Untested
Job knowledge	High	Low	High	Limited	Untested	Some doubts
Personality	Variable	Low	High	High	Low	Some doubts
Assessment	High	Very high	Fair	Fair	High	No problems
Work sample	High	High	Limited	Limited	High	No problems
Education	Moderate	Nil	High	High	Untested	Major doubts

This comparison indicates that:

- Structured interviews have excellent validity but limited transportability, and are expensive to set up;

- Ability tests have excellent validity, are useful in many different types of jobs, are readily transportable and are cost effective and easy to administer, but can potentially raise legal issues in the United States;

- Assessment centres have excellent validity and can be used with many different types of work and at different levels of seniority. Legally they are fairly safe, but are challenging and often time-consuming, and they tend to be expensive;

- Work samples have excellent validity, are easy to use and are generally quite safe legally, but are expensive, because they are necessarily specific to the job;

- Job-knowledge tests have strong validity, are easy to use and are cheap because they are commercially available widely. They have the potential to cause legal problems when they are paper-and-pencil tests but the use of paper-and-pencil tests is becoming less common with increased digitization;

- Personality inventories are useful in predicting a number of behaviours, but are not useful in predicting a specific skill. They are better used for predicting things like how quickly a worker will learn in training, how they deal with stressful situations, for example;

- References have only moderate validity, but are cheap to use. However, legal cautions are tending to limit their value but they can provide very useful information for a third-party without the bias implicit in self-report tests; and

- Results from similar studies, such as Arnold et al. (2005), suggest there is a fairly strong consensus on the efficacy of different assessment methods.

Assessing senior leaders

This is neither easy nor cheap. It requires skill, insight and time. As an example of how to do it well an actual method used by a government agency is set out below in seven steps:

1 First, a candidate has a one-hour unstructured interview by an HR professional with experience of the company. A detailed report of the observations is written;

2 Second, this report is given to a second similar person who prepares and then executes a structured interview based on the criteria/competencies that the person is looking for;

3 If the candidate is deemed suitable by both they are asked to go on a public assessment centre evaluations where they are investigated by a team of people and where the candidate is evaluated against others;

4 If they 'pass' this, they are required to give ten to twelve possible referees who know them well in a range of capacities (taught them, worked with them, etc.). Eight of these are selected and given a structured telephone interview covering some of the same points as the second interviewer (see point 2);

5 If the candidate is still judged to be a good candidate they are invited to a final interview of a board comprising a senior manager, and a HR specialist, the person's potential boss and an experienced outsider. This board is sent all the notes of the above: two written reports, the assessment centre report and the references;

6 They meet two hours before the candidate arrives to discuss their impressions and concerns; and

7 Then they conduct a two- to three-hour planned interview with three senior members of the organization and one outside independent assessor.

This is a very expensive procedure but with a history of picking high flyers and avoiding errors.

HPTI and senior leadership

Conscientiousness

Conscientiousness means strong planning, goal-directed behaviour and discipline. Strategic thinking is impossible without high conscientiousness. Low-conscientiousness leaders are those whose organizations will be governed entirely by emergent strategy. They may be brilliant negotiators of last-minute situations, of adapting to opportunities, and being decisive even when they do not know what is going on. But strategic leadership is next to impossible without high conscientiousness.

Adjustment

Adjustment is helpful, but also relative to the demands of the organization and situational factors. Greater demands, more intense pressures and hostile climates demand greater adjustment (emotional stability). Leaders must take responsibility, and the brunt of responsibility and consequences, which require emotional stability. The strategist must be able to overcome their own emotional (in)stability and focus on the values and strategy of the organization.

Competitiveness

Competitiveness is instrumental, but in moderation. Useful (instrumental) competitiveness focuses on the success of the organization, competitive advantage of teams, departments and the company. The moderately and adaptively competitive leader can channel their desire to succeed into realistic and conscionable objectives. The hyper-competitive leader wants to be seen as *the* success of the organization, whereas the completely uncompetitive leader may have difficulty focusing on strategic advantages and pursuing opportunities.

Curiosity

Curiosity is essential for strategy: the desire to learn and explore information is foundational for the strategist. Good strategy is rooted in a rich understanding of the company, the people in it, and what is going on outside of the organization. Continual learning informs the top-down strategy, helps to discover successful emergent strategy and to make informed decisions. It is difficult to develop a strategic understanding of any issue or company without intellectual curiosity.

Ambiguity acceptance

The oversimplified solutions are often the most appealing and the least successful. Those with high ambiguity acceptance seek out more information, even when there are conflicting opinions. Leaders must have the capacity to listen to unpopular or dissenting opinions, and those with low ambiguity acceptance have little tolerance for vagaries or complexity. But, a good strategy cannot form without understanding of complex issues. Simple, unambiguous and insincere solutions are frequently peddled by toxic leaders.

Risk approach

Risk approach, when it is constructive and conscientious, is required for leaders and strategists. The leader as a strategist must have the courage to explain why the strategy is important, even in the face of opposition. They must have the fortitude to stand by and explain their own values.

Conclusion

Assessment is about learning detailed and complex information. There are simple, standardized methods that are useful and comparable between people. Winnowing down large applicant pools into real groups of talent potential is challenging, but not impossible. Good information, valid criteria and strong tests lead to good selection decisions. However, at higher levels or for more specific or personal decisions standardized practices have limitations. People fake, deceive, manage their idiom and act in certain ways. More informal situations can show a range of informal skills, characteristics, values and attributes. Whatever the position, development opportunity or the intention of assessment, the most important thing is identifying the key criteria, the indicators of high potential, and finding the best way to measure or evaluate those indicators.

17

Methods for assessing people at work

All human error is impatience, a premature renunciation of method,
a delusive pinning down of delusion.
– FRANZ KAFKA

What can we know? or what can we discern
When error chokes the windows of the mind?
– SIR JOHN DAVIES, *NOSCE TEIPSUM*

Introduction

There is no ideal method, test or technique to fit a person with a work position. Job requirements always vary, based on 'ideal' employee criteria, and the reality of labour markets. I have heard descriptions of desirable employee characteristics only half sarcastically described anywhere from 'must possess a heartbeat' to 'willing to move heaven and earth'. The first is quantifiable and less than optimistic; the second is overoptimistic unless applied to a theologian or a geologist respectively.

Good assessment must compare the demands of the job with the candidate's competencies. Different methods of assessment have strengths and weaknesses. However, familiarity and personal experience can strongly influence work assessments. Practical concerns are also a factor, assessments are expensive and expense can be one of the greatest limiting factors. Interviews, CVs and personal statements are almost ubiquitous in assessing job candidates, but are far from the most valid methods for assessing success.

Six methods and approaches for assessing people at work

There are, essentially, five different methods that can be used to collect data about people. There are also a few quirky alternatives that don't fit nicely into the first five categories but are interesting nonetheless. These methods can be used for development and retention as well as selection, but tend to be most well known as selection methods. We will discuss them here, because although they can and should be used for development and retention, they are perfect for highlighting the best and the worst in employee selection. Then, there are issues we can discuss with development and retention that are more interesting without reiterating the particular concerns with techniques like interviews and references.

We discuss each of the methods in detail.

Self-report

Self-report methods are essentially what people say about themselves. Self-report methods usually ask people to describe themselves. *Rate your agreement with the following statements. Tell me why you want this job. Describe and provide an example of the last time you demonstrated notable valour or heroism in or near the London borough of Hammersmith and Fulham.*

Self-report methods can be open-ended, where the information is generated and framed by the person being assessed, typically a CV, cover letter or personal statement. Open-ended questions allow the person being assessed to influence the nature and type of information they present. The person is asked a question, and draws on their own experience and understanding of how to respond to the question being asked. An open-ended question could be, 'how do you see this job fitting in with your personal life'. Or self-report can be more guided with a closed-ended question like, 'do you have a car that you can depend on to get you to work every day?' Closed-ended questions are also very common, but tend to be used when selection is less conversational. Most personality tests or interviews ask people to respond to specific questions on paper or online. Closed-ended questions have a limited number of possible responses, so tend not to be used when there are opportunities for conversation, more open social interaction or opportunities to prove the nuances of the responses.

Self-report techniques can be structured or unstructured. Structured processes involve specific questions, rigid criteria and requirements or pre-defined instruments. Unstructured processes can be open-ended questions in interviews that lead to new, unplanned questions, 'tell me about yourself' and flow from the interaction. Structured processes use a standardized, unchanging list of questions that the interviewer is not supposed to deviate from (although the responses may vary greatly).

The advantage and appeal of self-report methods, when used for interviews and CVs, is their familiarity. Most people learn during their education or work experience how to write a CV, and are familiar with the format and requirements. Employers know what to expect from a CV, and do not need to explain why they are asking for a CV. Most employers are familiar with CVs, so feel able to write the requirements and job descriptions. Interviews are equally familiar, and most employers feel confident that interviews are an effective method and are useful for judging personal characteristics. Unfortunately self-report methods, and interviews in particular, are one of the least accurate and least reliable methods of assessing potential.

Despite the popularity of self-report techniques, there are two serious drawbacks that are often overlooked.

The first problem with self-report is about self-insight and social desirability. There are things people cannot or will not say about themselves, even if they wanted to. For example, it is common for interviews to ask questions like, 'what is your greatest weakness?' It is extremely unlikely for an interviewee to say something like: 'Well I'm a raging misogynist, but I'm not very good at relating to other people or communicating, so you probably won't pick up on that for quite a few years.' The issues surrounding self-insight and social desirability can be a particular problem with motivation. For example, in a job interview, the candidates might be asked, 'why do you want this job?' It is unusual for people to say, 'a paycheck'.

The second problem with self-report is the most obvious: people may not tell the truth. This is called malingering or dissimulation, but is basically lying. Most people know that people exaggerate (or deliberately lie) on CVs and in interviews. Yet, they are nearly always a requirement for job selection and promotion. It is not unusual for interviews and/or CVs to be the only assessment techniques. There are many reasons people may deceive themselves or others, especially when a potential job or promotion is on the line. In a self-report format the person may be tempted to answer the question in a certain way, even if it is not accurate. Or a person may add creatively to their CV. There are many different ways of telling untruths, so we will go into that in further detail.

Max Eggert, an expert on selection, has argued that there are many different types of lies. They make a good checklist for the potential interviewer.

1   **White Lies:** These are found in the short endorsements about themselves that may lack any substance or veracity. They are like a checklist of things one is 'supposed' to include in a CV, whether or not they are grounded in reality. 'I am a totally committed team player'. 'I have excellent social skills and the ability to read people'. 'I am utterly

trustworthy and loyal'. The question, of course, is, 'who says?' Where is the evidence? The best solution is to ignore all this flimflam and say, 'I will be the judge of that, thank you'.

2 **Altruistic Lies:** These are lies that attempt a cover-up, but look as if they are helping others. Rather than say they left their last job because their manager was a bully, their team was incompetent or the company was patently dodgy, they say they resigned to look for new challenges.

3 **Lies of Omission:** For many these are the most frequent and easiest of lies. People might omit details of school or university grades because they had poor marks. Whole periods of their life are obfuscated or 'forgotten'. The most common lie concerns dates, often to disguise the fact that the candidate seemed to spend a surprisingly short amount of time in a succession of jobs. A job tenure of '2011–2012' could mean two years, two weeks or two days.

4 **Defensive Lies:** The defensive lie is one that conceals by generalizations or vagaries. Ask a person about their previous boss's management style, their reason for leaving or their health record, and you are often faced with a string of vague expressions such as 'like others in the company'; 'much the same as my co-workers'; 'at that time'. Ask vague questions and you get defensive lies. People blame things like 'the recession' for things like their own incompetence, that are completely unrelated to trends in gross domestic product.

5 **Impersonation Lies:** This is also called the transfer lie and occurs mostly where people take credit for others' work: statements such as 'I doubled sales over the year' or 'I was responsible for a budget of over three million'. All others in the hierarchy are forgotten in these lies. And it is difficult to establish the facts often as to who exactly was responsible for particular successes (and disasters which are, of course, omitted). These are lies told by the people who take credit for everything, and happily forget everyone else's contribution in the process.

6   **Embedded Lies:** This is a clever subterfuge to confuse the interviewer. So 'I really enjoyed my time in Oxford' could refer to a brief course at the lesser known university, Oxford Brookes, just down the road. The idea is to suggest that an experience, qualification or achievement was very different from the actuality. 'It was good fun being with the BBC' could mean practically anything from an enjoyable experience in the Question Time audience to 'they filmed at my school'.

7   **Errors of Commission or Fact:** This is lying 101. They are explicit, verifiably, false claims. It is about claiming qualifications you don't have; describing work for companies that never existed; skills that don't exist. It is the most blatant form of lie.

8   **Definition Lies:** This is the sport of lawyers and of presidents. What precisely does it mean 'to have sex with' someone; what is a company turnaround; what does it mean to be in the latest group? This approach involves working with a very specific and obscure definition so that for all intents and purposes you are telling the truth. 'I had no "contact" with the Russians'. Or see Bill Clinton's statement, 'that depends entirely on what the meaning of the word "is" is'. Or perhaps a claim that inconvenient truths are fake news.

9   **Proxy Lies:** This is where the candidates get others to lie for them. It is usually referees but could be former teachers, coaches or colleagues. They may skilfully work on their previous employers' poor memory, vanity or other bribes to persuade them to obfuscate.

Deception and lying can be put into two further categories. The distinction is whether the deception is focused internally or externally. Some people lie to themselves while some people lie to others. And, of course, some people tell the truth.

(1) **Impression management** is when the person wants to create a particular image of themselves, their skills or attributes. Impression management can

be relatively minor, passive, by omitting or glossing over certain details. Accentuating the positive. Impression management is common in social situations, and work is no exception. Being successful at work always involves some degree of promoting oneself, and presenting the image of competence and skill. Omissions of information can vary in scale and severity though, and unmentioned errors can add up. Impression management can be very serious when a person lies, claiming non-existent qualifications or experience. Deliberate, conscious and continuous deception can have serious consequences for individual, group and corporate performance. Typically Eggert's types of lies involve some degree of impression management.

(2) **Self-deception** is when people genuinely believe something about themselves that is incorrect. For example, the person who would say (and believe) that they are a brilliant orator and conversationalist. They believe it so much they put themselves in situations where they can discuss their views, and would happily take a leading role in the conversation at a meeting, dinner party or bus stop. Because they are deceiving themselves, they can be completely unaware that all the evidence demonstrates that they are actually an insufferable bore. Yet, when asked they would honestly (in their own opinion) describe at great length the strength of their interpersonal skills and their excellence as a conversationalist.

Impression management and deception are not insurmountable obstacles for tests and assessments. Many personality and preference tests involve measures that are intended to pick up impression management or self-deception. They pick up people who are answering things in socially desirable ways; they attempt to pick up lying or inconsistency. The purpose is to detect patterns of responding that are not directly related to the primary purpose of the test. They are generally known as measures of response bias. However, it can be difficult or impossible to detect deception on CVs or interviews, and the best liars who are not detected can be much more destructive than the unsuccessful embellishers. Conducting interviews is a fine skill, and even the most practised interviewers can be influenced by many other factors. That's why it is important to verify self-report claims with other forms of information, whenever possible.

Observation data

Observation data is second-hand observation about a person. The purpose of observation data is to provide a (hopefully) more impartial view of a candidate's performance. The most typical observation data is either references or testimonials. The key assumption is that other people are more reliable than a person will rate him- or herself. This is not necessarily incorrect, but is not without limitations.

360-degree ratings (multi-source feedback) use observations about an individual from others who are familiar with that person's behaviour. They are

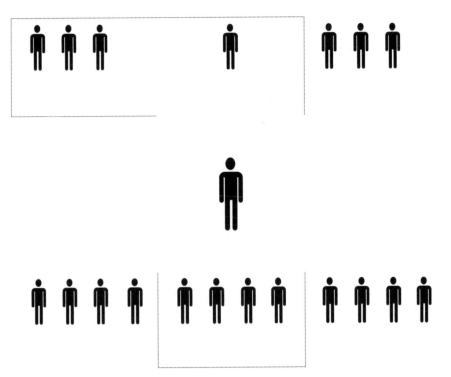

FIGURE 17.1   *360-degree (multi-rater) instruments.*

popular, because they appear to provide more 'objective' information about how a person thinks and behaves. The name implies a full view of the person's potential, taken from every angle.

Most organizations attempt to get reliable reports from other people who know the candidate. Many application processes ask candidates to list people who know them in a relevant setting, which may be education or work or possibly social or sporting clubs. These external raters may (and should!) be called upon to provide testimonial. There are also limitations with observation data which should be considered, but observation data can still be useful.

The first issue concerns what the observer actually knows about the person they are describing. A line manger knows about only a limited set of characteristics and behaviours from certain circumstances and experience which may be very different from a colleague or an employee. The behaviour and performance they see are coloured by the work environment, their relationship and their own perceptiveness. A school teacher or a university lecturer will have a different set of knowledge and experience than an employer because the relationship and environment are different. A spouse, partner or lover may have a *very* different frame of reference and set of observations. The question is *what they know*: the quality, and quantity of data on a person's ability, motivation, work-style and behaviour. People may also present themselves differently to different people. Some people treat their managers, their colleagues and their direct reports very differently.

The second issue is the extent to which the referee is prepared to tell the truth about an individual. Some organizations refuse to provide references about staff because they fear litigation. They worry an employee will take them to court for what they did or did not say. Some companies have policies that only allow them to confirm the dates the person worked at the company, but forbids them from describing what happened during that period. This is, of course, is largely ineffective because much more than that can be conveyed in a sentence. Imagine you are saying, 'Yes, Pascal worked here from January to July'. Think of all the ways you could emphasize the word *worked* to change what message that statement is actually conveying.

The third issue is that people choose their referees because they hope that they will present the most positive image of them. This is not to suggest people who provide testimonials and references are bad people or are deliberately disingenuous. But the relationships colour the result of the reference. People choose references they think will paint the most positive image, and references may feel obliged to emphasize the strengths of a person they already have a relationship with, and would like to see succeed. Many know the power of negative information, particularly when references are selected to give positive appraisals, and therefore try strongly to resist providing any negative information. It is therefore rarer and much more difficult to get very useful data on a person's weaknesses from references that the person selected.

Test performance

Test performance refers to how well people do on tests that measure some underlying characteristic or ability. Intelligence tests, for example, tap into a general capacity for information processing, retrieval and storage (see Part Three). There are many different tests that assess specific skills. Tests of vocational skills may focus on practical exams, to demonstrate competence in specific skills. For example a truck driver needs to be able to drive a truck: the best way to test that is to ask the candidate to drive a truck. Written or oral tests can be used to test theoretical or practical knowledge about a particular subject. Or, tests could be of physical ability. The military, police and firefighters all use tests of physical ability to ensure employees have the necessary ability to complete the job. Valid tests of performance are a much better predictor of success than self-report methods.

The range of tests available is vast with ever more being developed, and many people feel they are able to make up their own. Employers with little knowledge of testing or assessment may develop their own performance reviews, ability tests and practical assessments. This is where things can go very wrong when someone does not have the proper training and experience to develop a good test.

Another common issue is when supervisors or managers think up little tests of performance or ability, with specific criteria, but do not make the criteria clear to the employee. For example, an employer may assign a project without a specific deadline, but think to themselves 'they should have this finished by the end of the week'. This is almost always a mistake because poor testing produces useless or misleading results. Test development is not a place for dabbling if one wants useful and valid results.

A case study of practical testing

Tests of practical skills are regularly used in vocational careers, because the tasks appear to lend themselves to practical testing. If the job involves fixing an engine, styling hair or cooking a meal, ask the person to demonstrate their ability. Why is this so rare in white-collar occupations?

One of the authors was recently involved in selecting a candidate for a job that involved updating and maintaining an online database and basic customer contact. This person would be working off-site, so was required to be self-disciplined and able to work to deadlines (conscientious). Interviews would not have been effective to assess the required skills, especially the technical skills.

Instead, we used a brief simulated exercise very similar to the tasks required of the potential employee. There was a technical task and an interpersonal task. The first task involved developing an online database with a few, simulated entries. Candidates were given an overview of the *minimum* requirements and a specific overview of how they would be scored. They were given a few days to complete the assignment on their own time. Candidates were also given the opportunity to ask questions about their assignment. An extract is shown in Table 17.1.

TABLE 17.1 *Sample practical test scoring*

Element	Points	Points awarded
Task 1: Technical		
Completed on time	10	
Database created, and correct information entered	30	
Questions appropriate and timely	10	
Task 1 Subtotal	**50**	
Clarity	5	
Professionalism	5	
Obtains required information	10	
Task 2 Subtotal	**25**	
Total	**125**	

In their CVs all candidates said they were skilled, and would have repeated this had they been asked in interviews. From the CVs nearly all appeared to be equally qualified for the position. Yet, the practical testing revealed many clear differences between the candidates. First, there were clear differences in candidates' actual abilities. Some candidates could have just barely done the job, while others' work displayed a much greater level of proficiency. Second, it showed candidate's ability to work to a deadline, which was essential for the position. Some applicants never completed the task, others submitted it just before the deadline, while still others completed the task within hours of it being released. This provides some insight into work habits and ability to work to deadlines.

Of course some people will try to impress more when they know they are competing against others, or if they know the job is on the line. Third, the questions people asked revealed even more: candidates were encouraged to ask questions, and told that the task was designed to be an overall evaluation of how well they would work in the position.

Some job candidates asked no questions, which may be preferable for some roles, or it can also be a warning sign that the person is more likely to do something *wrong* than to ask for instruction or clarification. Other candidates asked questions about the specific requirements of the task, which is desirable in a position that requires precision and accuracy. In this task, one person asked more insightful questions about the scope of their responsibilities, about the scale of the workload and future directions of the position. Clear, well-thought-out questions showed a higher level of insight into the position and greater depth of thought about the potential challenges and opportunities in the job. There are qualities you can ask about in an interview but an actual task is much better at revealing these qualities.

The first practical task allowed the top candidates, those most likely to perform successfully in the position, to be short-listed. Then, candidates performed a second test, in a mock customer service–type task. This test of interpersonal skills helped to select the best, most well-rounded candidate for the position. Unsurprisingly, some candidates with the greatest interpersonal skills were less technically apt.

Practical skills testing can be a demanding process because it requires the development of specific tasks and an evaluation framework before the selection process even begins. It means required criteria must be established up front. It may be even more time-consuming if applicants have the opportunity to ask questions and more demanding or complex tasks increase the workload for assessors. A larger pool of applicants also increases the workload. But the information can be extremely valuable and help make assessors make more informed decisions, and greatly increase the probability of selecting the best person or people for the job.

Assessing performance on practical tasks can be much simpler in the case of retention and development. Work is the completion of practical tasks, so an effective leader or HR department will evaluate employee performance on the job. This can be done formally and informally, and provides insight especially when guided by clear performance criteria. Some elements of the job performance (e.g. completing the task well) predict their ability to complete similar tasks. Whereas others such as ability to meet deadlines (conscientiousness), ability to confront and overcome challenges quickly (courage) and ability to adapt to change, and logically solve problems (intelligence) can be indicators of potential to be successful in other positions and responsibilities.

Physiological evidence

Physiological evidence is probably the newest and most disputed of all measures, though there is a long history of people measuring various anatomical or physiological attributes like shape of the skull, finger length and head size. There are now tests of bodily function, like health, presence/absence of chemicals. Thus for some jobs, employees have to go through a 'medical check-up' which they may have to do on a regular (i.e. annual) basis simply to keep their job.

The UK Armed Forces have specific fitness requirements in their selection process, testing both cardiovascular fitness and muscular strength. Requirements are shown in Table 17.2. In the UK Armed Forces there are minimum requirements to qualify; then physical performance is evaluated and weighed with other relevant job criteria. In other jobs, such as working in the alcohol industry, it may be a requirement that people go through a *liver function test* to screen out people who may have problematic relationships with alcohol. Olympic athletes are tested for various substances that the body does not produce, but are thought to artificially enhance performance.

TABLE 17.2 *Fitness requirements in UK Armed Forces selection process*

Test	Male	Female
Beep test	Level 10.2	Level 8.1
Sit-ups	50 in 2 minutes	50 in 2 minutes
Press-ups	44 in 2 minutes	21 in 2 minutes

Science and technology is creating new and more efficient measures of physiology that make it quicker, easier and cheaper to test people physiologically. Blood tests and saliva samples can be used for various diagnoses, including drug taking and stress levels.

Physiological evidence is being used to greater extents and effectiveness in high-performance activities like competitive sporting. There are a wide range of physiological tests available to measure attributes like resistance to extreme temperatures, how efficiently the body can transport and use oxygen or muscular strength. Although interesting selection for physical performance is an entire field in itself (see Tanner and Gore, 2013) for a thorough review. The growth of this technology will soon raise a host of ethical, practical and legal questions for the everyday interviewer – something to look forward to.

For example, MIT Media Laboratory Group has been developing what they call 'sociometric badges' which are wearable electronic devices that are purported to measure a whole host of different social interactions. When one wears this badge it purports to track things like the facial expressions of others around them and the amount of social interaction with other people. They are also intended to measure movement and other social signals. These types of devices could then be used as part of a performance management system or to 'reward' employees based on the level and 'quality' of their social interaction based on the data the device collects. This may sound like fun to some, and terrifying to others.

Personal history/biography

A biography is the history of a person's life. In a biography you can look for clues about their intelligence, personality and potential behaviour, for instance *where* they were born and educated; the family from which they came and their present family and address. Some information is thought to be very important such as socio-economic status; does the person come from a minority race or religious group; how many brothers and sisters do they have and what is their place in the birth order; what was their schooling like and how successful were they at it. However, many of these are less important than the factors discussed in previous chapters like intelligence, personality, work experience and values.

There is an extensive literature on psychobiography which is a psychological interpretation of a person's personal history and experience. As a result there are a number of studies of such people as Steve Jobs and Richard Branson that try to understand the motivations of these remarkable people. Other than a list of developmental milestones described, there is no single life trajectory or sole experience that can serve as a marker of high potential.

Quirky alternatives

Management consultants and marketers too often feel the urge to add a bit of novelty and excitement to the recruitment and selection business. Every so often they think of daft activities to provide 'new and rich insight' into candidates' 'real abilities, personality and motives'. This goes well beyond asking some rather bizarre questions and may involve a rather odd task, perhaps with others, in a quasi-assessment-centre situation. Sometimes quirky methods are invented simply as a marketing opportunity.

Team games

Most people work in teams; they have to learn to co-operate and help others. But how to assess this? The following rather quirky methods have been suggested.

a   *The Ethical Dilemma Game.* there are hundreds of variants of this
game: the hot-air balloon; the lifeboat; the kidney machine patient;
lost in the desert, the arctic or the ocean. Essentially it involves having
to make some rather difficult decisions with no correct answer. The

ethical ones – which person to save or jettison – can cause the most problems as sensitive issues are touched upon. Some trainers revel in these; others studiously avoid them. The idea is that the participants learn to talk to each other, deal with conflict, solve problems. But precisely because it is a game and so far removed from real life, it has a very limited long-term impact and may not be any good at predicting likely behaviour.

b *The Questionnaire:* there are a few questionnaires that supposedly measure how an individual usually or preferably works in teams. Are you a modest company worker or a more natural chairman? This is a more serious and pseudo-scientific, introspective approach, carried out safely in a nice classroom. You fill out the questionnaire, look at the pattern of your team and try to understand why you have frustrations, conflict or, indeed, success. The idea is to maximize heterogeneity; have all the roles covered. Safe, semi-intellectual, some nice discussion and a bit of reflection, but overall pretty ineffective.

c *Fun and Games:* depending on the setting and the weather, groups make things or solve puzzles. Often the task involves balloons, lolly sticks, egg and spoon races and summer camp activities repacked into corporate retreats. The groups are in competition. Some people sit and observe and a week later it all seems rather daft and pointless even if it did seem like good fun at the time.

d *The Sadistic Ex-corporal Approach:* here flabby business people have to do a spot of outward-bound training, getting cold, wet and miserable on a Welsh hillside. The idea is to take you far out of your comfort zone, to experience life at the bottom of Maslow's hierarchy of needs, and discover how much you really need each other. But the ugly head of post-course, angry litigation for injury and insult soon makes this a rather unattractive option.

A good lunch

Why not simply invite a candidate to lunch? Social skills, emotional intelligence and charm can all be measured. Can the candidate do small talk? Do they understand the importance of turn-taking? Can they express an interest in others and be interesting? Sometimes informal situations where people can be more at ease give much more unique and interesting insight. Some argue a one-to two-hour lunch offers the opportunity to visit many issues that may seem inappropriate in a traditional stilted office atmosphere. A chat about previous jobs; bosses they admired; policies they thought innovative; what factors had most influence over their career; indeed their out-of-work activities. People drop their guard in such events, unable or unmotivated to keep up various pretences for all that time. Informal situations beget informal discussions.

It may also show their understanding of etiquette and politeness. Most would (usually) refuse alcohol, but what if the host said, 'I fancy a glass of wine, will you join me?' The skilled executive knows the power of mirroring when it comes to negotiation and general 'friend-raising'. Dealing with staff – it is possible over the course of lunch the candidate might interact with a range of serving staff. Do they treat them like 'plebs' or are they intimidated by them? Are they annoyed by over- or under-attentiveness? What do they think of how the restaurant is run? How do they react to tipping?

Peculiarities will be revealed at luncheon. Strong dislikes, intolerances and restrictions may reveal rigidities of one sort or another. It is quite possible to bring up issues of health over food, as well as other habits. Interesting behaviours like reacting to strangers, servers, delays, kitchen errors, noise, crowding, agreeing on appetizers reveal all sorts. If the job involves novelty like a lot of travel to foreign countries, entertainment and selling. Is the cost of time and money worth it? It depends on how good the lunch is. And what about the retributive, litigious interviewee who, having been rejected, is convinced it was pure prejudice against teetotal, vegans who insist on bringing their own cutlery to meals?

Some would argue this is highly unscientific and likely to introduce many biases, and it is. But it is also useful and interesting and might even be fun. Others argue that you cannot really get beneath the skin and the defences of a candidate at such an occasion and this also has an element of truth.

Of course, every interview should not take place over lunch. But when you're looking at developing high-potential people, mentoring relationships, succession planning, high value or strategic positions or particularly important recruitment or retention decisions, consider lunch.

18

Selection: Choosing the right people

Did you ever know a fool to choose a wise [council]?
– EDMUND WALLER

Introduction

There is always the fundamental question about whether to put effort into *finding* (recruiting, sifting, selecting) top talent (who are nearly 'fully formed') as opposed to coaching, training and teaching the early high potentials to become top talent. It is a question about *how much people can and do develop if they want to.*

There is really one simple question: *Do you have the resources to identify foundational potential, to train the corresponding skills and competencies, and impart the required knowledge?* Or, do you need someone to be high performing right away? Recruiting top performers is expensive. But investing in recruiting early high potential, and developing that potential into high performance is also expensive, time-consuming, and may involve considerable personal investment (Schmidt, 2016).

There are three key stages for developing an appropriate employee selection process (Berger and Berger, 2004; Cloutier et al., 2015)

1   **Identify the competencies.** The competencies are the skills, behaviour and attributes that are necessary for performance. These selection process must aim to identify these competencies which then can subsequently be used for performance appraisals and reviews, provide a clear framework for employees to understand what their responsibilities are and align staff with organizational values.

2   **Define how to measure the competencies.** The definitions are important, and then draw on everything discussed in the previous chapters on assessment. These may be particular rating scales for interviews, tests of individual characteristics or behaviours observed in an assessment centre. The measurement definitions describe exactly what is meant by the competencies, and how best to assess them. The measure should use the best available evidence to appropriately measure the competencies.

3   **Develop the assessment process.** This may involve using the scales to structure and interview, but interviews are far from the optimal selection method, and different competencies are best measured in different ways. The third key step is designing the selection process, from how the tests will be administered, who will be doing the interviewing, how interviewers will be instructed, trained and supervised, and where and when the selection process will occur.

The ubiquitous interview

We have already mentioned interviews in the 'self-report' section of Chapter 17. Interviews are far from the best selection method, but there is no getting past how widespread their use is. The interview is not going away any time soon.

Interviews have the dubious honour of being one of the mostly commonly used and least reliable selection techniques (Levishina et al., 2013; Huffcutt et al., 2013). There are many variations of the job interview: how long they last; how many interviewers they have; whether they are panel or board interviews and, most importantly, whether they are structured or not. Structured interviews are predesigned, formulaic, and ask specific questions of every candidate. Unstructured interviews are guided by the skill, judgement and focus of the interviewer.

There are many sources of inconsistency and uncertainty in what questions the interviewer asks, and the conclusion that the interviewer makes. One important question is, do interviewers agree? How similar would the judgement of two different interviewers be about the same job candidate? The most well-structured interviews have about 50 per cent overlap between ratings of interviewers. Ratings between unstructured interviewers of the same candidate overlap only about 11 per cent.

This is hardly reliable enough to be used as a sole source of information for hiring into a pivotal position. The more important the position is, the more important it is to supplement the interview with other assessment methods which predict potential. One of the major problems is that in an unstructured interview, there is little similarity between how different interviewers would judge the same person. This means that interviewers of the same person do not agree very much on their assessments. One interviewer may have been very impressed while another thought the candidate would be a terrible fit.

The major implication for this is that job interviews are not very useful at predicting success (or failure) on the job. They are insufficiently reliable to use as the sole source of information for hiring (Frauendorfer and Mast, 2015). If two different people come up with wildly different evaluations of a person, it is not reliable, and not a great way to learn about people.

Only planned, structured interviews conducted by skilled interviewers offer relatively good data, and can still vary significantly between interviewers (Nolan et al., 2016).

Essentially, interviews are not very effective alone for assessing potential, particularly for important positions (but later in this chapter we provide an example from a case study for improving the interview process). However, interviews are popular and widespread. On the surface they seem to be the easiest – schedule a conversation with each job candidate, see which one appears the most impressive. It's not surprising that they don't consistently predict potential when there is not a clear definition of potential, or no framework for asking questions. Few employers go through the processes that are really necessary to design a good job interview. There are many different things interviewers should look for, problems which create many sources of error in the interview process. Sources of error in the interview process come from:

- **Interviewers have different values, motivations, beliefs and preferences.** Interviewers with common values or beliefs or preferences may prefer certain candidates, despite their actual ability. It is not uncommon for job candidates to establish rapport over shared interest in sports teams, television shows or recreational activities, and suddenly become the preferred candidate;

- **Interviewers vary in skill.** Getting information from people is not always easy, and some interviewers are better at detecting deception, are more skilled at making job candidates feel at ease and getting honest, truthful answers. A quick joke and a kind comment can change an entire interview. Similarly, a bad joke and an awkward comment can change an entire interview;

- **Interviewers' motives, attention and need for justification of their decisions differ.** While some interviewers are dedicated to the selection process, and its success, others may be disinterested or disengaged. Some interviewers may want the highest performers; some managers look for employees they can control, they find likeable, interesting or attractive. There are many reasons interviewers choose people, many of those reasons unrelated to potential at perform well at work;

- **Interviewees try hard to manage a positive (not totally realistic) impression by self-promotion and self-enhancement.** Some interviewers are better at detecting self-promotion or deception; others can be caught up in real or feigned enthusiasm, self-aggrandisement or flattery. Likewise, some interviewees are much more skilled persuaders;

- **Interviewees may be coached by a range of different sources on how to behave in interviews.** This could be from friends, coaches, mentors, education or even interviewers. Many jobs skills courses teach interview skills. Some candidates may have high potential but not know how to interview well, putting them at a disadvantage;

- **Interviewees (and interviewers and referees) can lie.** The better the liar, the more severe the consequences can be, but the harder it is to detect. A candidate who is a skilled liar may interview very well but could be a terrible employee;

- **Variations occur in how interviewers use rating scales or other measurement techniques.** Variations can be innocuous, and unintentional (misunderstanding). Or, when criteria are not clearly documented, some interviewers will use more creative criteria;

- **The interviewer is trying to predict how the interviewee will perform in an entirely different setting than the interview, under different conditions and circumstances.** People who find unfamiliar situations and people challenging or stressful may perform very differently in the role compared with in the interview or test;

- **Interviewers tend to rate interviewees within a more limited range than is really necessary.** They do not discriminate/differentiate clearly enough between the different candidates. In other words, if each interviewee is scored between 1 and 100, it is extremely unlikely the lowest-performing interviewee will be scored 1 and the highest at 100;

- **Interviewers can, and do, make up their mind before the interview.** Sometimes there is already a preferred candidate before the interviews begin. There may be a preferred internal candidate who will automatically get the job. One person's CV may be the overwhelming favourite or perhaps there is nepotism at play. Interviews may be a mandatory pre-requisite to hiring, but are not always conducted with an open mind;

- **Interviewers are susceptible to forming a first impression and ignoring subsequent information** (or view all subsequent information through their initial perspective);

- **Reasons-to-reject (i.e. select out) factors have disproportionate weight compared to select-in factors.** This is particularly true when characteristics are salient and easily dislikeable, like bad breath, awkward behaviour or other social errors;

- **Interviewers have their own (wrong, unproved, bizarre) implicit personality theories.** These could include factors such as people with a background in sports work well in teams and a person's date of birth predicts their personality and compatibility with a job.

Interviews can be improved to increase their reliability and validity by relatively simple steps. But, anyone who is conducting interviews or relying on information from interviews must remember that interviews are not the best assessment method. Interviews should rarely (or never) be relied on as the sole method to obtain information about hiring, development or retention decisions; the more important the decision, the greater the importance of including other sources of information to make decisions.

Twelve Best Practice Tips for Interviews:

1 *Base questions on a thorough job analysis.* make sure the clear, desirable traits and behaviours are identified ahead of time, and are true indicators of performance and potential;

2 *Ask exactly the same questions of each candidate:* don't give 'hints' to certain people, use follow-up questions and make sure all candidates are provided with the same questions, with the same amount of information;

3 *Use relevant questions*: design questions as situational, competency-based, biographical or knowledge questions. Make sure questions are assessing valid skills in the best possible way. Ask people to demonstrate their knowledge or understanding, instead of asking whether or not they have the skills (Ingold et al., 2016);

4 *Use longer interviews or larger number of questions:* make sure information from other sources does not influence the interviews. For example, it can be useful to have different people reading CVs and references, so interviewers are making decisions solely on the basis of interview performance. Those who have reviewed other information can compare evaluations once all interviews are complete;

5 *Do not allow questions from the candidate until after the interview:* that is when the data has already been collected. That way all candidates can be given consistent information and proper feedback (if it is to be provided), based on their relative performance;

6 *Use detailed anchored rating scales and take detailed notes*: (e.g. 1–10). That way candidate responses can be rated numerically and can be compared more objectively with other candidates;

7   *Rate each answer using multiple rating scales:* particular questions may
    have multiple desired criteria. A line of questioning about a person's
    knowledge may be rated on the accuracy of knowledge, the ability to
    apply knowledge to the work, or both;

8   *Use multiple interviewers where possible:* multiple interviewers can
    compare evaluations and see which candidates they rated similarly or
    differently and why;

9   *Consistency:* use the same interviewer(s) across all candidates and
    provide extensive training to enhance reliability. Well-trained
    interviewers will be better able to compare candidates when they
    interviewed all candidates. Furthermore, when possible keep interview
    times consistent. The same interviewer may have different feelings
    about people Monday morning, Wednesday at midday and Friday
    evening;

10 *Use statistical, rather than clinical, prediction:* use research and
    evidence instead of your own personal experience to make decisions
    about potential. Both are valuable, but individual experiences (your
    own, or anecdotes from others) are far less reliable than large-scale,
    high-quality studies;

11 *Don't ask unrelated or inane questions:* if you were a fish, no one
    cares what type of fish you would be. There may be the temptation
    to surprise or embarrass interview candidates with ridiculous
    questions. Your time, and the interview candidate's time, are
    valuable. Ask questions that are specific, relevant and targeted to
    the job;

12 *Be kind:* many interviewees put time, effort and personal energy
    into the application. Acknowledge unsuccessful applicants and be
    respectful to all. Present the same consideration you expect from the
    successful applicant.

Personal or professional references

References are an attempt to get some objective, independent evaluation of a person's skills. References are commonly used, requested, and are rarely checked. Despite the frequency references are requested, it is surprising how rarely they are checked. Furthermore, although references give a perspective that is external to the applicant, they are rarely independent and never objective. People choose referees based on what they think (or know) they (referee) will say. When people provide references, they select people who will be most complimentary, and least likely to be aware of or describe the applicant's weaknesses.

There are advantages to references, but there are equally serious drawbacks. References, like interviewers, can be open-ended where references are provided, and interviewers or assessors can contact the reference and ask questions. Closed-ended references are more flexible and may ask the person to describe their own skills or characteristics. They can be helpful to provide some reference point for a person's skills or experience (and also their ability to develop positive relationships) but there are serious limitations. Typically references involve free response or ratings that an observer reports on another. The person giving the reference is providing an observation based on what they know of the candidate. They are both common and popular in both worst and best senses of the word.

Essentially, it should be simple to find a positive reference. Anyone who has ever met (and made a positive impression on) another human should be able to get a positive reference. References are massively subject to experience and social position and personality. References are supposedly dependent on performance, but the ability to get positive references is based on persuasiveness, connections, charm and assertiveness.

The critical evaluator of references tends to be more sceptical of references and believe they are unreliable and of poor validity. The main concern with references is that they require the evaluator to evaluate many more aspects than just the attributes of the candidate relevant to the potential job position. References require an evaluation of the candidate, the referee, the relationship between candidate and referee, and the information provided. This evaluation involves far more complex analysis than most assessors really have the time or resources for. The most frequent errors made when examining references are:

- *Leniency.* Most references are indiscriminately positive. Candidates select who they believe will give the most positive references; references worry about the interpersonal or legal implications of giving bad references; respondents have no incentive to take the time or tell the truth.

- *Idiosyncrasy.* People can describe and evaluate others in strange ways, and on wildly different criteria. This can make it difficult to apply some references to specific definitions of potential at work.

- *Free-form references.* Reference writers are often offered no guidelines or requirements. In many cases, references are listed just as a name, title and contact details, or as testimonials. These can vary wildly when referees are not provided guidelines.

It is possible to improve the validity of the reference by explaining fully the purpose of the reference; using rating scales or a forces choice format. Using well-designed rating scales also helps a great deal. For example, ask referees to rate the candidates using the following chart: The candidate is applying for a job where they have to meet with many clients around the country and promote our services. Please rate the characteristics of the candidate as they relate to this job.

The information in the chart is useful, because it can be compared with other people. Although referees are likely to give high ratings, and may be happy to exaggerate, the chart shows a clearly lower rating on 'punctuality'

TABLE 18.1 *Sample ratings of job skills*

Characteristic	Rating (1-Poor, 10-Excellent)
Interpersonal skills	9
Sales ability	9
Punctuality	7

than sales ability or interpersonal skills. This type of rating system also can allow for referees to say they don't know about certain skills a candidate may or may not possess. Referees are best when the employer chooses the referees; those referees are peers who know the candidate well; the referees are asked specific questions and are guaranteed anonymity.

Improving selection processes

Below are a few recommendations to improve interviews as an assessment method:

Define potential. As is a common theme in this book, define exactly what qualities, traits and competencies are required to successfully perform the work. Make sure the advertised job description is clear about the requirements, and that any interviewers or assessors have a clear and precise understanding of what is required, and how to evaluate it. If there are multiple desired criteria, define and rank their importance up front.

Increase objectivity. It is impossible to completely remove subjectivity in the assessment process. Every job and company has slightly different requirements and different positions, different potential career trajectories. Yet all possible efforts should be made to ensure the process is as objective as possible. Once potential is clearly defined, this should lead to a few, clear, assessment methods.

If the job involves selling a product, a mock sales call is a better assessment measure than a standard interview.

A one-size-fits-all approach to selection is a quick way to get the right people into the wrong jobs. Finding better ways to assess the actual skills and abilities should be of constant interest to those in charge of selection. For an administrative position, give a brief administrative task before the interview. Then spend the interview discussing the process and results of the task.

Establish reliability. Make sure assessments are consistent between interviewers and interviewees. If multiple interviewers are being used, make sure all interviewers are briefed in the same way, have all the same information and all interviewing based on the same assumptions and criteria. It may seem simple, but make sure every interviewer has read and understood the job description, and is evaluating based on the job description (it is surprisingly common for interviewers to make assumptions about the position that are unrelated to the actual, official job description).

People interview based on what they want or what they think they want at the time. If there are multiple interviewers or evaluators, it can be useful to split the interview/assessment process into multiple steps. For example, if candidates complete a practical skills evaluation, followed by an interview with questions, it can be useful for a different assessor to evaluate a different assessment method related to their area of expertise. When possible, candidates should be assessed the same way, by the same person or people so scores or rankings are fair between interviewees.

Remove barriers. Remove all barriers to employment that are unrelated to actual job performance. This has the dual advantage of promoting employment equity and increasing the potential talent pool (making sure high-potential candidates are not overlooked). Barriers can be anything from gender, class, ethnicity, geographical distance, nepotism or others. For example, most companies overlook the possibility of hiring someone who cannot have a physical presence in the office. More and more jobs and evolving information technology mean there are more jobs that can be done remotely.

Some jobs do still require a physical presence, but not all do. If communication is viable, proper oversight and quality controls are in place, geography should not be a barrier to work. This is, of course, not true of every job. A mechanic or surgeon cannot telecommute. Yet, more competitive companies are finding ways of finding and hiring the highest-potential person, even if they never meet.

Develop Validity. Validity, in this sense, means optimizing the process to make sure the highest-potential person or people are successfully identified. The more valid the process is, the better able to discern a person's actual potential. Validity encompasses all of the above steps along with the subtleties and peculiarities that will arise from a process that involves working with people. It means adapting approaches to fit within the business context, the requirements of the job and what potential means for a particular position or career path. It means constantly considering and re-evaluating the question *potential to do what?*

Conclusion

Selection is commonly associated with assessment, and selection tends to be used for hiring new people. However, selection is ongoing in many ways. Good selection involves the selection of new hires, selection of people for development, for retention or redundancy.

Basic methods like interviews and references are both least reliable and most common. That does not mean they should be scrapped outright, but more sophisticated tools should be used, particularly in high-value positions and when the risks of derailment could be severe. Build a list of desirable characteristics and competencies, and then choose the best assessment methods. Proper selection processes can be difficult, expensive or time-consuming, but greater accuracy brings greater rewards. And letting the wrong person through with dark side or derailing traits has severe consequences, as everyone who has worked with one of these people knows.

19

Training

Try to learn something about everything and everything about something.
– THOMAS HUXLEY, QUOTED IN *NATURE* VOL. XLVI (30 OCTOBER 1902), P. 658.

Opportunity is missed by most people because it is dressed
in overalls and looks like work.
– THOMAS A. EDISON

Introduction

Development can mean the difference between the great and the good; the transformation of the mediocre into the good; the improvement from the inadequate to adequate; it can be the difference between failure and success. 'Executives who consider a job to be a set of tasks, miss the importance of developing people' (Berson and Stieglitz, 2013, p. 93).

Development is a lifelong progress that starts with the earliest human learning. Babies, children and adults all develop at different rates based on their genetics and their environment. Some people are more predisposed to picking things up, understanding other people and their surroundings. Some people learn very quickly while others need practice. In psychology, development just means change in a person over time. For example, physical growth and learning are developmental. In the context of human resources and performance at work, development typically means deliberate effort, training and learning that are intended to directly or indirectly improve performance or realize potential.

In common usage, training is different from development. The focus of this chapter is to discuss training and experience; then the next chapters discuss development and how to develop high potential. Training is part of development, and is important but is less interesting from the perspective of this book, and you'll see why in a moment.

The lessons of experience

There are many ways to develop talented high-potential people. Experience and training can vary widely and not all is made equal. Talented leaders report similarities in what experience contribute to their growth and development. Studies across organizations in different sectors as well as those within big corporations and across different corporate and national cultures and even different historical time periods reveal the same story. Successful leaders who have proven to develop their talents mention six powerful learning experiences.

1   **Early work experience**. Early experiences with work are consistently reported as a factor in shaping the early development of high potential. This experience may be a part-time job at school, a relatively unskilled summer holiday job at university or one of the first jobs they ever had. These experiences may be positive or negative. Bad experiences can shape someone as much as the good ones. For some it was the unadulterated tedium or monotony which powerfully motivated them because they never wanted to work in that environment again. For example, one of the authors once worked at an unimaginably tedious

job where the sole task was stacking newspapers into piles of ten as they came off a conveyor belt. For others it was a particular work style or process in a particular job or organization, the memory of which they have retained all their lives. This is something to select for: what type of work experience they had while young and, more importantly, what they learnt from it.

2   **Experience of other people.** Working with other people can always provide more useful experience. The most common example of early experience with working with others is nearly always an immediate boss, but can be a colleague or one of the serious grown-ups. The high potentials almost always remembered this person as either very bad or very good: both teach lessons. Usually the lessons include experience about how to treat others, or how *not* to treat others. The lesson here, from a development perspective, is to find a series of excellent role models, mentor-type bosses for the talent group.

3   **Short-term assignments.** These assignments can be project work, standing in for another or interim management. Short-term assignments are most effective when they take people out of their comfort zone and expose them to issues and problems they have never before confronted. They force people to learn quickly and adapt to new challenges. For some it is the lucky break: serendipity provides an opportunity to find a new skill or passion.

4   **Major line assignment**. This is often the first promotion, foreign posting or departmental move to a higher position. It is often mentioned as important in shaping development because suddenly the stakes were higher, everything more complex and novel and ambiguous. There were more pressures: the buck stopped here. Accountability and personal responsibility are greater than ever in this role. The idea, then, is to think through appropriate 'stretch

assignments' for talented people as soon as they arrive. They should be challenging and success should be feasible.

5 **Hardships of various kinds**. Intelligent, high-potential people learn from difficulties. This type of experience is about attempting to cope in a crisis which may be professional or personal. It teaches the real value of things: technology, loyal staff, supportive head offices, personal values or experiences. The experiences are those of battle-hardened soldiers or the 'been there, done that' brigade. Hardship teaches many lessons: how resourceful and robust some people can be and how others panic and cave in. It teaches some to admire a fit and happy organization when they see it. It teaches them to distinguish needs and wants. It teaches a little about minor forms of post-traumatic stress disorder and the virtues of stoicism, hardiness and a tough mental attitude. Learning and persevering after failures are an essential part of long-term success.

6 **Management development.** Different types of training, education and experience are usually a part of development. Some people remember and quote their MBA experience as useful; far fewer some specific (albeit fiendishly expensive) course. One or two describe the experience of receiving 360-degree feedback. More recall a coach or mentor, because they were either so good or so awful.

To the extent that leadership is acquired, developed and learnt, rather than 'gifted', it is achieved mainly through work experiences. Inevitably some experiences are better than others because they teach different lessons in different ways. Some people seem to acquire these valuable experiences despite, rather than as a result of, company policy.

Experiential learning takes time, but timing is important. It's not a steady, planned accumulation of insights and skills. Some experiences teach little or indeed bad habits.

But three factors conspire to defeat the (good and rather valid) experiential model:

- *First*, both young managers and their bosses want to short-circuit experience: learn faster, cheaper, better. Hence the appeal of the one-minute manager, the one-day MBA and the short course;

- *Second*, many HR professionals see this approach as disempowering them because they are 'in charge' of the leadership development programme;

- *Third*, some see experience as a test, not a developmental exercise.

A large component of leadership potential should be defined as the ability to learn from experience, and apply that experience to the work. Those with the optimal personality traits to work hard, persevere and overcome stress and difficulty are more likely to have high potential. Equally, every move, promotion or challenge should be evaluated by its learning potential.

Training and competencies

Training is about teaching an employee how to do a certain task or job. It relates specifically to competencies (training is essentially the process of acquiring competencies). Competencies have been popular since the 1980s, and can be seen as the fundamental building blocks of any careers (McClelland, 1973). Competencies are the basic things a person needs to get their job done. Competence implies the minimum level of performance, whereas other words such as 'expertise' or 'mastery' imply optimal skill levels. Consider the definition of competencies by the Employment Department and National Vocational Qualifications' definition of a competency: 'something which a person who works in a given occupational area should be able to do'. A bit vague, but it means the right behaviour to get the job done.

Competencies can be broken down into elements of competency, and each can be assessed, using a practical or theoretical assessment, where people demonstrate the appropriate behaviour and performance. The following elements of a competency (Table 19.1) are taken from a competency-based model for Aircraft Structural Technicians and Utility Arborists. Competencies lead into training programmes, because there are specific, limited and clearly defined outcomes of training, that can then be tested and measured.

TABLE 19.1 *Sample of competencies and occupations*

Aircraft structural technician		Both	Utility arborist	
Aerodynamics	**Metal routing**	**Regulations and safety**	**Climbing**	**Hand tools and small power tools**
Explain why an aircraft can fly	Describe routing principles	Identify relevant legislation and regulations	Select and inspect climbing gear	Use and maintain hand tools
Explain lift, thrust, weight and drag	Demonstrate hand routing	Identify potential workplace hazards	Conduct pre-climb assessments	Operate a variety of small power tools
Explain axes of flight	Demonstrate computer-controlled router	Use personal protective equipment	Climb using various techniques	Use and inspect ladders
Explain aircraft control			Conduct post-climb job and gear inspection	

Adapted from ITA (2013a), ITA (2013b).

Every occupation is made up of a limited number of competencies (McClelland, 1973). Each competency may be, but is not necessarily, exclusive to a single occupation. For example, as was shown in Table 19.1, two very different occupations at Aircraft Structural Technicians and Utility Arborists have many different competencies. However, there are similar competencies in understanding the relevant regulations, workplace hazards and personal protective equipment. The key idea is that each competency is important, and every competency is necessary. The limitation to competencies is the chasm between the basic level of competence and excellence of high potentials.

Planning training and development: An example

Take the example of local community development offices. The development office works with small and medium-sized local businesses. Its purpose is to help those businesses grow by providing funding or other business support. One of the important jobs in the development office is an accountant. The accountant assesses proposals and business plans to make sure the development office is supporting financially viable businesses and plans. If we assume selection was done well, an accountant for the community development office will start the job with strong qualifications and will be fully capable of assessing financial plans and providing financial advice. The accountant would be intelligent, conscientious and hopefully have similar values to the organization.

However, as many people quickly learn when moving from education into the workplace, there are more demands, complexities and challenges in work than education or training can prepare you for. A good leader can prepare people for this shock, and, in the ideal cases, development starts with this realization. For the new accountant in the community development office, numerical and financial acuity is a fundamental competency, but improving performance involves interpersonal skills and the ability to build relationships that some accountants may need and may not have learned at the start of their career. Part of the work of assessing small businesses is getting to know the people in the business, understanding their motivations, goals and abilities.

Thus, a development opportunity for the accountant would focus on building up skills that are important for successful performance, improving performance or potential. It may start with formal training on orientation, workshop or course, and then would involve practicing more informally. Perhaps teaming up with a colleague who already has those skills so can provide some informal help and guidance, with on-the-job learning.

There are many ways to develop staff with potential. There are two primary dimensions of development that are helpful for understanding the range and breadth of development:

Formal vs. Informal which distinguishes between whether the development is formal, explicitly part of the job and monitored/recorded formally. Informal experience can occur inside or outside the company, but tends not to be explicitly recorded or rigidly structured.

Knowledge vs. experience distinguishes between abstract learning and theory compared to actual practice. For example, it is the difference between learning about business plans and business models versus actually applying it, which involves getting to know and understand the person behind the business.

Table 19.2 shows a matrix of development types comparing knowledge/experience and formal/informal. The most effective development draws from each of the quadrants, and uses various aspects to build on each type of development.

TABLE 19.2 *Examples of knowledge vs. experience and formal vs. informal development*

	Formal	Informal
Knowledge	Teaching, training, orientation	Coaching, mentoring
Experience	Task force assignments, rotating assignments, job placements	Teaching (as learning), activities outside of work, deliberate practice

Formal development of knowledge (typically training) can provide the foundation for development, teaching the basic skills necessary to be successful in the job and to teach employees strategies for enhancing their own development. Formal development experience gives people a chance to apply their knowledge and hone their skills and apply those skills to familiar and novel situations.

Formal development of experience involves structured and targeted applications of knowledge and experience. When done right, it usually has formal objectives, clear requirements and success criteria. Essentially, it should be a method of directing and applying skills learned in training. It serves to reinforce the training, and should be a strong indicator of whether or not the training was successful. If a training programme does not improve performance, either the training was useless or the person did not really learn from it. Good training (formal) should provide direction for further experience to develop the skills: skills learned in training should be transferrable to the workplace.

Informal development experience can provide a novel or interesting environment for experimenting with new skills (potentially outside of a work environment), or to develop skills further, such as teaching colleagues. 'Teaching as learning' is an excellent example of this. After training, the person teaches one or a few colleagues the skills they have learned. It is less formal, because it does not happen in a classroom and may not be directly supervised. It's a chance to practise the skills and apply them to a new and different set of circumstances.

Informal development knowledge can be imparted by coaching or mentoring. Coaches or mentors can be provided in an organizational environment, or can come from outside the organization. Mentors can provide insider knowledge, advice and guidance. Mentors can help to bridge the gap between previous knowledge and experience and future development. A coach can help a person to make sense of previous experience, and then can guide the person to future development opportunities that would be of the greatest benefit given current skills. It requires greater knowledge of the person, their abilities and history, and is an ongoing benefit.

The key to successful short- and long-term development of high potential is integrating all types of development into an employee's work life. Successfully combining these will improve development. Quick fixes are common practice, but are not necessarily effective. It's common for development to be done on an ad hoc basis; development is done in a quick course to check a box off the good HR manager's 'to do' list. Or, when a department has some money left over at the end of the year, it is shovelled into training exercises.

The reality is short courses, workshops and training exercises *can* be useful, but are not *necessarily* valuable. Effective salespeople generate excitement about a course or workshops, making the training seem interesting, fun and promise results. It's easy to justify the expense by imagining *any experience is valuable* but that is just not true. Development efforts should be focused, and integrated into performance objectives and long-term development efforts. A quick checklist:

A great, rule of thumb for testing out whether a development opportunity is valuable is to plot it in the development matrix. Use the question *potential to do what?*, keeping it firmly in mind. Does the development fit broadly within the context of the employees' potential?

First, put the development opportunity into the appropriate quadrant of the development matrix (e.g. formal + knowledge). Are there applications where the knowledge can be used in the workplace? It should fit into the framework, and be reinforced by further formal and informal development, such as follow-ups and practicing on-the-job to test out the knowledge or skills.

If the development opportunity doesn't connect with all quadrants of the development matrix, one of two things should happen. One, drop it. Save yourself the time and avoid the glibly packaged schoolyard activities. Two, ask more questions and learn about the *realistic* outcomes. If it is unlikely it will translate into valuable experience, or have any effect on performance or potential, refer to one.

Not to say that something that is not directly related cannot be valuable experience – but there should always be a cost-benefit analysis. If something is sold as a great development experience, and comes with a high price tag, it needs to be able to demonstrate direct links to performance. Many informal (and low-cost) activities – even hobbies or 'extracurricular activities' – can lead to strong connections with other development efforts. Hobbies can lead to developing new skills, or developing informal networks that can be a source of experience or a place for informal coaching.

Why training and development fails

Despite the effort, money and time some companies dedicate to talented people, many feel it frequently fails. But why? Below are a number of reasons for this all-too-common event:

- Failure to predetermine outcomes relevant to business needs of the organization. Unless one sets out a realistic and specific goal or outcome of training, it is very difficult to know if it has succeeded or failed;

- Lack of objectives, or objectives expressed as 'will be able to' rather than 'will'. There is a difference between 'can do' and 'will do', often ignored by evaluators;

- Excessive dependence by trainers on theory and chalk-and-talk training sessions. This method is least effective for the learning of specific skills;

- Training programmes too short to enable deep learning to take place or skills to be practised. The longer and more spaced out the programme, the more participants learn and the more it is retained;

- Use of inappropriate resources and training methods which have to be considered beforehand, particularly the fit between the trainer and the trainees' style;

- Trainer self-indulgence, leading to all sessions being fun sessions, rather than actual learning experiences;

- Failure to pre-position the participants in terms of the company's expectation(s) of them after training. This means having a realistic expectation, per person, of what they should know, or should be able to do after the training;

- Failure to debrief participants effectively after training, particularly as how best to practise, and thus retain the skills they have acquired;

- Excessive use of 'good intentions' and 'flavour of the month training', rather than those known to be effective;

- Use of training to meet social, ideological or political ends, either of trainers or of senior management. That is, training is not really about skill acquisition but rather about a fight between entrenched and opposed colleagues, or a fight between various departments.

When it is done well, experience is a fantastic teacher for those who are receptive to its lessons. Training will inevitably be part of development systems, but a broader range of development programs must be integrated for high potentials to reach the upper heights of their potential. The next chapter discusses this in more detail.

20

Development systems

There is the greatest practical benefit in making a few failures early in life.

– THOMAS HENRY HUXLEY, ON MEDICAL EDUCATION

All men dream, but not equally. Those who dream by night in the dusty recesses of their minds, wake in the day to find that it was vanity: but the dreamers of the day are dangerous men, for they may act on their dreams with open eyes, to make them possible.

– T. E. LAWRENCE , *SEVEN PILARS OF WISDOM*

Employee development processes

As opposed to training, which has specific timing and focuses on specific skills, knowledge and competencies, development is more broad and wide-ranging. While training is primarily to get up to minimum levels of performance, development is to maximize potential. It used to be that training was for entry and 'low'-level workers, while development was for higher-level managers and professionals (Winterton and Winterton, 1999). Table 20.1 highlights key conceptual differences between training and development.

TABLE 20.1 *Selected differences between training and development*

Element	Training	Development
Timing	Fixed (e.g. 500 hours)	Ongoing
Objective	Competence	Expertise/mastery
Structure	Primarily formal	Primarily informal
Application	Specific	General
Relevance	Current role	Future opportunities

Development is fundamental to moving from competence to excellence, from high potential to high performance. Development is the most important vehicle driving the development of potential; from the potential (possibility or likelihood) to do well, into actual performance when required. It involves developing new skills, applying old skills to new environments or tasks and refining and honing other skills.

Typically the objective of development is to improve work performance. Many high performers (or high-potential people) want development opportunities because they want to improve their own performance and self-actualization. A further benefit of development is that it can help retention, as will be discussed in the next chapter.

Developing people is an opportunity for individuals to improve, but it should be equally seen as an opportunity for the company to develop people – to increase the capability of workers, with higher performance as a consequence of development. Approaches to development vary widely. Some employers are interested in providing (or selling) 'transformational experiences' and self-awareness. But when it comes down to it, most competent leaders will assume if they've managed to find and hire you, you have already managed to 'find yourself'. The key to development should be that it is based on a clear conceptualization of potential, realistic objectives and a plan.

The Goldilocks Zone of development

Development is the process of directing, targeting and applying experience to maximize potential. As discussed in Chapter 5, experience is a fundamental part of high potential. Experience is central to development, but all experience is not developed equally. For people to develop they need opportunities to practise and learn. They need challenges to learn from, but not to be thrown in, the 'deep end' without any help or support.

Good development occurs under conditions that are not overwhelmingly difficult, nor underwhelmingly dull and uninspiring. It could be described as the Goldilocks Zone of development: not too easy that it's effortless; not too difficult that it's impossible. It's similar to the idea of deliberate practice, but deliberate practice under the right conditions; both the internal dedication and right levels of difficulty; too easy and learning cools off; too demanding and burnout is imminent. The Goldilocks Zone is what astronomers affectionately call the circumstellar habitation zone – the narrow set of conditions in which life can develop.

Whereas practice can be completely focused, and rehearsed, the Goldilocks Zone of development can be in new and unfamiliar conditions, and learning new skills while using current skills. It's not too hot, creating too much pressure to really be able to learn from successes and failures. Nor is it too cold, slow-moving, sluggish and unchallenging to promote any learning. Colvin (2011) refers to it as 'effortful activity': it is activity that is conscious, effortful, challenging and deliberate. Lev Vygotsky (1968) described it as the 'Zone of Proximal Development'.

That Zone is something that is fostered internally by the person, and externally by leaders and organizations. One has to be focused, dedicated, engaged in the activity, continually thinking and reflecting upon the new challenges and experiences. At the same time, a strong leader or mentor will help the high-potential person to understand and make sense of situations. An organization can encourage (or inhibit) people's desire to learn new things, explore new techniques and take risks and allow people to learn through successes as well as failures. Of equal import is the ability to distinguish between individual error, and failures that affect the organizational goals.

Thus development should be a *co-operative process*. The employee, the person being developed, should be actively seeking that Goldilocks Zone, where the work is *challenging, engaging, and helps to improve skills*. It is the person's responsibility to not just participate, but focus on learning from the work and to be part of the development process. To be thinking about the challenges, seeking support where required, reflecting on lessons learned and lessons that still need to be learned.

The person who believes they already know (or can do) everything, who believes everything is easy because of their overall mastery, will stagnate. They are in the 'too easy', too cold zone, and can't see that there is a more challenging area that is waiting to be explored and developed. Overconfidence, arrogance, fear or a leader without a strong vision and ability to push/inspire can cool off development.

Leaders, HR departments and colleagues contribute to the development process (and depend on the size, structure and particularities of the organization). They create opportunities for development, inspire people to push themselves where appropriate, and support and coach them when and if they become mired in challenges beyond their current ability. They provide a structure for guiding development, and a support system to push the boundaries of the Goldilocks Zone.

It's not uncommon for people and organizations to languish in either the too hot or too cold zones. Some organizations and people get comfortable in the cold zone, where things are going well, minimum performance is sufficient, sales are good enough. Some people who don't see their personal development tied up in their work may be content to have steady, consistent, reliable performance in the cold zone, to save energy for their personal or family life. Organizations, too, can become complacent.

It is also surprisingly common for people and organizations to stick in the 'too hot' zone. Instead of consistently meeting minimum performance standards, many organizations are in a constantly reactive state. Every day, every task is a fight against the newest, most pressing challenge: customer complaints, legal challenges, staffing problems, leadership difficulties and insufficient funding, poor sales.

There are innumerable problems that create an environment where the company and the people are constantly jumping from place to place, fighting fires, extinguishing emergencies, but never really settling down. Yet, the lessons are never learned, the major problems are never resolved and the bigger picture, systemic problems are never really dealt with or given the appropriate time or attention.

Many hospitals have physicians and nurses running from emergency to emergency, always with many things to do but emergencies, quite rightly, taking priority. Yet sometimes this means key problems with the organization go unresolved and unaddressed. Politicians can become embroiled in the most populist current issues, the controversy of the moment, and react to the short-term concerns instead of meaningful, strategic and long-term planning. Employees, leaders or companies sling mud at each other in what can quickly become a race to the bottom, instead of developing and (improving) potential.

New managers will often micromanage, taking control of minor details instead of their key responsibilities. They take control of the things they have done well in the past, but neglect their new responsibilities. There is always something or someone who needs to be instructed and monitored, but never enough time to get everything done. This 'too hot' zone also inhibits development, because there is not time to think, learn and reflect from the experience. People who are feeling the pressure, fatigue and excitement tend to jump to dealing with the most pressing problem that they are already best able to resolve. There appears to be no time to consider priorities, take the time to learn how to do something new, and the cost of failure is perceived to be too high.

Good development is a dynamic process that requires co-operation and interest from the individual being 'developed', the organizational culture and relationships with colleagues or leaders. Personal relationships are an important part of development, particularly in the coaching or mentoring process. Not all development is based on relationships, but it will be challenging for anyone to continually develop within one organization without strong social ties and respectful trusting relationships. Disconnections between cohorts, generations, organizational groups, departments and management levels can easily develop when information is provided (feedback, recommendations and advice) without trust or respect. It's hard for anyone to hear criticism or their limitations described, and, when it comes from a colleague or leader where there is no relationship, it probably will not be well received.

Berson and Stieglitz (2013) describe how 'leadership conversations' are important to help new employees, or employees in new positions, develop plans of action, define expectations, clearly communicate performance standards and develop relationships. They suggest that leaders should work to have 'conversations' in order to develop personal relationships and regular contact. The interaction should be about developing the relationship; contact is not just about listing tasks. Building relationships can lead to opportunities to use people's skills and networks – both to achieve the organization's goals and to develop people. But, leaders need to stay in touch and be up-to-date to know who has the unique knowledge, expertise or contacts – and need to have built the trusting relationships so that people are willing to disclose and use their talents and knowledge.

Not every characteristic can be developed. For leaders, learning to ask the right questions in the right way and learning to build honest and trusting relationships can be developed. Many characteristics cannot be developed.

Personality, for example, cannot be changed without serious psychological intervention. Experience and motivation build on intelligence, but intelligence cannot be drastically changed (except in extreme cases like brain injury). Development is primarily directed at broadening range, depth and suitability of experience.

Consider the following three stages of development:

1st – Before: Before training or development starts, it needs to be planned. One needs opportunities for new experience, whether they are specific training courses, or new on-the-job projects to learn new skills. It can be self-directed, when the person chooses training that will improve their own performance or potential. Opportunities for experience help to hone skills, applying them in new situations and to learn more about the job, other jobs, other people and one's own attributes.

Before the training begins, this may be choosing a task for a specific person, matching a group of people with a training or development programme, or designing a specific development activity for a group with a specific type of potential development in mind. Individually, it also involves understanding what motivates people to be part of development activities, what they hope to get from it, how important they believe it is and how important the development is to their supervisor.

2nd – During: Learning from training is the intended part of any training or development. But people always bring their previous knowledge, experience and expectations into development. This is an advantage, when people are curious and interested, considering how the new experience fits into their own career. Integrate their new experience into their current knowledge. However, expectations can be a double-edged sword. Resentment, scepticism or mistrust of a supervisor who assigned the development activity can bring in negative expectations and preconceptions that inhibit development.

3rd – After: Good development never stops. After completing a specific training programme, contemplate the lessons learnt and reflecting upon them helps to improve the outcomes of the training. Reflection is useful, whether or not the training or development was successful; it is useful to consider *why*. Reflection is important because it means carefully considering and reinforcing the lessons learned from previous development. It also gives a chance to direct future development. Good learning experiences mean challenges. They should not be *easy*. Good development opportunities will show the individual where their skills gaps are – and should help to shape objectives for future development.

Each of these factors links, and should be a dynamic process that incorporated continual opportunities, planning, learning and reflecting on each stage of the process.

Types of development

The first part of development in any organization is getting oriented, learning what to do and meeting colleagues. In human resources this is called onboarding; psychologists would call it socialization; most people would call it orientation. Essentially it's a process of learning about the job, learning about the company and learning about the people with whom they will be working.

Orientation and 'Onboarding'

Most jobs involve an initial period of formalized training that involves learning about the specific skills required for the job, the expectations of the organization and the future colleagues. It usually has a specific time duration (e.g. a half-day, one week, one month) and may be followed by some sort of testing or assessment of characteristics or skills, to make sure they are ready to start work. A more detailed orientation process that involves introduction to both the systems, people and social context of the organization (referred to as onboarding) introduces new employees to the work. This should be an introduction to the organization, but also the development process. What the employee has to do to initiate further development (document process), whom to work with, ask questions about various things.

Allen and Bryant (2012) describe six important recommendations for improving the 'onboarding' process, based on Van Maanen and Schein's (1979) pioneering work in socialization:

1 *Formal.* Specific activities that are designed to help new employees become accustomed to the organization, the groups and colleagues. Special groups and activities arranged formally, with specific purposes. These help new employees to learn and reduce anxiety, by providing easy steps to learn about the job demands and the group. They are planned new hire lunches, on- or off-site activities. These should have clear and consistent messages to convey job responsibilities, expectations and culture;

2 *Collective.* Combined groups of new hires help new employees to get to know each other, and to feel a sense of camaraderie that may not be initially possible with entrenched employees. These groups should be designed to create a sense of excitement about opportunities to work within the organization, and the organization is supportive of their development. Otherwise, informal, unstructured and unsupported groups may develop a feeling of 'us vs. them'. When done well, this creates a connected group who feel supported, and accepted into their new role;

3 *Sequential.* The order of events should be pre-arranged, designed and clearly described. This helps new hires know what to expect of the initial onboarding process, and feel more prepared to start. When new employees are able to prepare, they are more likely to feel greater control, and able to meet the expectations;

4   *Fixed.* The timing of onboarding events should be clear, not just the order. For example, a group of new hires would receive a specific schedule of events for new hires. All the various elements have a time and date, with clear description. Many people are anxious about new jobs, so fixed times and dates allow people to prepare, reducing anxiety and uncertainty;

5   *Serial.* People already experienced in the organization, such as experts or leaders, are part of the introductory process. These should allow opportunity for interaction, and building relationships with these 'insiders'. It helps people feel that they are really part of the organization, understand the inner workings and are getting the right contacts and building the right connections early on. It helps to learn who to ask questions and who can help solve problems. It also helps new employees identify possible mentors and role models;

6   *Investiture.* When the process involves early feedback and information about the position, along with clear social support, it helps new employees feel like a welcome and important part of the organization. This helps the new employees feel willing to provide their own contribution to the organization, as compared to *divestiture* socialization, which encourages conformity, but not integration into the team.

Onboarding, of course, must be relevant and appropriate to the position and the organization. It sets the tone and is an opportunity to convey performance and social expectations. It also leads into further development opportunities – lack of onboarding, or poorly planned onboarding, conversely signals there may not be a strong or coherent development path.

An example of exceptional onboarding actually comes from particular university student unions. Most university student unions organize a series of events for new students, in the sometimes infamous 'freshers' weeks. Some who work in university unions have learned the importance of starting off well. The onboarding and orientation events set the tone, and for students the transition can be a huge change. The transition into a new organization is often less drastic, but the importance of a smooth transition should not be underestimated. The Courtauld Institute of Arts is a good example of this, because it's a specialist and elite institution, well known for producing high flyers in the art world. Róisín O'Connor, president of the Courtauld Student's Union, describes the importance of these events:

> It is a chance for new students to explore the city and what's available to them. It also allows them crucial bonding time – peers must become family away from home and they can learn whom they want to spend their time with. Good fresher's events are very important for building what can become lifelong friendships.

Similarly, in companies new recruits must be given opportunities to develop relationships and meet prospective colleagues, leaders and mentors. It's a time to explore the organization, the systems, the culture and the opportunities. A strong start helps people develop the connections, knowledge and social support needed to be successful at work. Yet, it's not a simple or easy process.

> The success of fresher's relies on how comfortable the students feel about the Students' Union; how excited they are to become part of the wider student community; how interested they are to partake in societies; how confident they are in feeling that their voice will be heard and appreciated.

> It depends on the organizers, as well as the new 'recruits'.

Like any organization, the Courtauld has a unique history, culture and mission. It is a small university with about 250 new students in 2013 (mostly postgraduates), and its reputation for excellence means expectations are high; and this is true for any organization or company renowned for high quality. The orientation sets the tone, so disappointing students or new employees before they even began can be extremely demoralizing; an excellent onboarding experience can be invigorating and starts people off engaged and excited. Although student onboarding involves more 'fun' and typically involves significantly more alcohol than one would want to introduce to the workplace, other organizations can learn from student unions like that of the Courtauld to provide informal and engaging experiences. A sample of the Courtauld's 'onboarding' events is given in Table 20.2:

TABLE 20.2 *Extracts from Courtauld's 'freshers' events*

	Mon	Tues	Weds
Events	Breakfast, lunch and afternoon tea to meet colleagues, professors and professionals	Cocktails at bar in Shoreditch to meet fellow students	Pimms reception film screening, followed by evening at the pub with fellow students

The culture values and purpose of each organization will influence what types of events are useful, entertaining and appropriate.

Training/workshops/classes

These can be either internal or external, but have a specific time period (e.g. half day, day, weekend) and typically have a specific purpose. They are intended to teach a specific skill, or knowledge about a certain area. Good training exercises have a specific purpose, clear time period, and are geared towards a specific outcome. For detailed information about planning training, see Berger and Berger (2004). Ideally there should be direct linkages to future work, along with practice and follow-up evaluations.

Task force assignment

Specific tasks at work can be either directly related to a person's current job description, or outside of their current job scope. A task force is a good way to develop skills that were learnt in a workshop or class. The purpose of a task force assignment is typically practical skill development. In other words, there should be a specific, well-defined task along with success criteria (both of the task and of the development). To be successful, the person assigned to the task should be:

- Capable of succeeding (i.e. high potential on that task);
- Able to develop new skills, or hone existing ones;
- Willing, or motivated, to succeed.

The task should be limited in both time and scope. It has clear and specific objectives, and the person knows when, why and how the task will conclude. For example, if the task force assignment is to recruit three new employees, with a specific set of skills and characteristics to the department by the end of the month.

Rotating assignments

Rotating assignments are thus named because one is moved between positions or locations. Unlike task force assignment, it is not limited to a specific outcome or objective; one is required to fill an entirely new position (although the position may be similar). Of course, all of the concerns with putting untested or unknown people in unfamiliar positions are relevant here. Before placing people on rotating assignments, it is essential to ask the same, recurring potential questions. *What characteristics predict potential in the new assignments/positions? How much overlap is there between the current position and the prospective position? What is the potential (and consequence) of failure?*. Greater similarity of position reduces uncertainties of a person's potential to perform well and learn from experience, but similarity provides fewer opportunities to learn new skills and adapt to new situations. Rotating assignments require excellent assessment of potential, clear goals, 'areas to develop', and should target the Goldilocks Zone, getting the assignment and the person 'just right'.

Teaching (as learning)

Teaching other people about the job, the work or skills is an excellent way to practise skills and develop them with other people. It is not simply a lecture or description, but working with others personally and interactively to impart skill. It is real and practical training. For example teaching through learning can be an important part of learning a new language. Teaching others the vocabulary and grammatical rules helps to reinforce the knowledge and understand the knowledge in a social context. It also helps to identify any skill gaps, sometimes, when teaching (or trying to teach) one begins to realize both the extents and limits of their own knowledge and ability. Successful training and development naturally should lead to pride and satisfaction of achievement, as well as competence. Teaching others is a great way to demonstrate experience, and to reinforce previous experience. It is a natural reward for successful development because it recognizes the success of those who have it.

Activities outside of work

Development is not always limited to work, and is not always something leaders, managers or HR departments can oversee. This can be much harder to define, guide and manage, but is equally important. Activities outside of work, unlike most other developmental processes, are primarily the responsibility of the individual, not the company's.

This could be learning leadership skills on a club or sports team, meeting new and interesting people in community or non-profit groups, clubs or charitable works. Or it can be when seemingly unrelated activities provide new knowledge which eventually translates into insight at work.

Coaching and mentoring

Coaching is one-to-one advice and support for a specific task or issue. It is relatively short-term but is intended to be a closer, deeper look with specific advice and action planning. Mentoring is a longer-term relationship for advice and recommendations that may be less focused on specific issues, but the mentor is available for guidance or advice and general support.

21

Developing and coaching high potential

Being entirely honest with oneself is a good exercise.
– SIGMUND FREUD, *ORIGINS OF PSYCHOLOANALYSIS: LETTER TO FLIESS*

There is nothing more difficult to take in hand, more perilous to conduct, or more uncertain its success, than to take the lead in the introduction of a new order of things
– MACHIAVELLI, *THE PRINCE*

Introduction

Potential, of course, varies. People with high potential, by definition, have a greater capacity to develop from development opportunities and will learn more quickly. People with lower potential should not be excluded from development. Even those with more limited types of potential can still learn to do certain tasks, better or more efficiently, and occasionally those judged to have low potential *will* rise to challenges and surprise even the most experienced assessor. Stifling opportunities drains the talent pool.

One way to look at development is to compare foundational and growth potential. Those with low foundational potential are likely to struggle with many of their responsibilities; those with higher foundational potential will be more successful at the core elements of their job. Those with low growth potential are unlikely to greatly improve their skills or their performance in their current role significantly. High growth potential means that person is likely to learn new skills, improve their performance and may be able to use that growth potential to advance into new positions.

The focus inevitably falls on those judged to have the highest potential: the rising stars. The high flyers of the organization have all the right traits, who learn quickly from experience, are motivated to excel and have seized opportunities available to them. Most people in the other three categories can still benefit from development, and the majority of people are 'average', in the middle, who are competent, mostly do a good job, but are often forgotten as people who can benefit from development.

Thus, people can be classified (broadly) into four development groups (see Table 21.1).

1   *The Underachievers* barely (or do not) meet the minimum requirements for the job. They don't have the basic skills or abilities, and are unlikely to greatly improve. At best, this is because of a mismatch between person and position, and they *may* have higher potential in a different type of job within the same organization. At worst, there may not be a position for them in the current organization. Development for this group may focus on learning the skills for a different position, or low-risk task force assignments to discover what jobs they are suited to;

2   *The Strong and Stationary* are fully competent in their current position, and have a high potential to continue to perform well in the same position. They will benefit from some development opportunities, to

improve their current performance, but their performance is unlikely to change greatly. This can be seen as a weakness or a strength. Development for this group is for retention as much as it is to improve capability;

3   *The Poorly Placed* have a high probability of learning new skills and improving their performance, but they may have challenges with the core tasks. This could be because they have not yet learned the skills, or because their attributes are not a good match with the position. Typically development activities for the poorly placed should focus on finding a better job match, giving people the opportunity to grow and develop into new positions.

4   *The Rising Stars* are the future high flyers. They have all the right traits to do their job well, likely already have strong performance and are likely to improve their performance, learn new skills and be capable of moving into other positions. This group should get the full suite of development opportunities, either with the aim of improving performance, training experts and specialists, or with the purpose of moving the rising stars into managerial or leadership positions.

TABLE 21.1 *Matrix comparing development objectives for growth and foundational potential*

		Foundational potential	
		Low	**High**
Growth Potential	High	3. **The Poorly Placed** Development, possibly leading to more suitable positions.	4. **The Rising Stars (High Flyers)** Development is critical and wide-ranging.
	Low	1. **The Underachievers** Development has minimal effects	2. **The Strong & Stationary** Development focuses on current position, responsibilities.

A critical component of potential is the *ability to learn from experience.* Equally, every move, promotion or challenge should be assessed by the learning potential. The capacity to meet and learn from a challenge is more important to potential than past experience at an identical task. While others may be focused on getting the job done, high flyers are continually interested in new experiences, and developing their own potential. In a study of high flyers, Galpin and Skinner (2004) found that high flyers were clear about the value of developmental processes. They noted the order, *from most to least valuable*, processes were:

1 Mentoring;

2 Job Rotation;

3 360 Degree Feedback;

4 Qualifications Support;

5 Coaching;

6 Interpersonal Training;

7 Management Development;

8 Technical Training;

9 Career Counselling;

10 Buddying; and

11 Career Development Resources.

It is important to note that formal training and basic institution resources are not the most valuable developmental tools. The highest-rated development processes provide honest and constructive feedback and advice (mentoring) or direct and applied experience (job rotation). These are some of the most complex and most difficult developmental processes to administer, but are also the most valuable.

Galpin and Skinner (2004) noticed that high flyers had very strong views about what they believed was good for their own development and wanted to be 'in the driving seat' of their development. 'Clearly, there is a need to ensure that there is a healthy balance between the organizational performance and the individual's development, and that the high flyer does not get rewarded for leaving a trail of destruction behind them' (p. 114).

Development, particularly for demanding, engaged, and career-mobile high flyers, is not easy, but it's necessary, and is one of the most important activities to keep the best and the brightest.

Students of the magical (but occasionally disillusioned) MBA or the part-time degree know the sacrifice that is involved there. If there are twenty-four hours in a day and you sleep another third, how much of the remainder do you give to your friends/family and work? The mastery of any skills comes easier to the talented but all skills take practice. This includes all those skills one goes on training courses to achieve: presentational skills, negotiation skills, counselling skills and selling skills.

Measuring development

Traditionally, there are four measures of development success. The *first* and easiest is the 'happy sheet' method where trainees report on their reactions and also perhaps how much they did and didn't learn. These are not always reliable. Trainees can be deluded as to how much they learnt. Others are ingratiating or sabotaging, giving unrealistically positive or negative feedback on all or specific aspects of the course.

The *second* is the classic before and after examination; test (for knowledge/skill) before the course, and then immediately afterwards. Make the test hard before and easy after and you can ensure impressive results. Or the other way around of course if you want to prove the course didn't work.

The *third* is to get others to rate the trainee who works with or for them. Thus they make a before-training-assessment and an after-training-assessment. They may be accurate and honest but of course they may not.

The *fourth* and best method is, of course, to measure not what people say, but what they do, or better still, what they produce. This makes the sponsors really sit up. Imagine sending people on a five-day sales course which increases sales revenue by 20 per cent over the next six months. Now you are talking! But there are two major problems with this ideal solution: having really good measures of an individual's performance and being sure their output is uniquely due to their own ability, effort and knowledge.

Another issue is whether training actually applies to different situations. The issue is called *transfer of training* and it may be the Achilles heel for trainers. Put people in a safe, supportive, comfortable environment and they may learn and readily display a variety of skills salient to a business. Pluck them out of that safe cocoon and three weeks later they appear to remember nothing. But something can be done. Four features considerably improve transfer of training.

Feedback

Feedback is a central component of all learning. The question is how to obtain honest and accurate feedback after the formal training has stopped. Trainees need to learn to ask for feedback or the signs of feedback. Certain tasks can have feedback mechanisms built into them. The microchip can be used to signal to people that they have been sitting or standing for too long or short a period of time. More importantly perhaps, new programme attendees need to be told it is their duty to help those on courses to maintain, even improve, their skills. All too often people who return from skills-based courses are ignored, even punished. Skills need to be practical and reinforced. In this sense the whole organization needs to be 'on the course'.

General principles

Teaching *general principles* is essential for generalization. This means giving the *big picture,* and even the *theory.* The idea is to provide a framework for learning – the greater understanding of why. If people do not know the general principles, they cannot easily adapt or see how differences between the training and work situation matter or not.

Identical elements

Identical elements is a great help, though not always possible. This refers to the self-evident point that the closer the training is to the real situation, the better. Given the correct identification of the situation (perception), training should mean learning how to respond most appropriately. It's about making training as realistic as possible and tying it directly into work tasks. And that refers to selling equipment, people and the like. Posh country hotels and cosy training rooms don't quite cut the mustard.

Overlearning

Overlearning is about achieving automaticity; doing something with little thought. Surgeons, pilots and the like can act quickly and thoroughly on extremely complex tasks without apparent thought. What they do has become second nature to them. And this requires serious practice. Transfer or generalization of training is a complex issue. And there are many different types of generalization. There is:

- generalization over time;
- generalization from the training time to the future;
- generalization over situations: from the safe and cosy training room to the complicated hard world;

- generalization over skills: from one set of particular skills (negotiation skills) to a similar set (selling skills).

All are important, though the first two the most significant and situation generalization may have many subtle features. This is because work-based behaviour depends not only on individual skills and motivation, but also, crucially, on group norms. There are famous cases of individuals trained to do x things in x minutes comfortably (type 100 words per minute or deal with one customer every 3 minutes), but who struggle when faced with the much higher output rates that the work group finds acceptable. This is not a training issue, but something much deeper embedded in organizational or cultural values.

Does coaching work?

Coaching has become increasing popular and is no longer just for athletes. Everyone from an entry-level employee to the CEO can get a business coach. Sometimes these are provided by the company. Other times ambitious people pay a coach out of their own pocket in a quest for self-improvement. Clearly it is filling some sort of need. Is it just that people need someone to talk to or encourage them? Does coaching actually improve performance?

Coaching has been defined as 'unlocking a person's potential to maximize their own performance. It is helping them to learn rather than teaching them' (Whitmore, 2009).

Like most topics in the workplace that command a great deal of money, the topic has been researched, so we would hope to have good evidence to answer the question about whether coaching works. Unfortunately, the scientific evidence about coaching and productivity in the workplace is mixed at best.

Theeboom and colleagues (2013) say that 'Whereas coaching is very popular as a management tool, research on coaching effectiveness is lagging behind'.

One of the main issues is that when we're asking if coaching 'works', it is necessary to add additional follow-up questions. What is the purpose of coaching? If the purpose of coaching is to improve performance, then what type of performance specifically? (Fillery-Travis and Lane, 2006).

Some of the results are encouraging, because Theeboom et al.'s (2013) meta-analysis suggested that coaching can be related to positive effects like improving coping abilities and goal-setting. But with this myth, it is essential to think about the outcomes or results as well as the process.

Questions to consider for coaching

When people talk about coaching, keep in mind how the question is being asked. For example, if someone is asking, 'does coaching work?' then they are not being specific enough. It's like when scientists ask the question, 'does alternative medicine work?' the question is not being specific enough to get a meaningful answer. Like any process that tells people it 'should' make them better, they are likely to feel at least a little better (Rajagopal, 2006). The same could be equally true for homeopathy or coaching. There are three things to keep in mind for a good, well-tested intervention that is as applicable to researchers as to practical interventions in the workplace.

Randomization

In scientific research participants or patients are randomly assigned to a group, each with different conditions. At work, this could mean that a pilot test of coaching effectiveness would involve people randomly assigned to different coaches, with some not assigned to any coach. This is important, because it helps to see if there is any benefit to the coaching at all. Sometimes in organizations the highest-performing group has access to the most resources. But what if the high performers are the most (or least) likely to benefit? Randomization also controls for the volunteer effect. We know that all sorts of variables in the doctor–patient or the coach–manager relationship can affect results. It can be the age, education or physical good looks of either party in the relationship that affects outcome, rather than the process itself.

If coaching works, should it work for all managers? And it should work for all (trained) coaches who follow the process. If it works only for certain types of people with certain coaches, then we need to know why and whether some specific factor (other than the coaching process) is having an effect.

So a manager has to be (randomly) assigned to their coach. Neither party likes this much but that is too bad. We know that some psychologists have a selection interview to decide whether both parties feel they 'can do business with each other'. The scientific question is why the treatments only work for certain combinations of giver and receiver. If it does this needs to be in the small (or indeed big) print.

Control groups

The second feature of the scientific approach is that there needs to be one or more control groups who do not receive the treatment or, in this case, the coaching. Obviously it may not be desirable to exclude some employees from a program that they might benefit from. In other cases there may be a strong budgetary argument to testing the program out on a limited group before rolling it out across the organization. In addition to that, ideally some participants will receive some type of coaching or training they may benefit from, but not directly related to the outcomes being measured. What this could mean is that some managers are assigned a real management coach. Another group may be allotted to a physical coach or another manager. Perhaps colleagues are asked to discuss their work with one another while others receive professional coaching sessions. Coaching may be beneficial, but is it really any better than advice from a manager or colleague? There are essentially two types of control groups: one in which the patient manager does nothing at all and sees if the coach experience is better than nothing. The other is where the manager does some other activity quite different from the coaching.

Control groups with no treatment will indicate to the evaluator whether changes in the managers' performance would have happened anyway naturally over time. It's called 'spontaneous remission'. Sometimes people just naturally get better. The body (perhaps the mind) can sometimes heal itself. Time can heal. But the control group can also show which condition is the most beneficial. Control groups really tell us about the process itself. It could be that just getting out of the office and talking to someone is helpful. It could be that being selected for a 'higher performer coaching program' makes people feel more confident. If this is the case, perhaps a lunch with a senior management would be just as effective.

Blinding

The third component of the process is just as important, but sometimes more difficult to do in a workplace setting. Blinding means the subject does not know if they are in the control group or not. Ideally, the evaluation should use double blinding: neither the experimenter knows which participants are assigned to which group. In medicine this means neither the doctor/nurse nor the patients know whether they are getting the (real) drug or a sugar pill. The reason for this is that often when people know which group they are in; it changes their opinion of the effectiveness of the treatment or the program. Equally, the experimenter or HR manager can influence the outcome in a number of different ways either intentionally or unintentionally.

So after two or four months of 'something' (executive coaching, exercise, lunches with their manager, nothing) the employees of the managers in the trial are required to rate them on their performance. Better still, some hard behavioural data can be used to see whose performance improves the most or the least. Managers' self-reports may be produced, but they may be completely delusional.

Does coaching work? Perhaps. But the only way to know is to test it out in your organization. Run a pilot test and measure the differences. Make sure to be very clear about what type of performance the coaching is meant to improve. Perhaps make the bonus for the coach conditional on actual improvements in performance. When a coach promises results, they should be able to specify exactly what type of performance they are intending to improve. Measure it.

If, and only if, the coached employee has statistically different and better evaluations than those of the other group can it be justified, or say that it 'works'. If it doesn't work (or works no better than other interventions), it may just be paying for very expensive conversations.

Having expensive conversations

There are all sorts of ways of having expensive conversations and work coaches. Senior leaders have executive coaches; people with psychological difficulties have psychologists. Rarely do these conversations come cheap, so it's important to think of the return on the investment. If coaching produces only small improvements in performance or productivity, is it worth a large piece of the training and development budget? Let's say a coach improves the effectiveness of the sales team which results in each employee selling £500 more per month. If the coach costs £2500/month for each employee, is the coaching still worth it?

What about the downsides? Is the therapist or advisor acting as a coach or a crutch? Do they create a psychological dependency that leads the person to rely too much on the external advisor to make decisions?

A useful way to examine this is to look at the different types of coaches that can be available.

The therapist-counsellor

Many coaches act almost like a therapist or counsellor for the employees they are working with. Many coaches, too, have received training in psychology or counselling. Of course, therapy and counselling are the same thing. Therapy is problem-orientated, counselling is person-orientated; therapy focuses on both the past and the present and is interested in significant change, while counselling focuses on the present and is more oriented towards gradual change. Therapists treat, interpret and intervene to develop new ways of solving problems and improve functioning. Counselling is about caring, enabling, facilitating, supporting, exploring, discovering (blah blah) to alleviate suffering, find solutions to problems and deal with crisis.

Do CEOs or everyday workers need therapists any more than front line supervisors or entry-level workers? It may be helpful to have someone to talk to, to help to relieve stress, but it may always be necessary. Senior leaders in high-pressure roles are also typically selected for their resilience to stress and ability to work well under pressure. This form of coaching can be seen as either a luxury or a necessity.

Remember that it's important to frame the question in a way that asks about outcomes. We're not saying that having a therapist is not valuable, and if it helps to make employees feel better that is certainly one measure of value. That is completely distinct from the question about whether or not this type of coach improves employee productivity or effectiveness. But perhaps if a worker is having psychological problems they need help with, a psychologist would be more helpful than a coach.

Confidant/friend

It can feel lonely at the top. Sometimes people forget that very successful people have problems and difficulties just like people who struggle to succeed at work. CEOs and presidents are expected to be discrete, and not to blab trade secrets or national secrets to competitors or random people they want to impress.

Those at the top of the career ladder are not the only ones who may need to apply some discretion to what they say and to whom they say it. But the consequences can be more extreme. It is helpful for everyone to have support from trusted friends, and someone to discuss sensitive issues with. But the pool of these people can be much smaller for someone like a CEO.

It might be a friend, and is often a spouse that people talk to about these types of things. However a coach can fulfil this much-needed role as a confidant. It is often encouraging to know that the coach has signed a strict confidentiality agreement and professional ethics also forbid the person from disclosing the discussion. Then for some, the coach is similar to a priest and confessional. The role of this coach, then, is to be there: to be a sounding board, a shoulder to cry on; a non-judgemental support in good and bad times. They might understand the business, but paradoxically they may do better if they don't. The naïve questions sometimes provoke the most useful thinking, particularly if they are about people or products.

The trouble with the friend model is that the relationship has no natural beginning or ending. The friend is paid to be a friend, which is a contradictory arrangement in itself. Confidant, confessor, sounding board, perhaps: friend no.

Again, there is the question of value to the company. Many very well-paid CEOs hire a coach personally to act as a confidential confessional. If it helps to make them feel better, ease their mind about the issue of confidentially and disclosing professional information, then there's nothing wrong with that. At the price tag of executive coaching, the executive coaches would likely agree quite strongly. But again, if we're asking the question about whether coaching works, consider what the specific outcome is.

The educator/tutor

There are many reasons why people climb or meander to the top. Sheer ability and knowledge of the business are often complemented by an ego, ambition and sometimes a temperament that may be useful but not necessarily ideal.

No CEO can really pretend to know everything about the business or how to take it forward. Wherever they come from and whatever their experience, they need to keep up with technical and legal changes. They also need to have a strategic vision for the business and its future in local or global markets. A helpful coach from the corporate, academic world may be very helpful. This can help to give impartial advice from an external, intelligent source. This can help to provide some much-needed advice and content from an impartial outside source.

This model essentially makes the coach an educator or teacher. It assumes that the coach has unique insight that will be valuable. The CEO expects wide knowledge. He or she has no time (or even inclination) to read burgeoning academic tomes and academic journals dedicated to the business. They do, however, expect the coach to do so and to provide an expertise and critique. They may want a revered Oxbridge professor to do their homework for them.

The educator may or may not be supportive and friendly. Some want a no-nonsense approach where the educator provides them with direct and sometimes harsh advice. It may be a soft touch or it could be the academic version of boot camp. This type of role is not about the coach listening; it's about speak. The coach is supposed to update and (often very directively), to advise.

The wise judge

Wisdom is about general enlightenment and respected expertise. It is the thoughtful application of learning in combination with insight intuition and good judgement. The word 'wisdom' is bandied about in business, but quality is hard to find. Wisdom may or may not be related to emotional intelligence, IQ or personality.

The wise judge would tend to have to be more respected for wisdom that comes from extensive personal experience. It is easier to recognize than to describe which can make it a bit of a dodgy concept. It's also fraught with problems about whether or not the expertise and judgement is correct or truly good judgement.

Who is the wise judge? It's hard to say, and for many it depends on political or ideological beliefs. It's the trusted talking heads that are always wheeled out by journalists to be the expert on a subject. Perhaps Gore Vidal or Kenneth Clarke (either the art historian or the MP). For some it might be Noam Chompsky or Shirley Williams, while for others it might be Ayn Rand or Ann Coulter. In these cases, the judgement you want and receive is probably very dependent on your views and the type of advice you want going in. Some people go off wandering around India or Australia to 'find themselves'; others just want someone to tell them where they are.

The wise judge tends to be seen as someone who doesn't 'do emotion'. They are not therapists or friends or tutors, though they might offer some of the benefits of the other three. Wisdom is not flighty or issue-specific. And it is very difficult to find.

The problem is negotiating a contract with a wise judge. Many require intrinsic, not extrinsic, rewards and they may easily express irritation with a dim, self-indulgent, psychopath posing as a CEO. Many are wise enough not to get involved in these sorts of commercial wisdom enterprises.

Whatever model you choose or have, coaching is expensive. It may be intellectually and emotionally taxing. It may eat up valuable time. But it is bound to be costly. The trick is to distinguish between a merely expensive conversation and a seriously good investment in improving performance.

Conclusion

Development is a lifelong process that has a greater span than any individual career or job. Some people are extremely 'developable' whereas others are resistant or unable. There is one way to develop people, because development is a process that builds on already available skills, and uses key traits like intelligence and personality.

Employers who want to develop high potential must begin development from the very first day with effective orientation procedures, ongoing training and real knowledge of employees along with constructive relationships. Development cannot always be structured and formal, and the 'good lunch' method described previously may be one of the best ways to assess and direct development opportunities.

22

Retention: Keeping the best and the brightest

Love truth, but pardon error.
– VOLTAIRE, *SEPT DISCOURS EN VERS SUR L'HOMME*

Those who deny freedom to others deserve it not for themselves, and, [...] cannot long retain it.
– ABRAHAM LINCOLN

In this country we find it helps, from time to time, to shoot one admiral to encourage the others.
– VOLTAIRE, *CANDIDE*

That is why I have resigned. In doing so, I have done what I believe to be right for my party and my country. The time has come for others to consider their own response to the tragic conflict of loyalties with which I have myself wrestled for perhaps too long.
– GEOFFERY HOWE, RESIGNATION SPEECH TO THE HOUSE OF COMMONS, 30 NOVEMBER 1990

Introduction

Losing the 'right' people for the 'wrong' reasons is a problem that, at best, is unnecessary and inconvenient, and at worst can cause entire systems and organizations to unravel or derail. High employee turnover rates are not just inconvenient; they are expensive and demotivating

There are many reasons that people choose to leave or stay with an organization, and some are entirely uncontrollable from the manager's perspective. Yet, while some people leave for 'personal' reasons, many people choose to leave very specifically because of colleagues, bosses, leaders and their organization. Most people have probably had the experience of working with people and thinking: 'I just don't have time for this; I don't need this'.

People join organizations but leave individual managers. That is, their decision to *leave* is based on 'push' rather than 'pull' factors. Many employees' decision to leave is based on unhappiness with the way they are managed rather than other factors. Similarly, most managers will have experienced an employee that is performing poorly, or manages to cause most of the trouble and chaos in a team or department. There's almost always one. They can be the most challenging to work with, and sometimes are the most difficult to get rid of.

There are inevitably two parties involved in retention: the organization, which may or may not want to retain a person or group of people; and the employees who may or may not want to stay. Many organizations have some idea of a typical employment period. For some fast food restaurants they may work on six months, while for some consultancies it may be three to five years. This is the idea of a normal or optimal 'stint', meaning a typical period that a person chooses to work for an organization.

Most organizations invest a lot in individuals: recruitment, training and development. Typically the more highly skilled the position, the more the organization invests in them. Individuals also feel like they are investing their time, efforts, energy and lives in a job or organization. As a result both want a *return on that investment*. Naturally employers want to retain people they have invested in and judge to be high flyers. Equally many employers have their own 'game plan' and are eager to move on to maximize the training and experience.

Organizations are most concerned when they see their high potential leaving and those with less potential choosing to stay. In this case, the question to ask is, why are the best leaving: is it push or pull? Are they being lured or enticed by other organizations eager to attract talent or are they being pushed by dissatisfaction with what they have?

Assessment for retention

Using assessment for retention is challenging because, as with recruitment, it depends on the position, the employee and the requirements of the organization. A good retention strategy involves clear and measurable objectives. Once the *short- and long-term objectives* of employee selection and development are documented, the appropriate assessments and instruments can be selected and deployed to *meet the objectives.*

Using assessment for retention requires a good understanding of the different assessment tools that are available. Regular assessment is useful only when the assessor is measuring the right constructs in the appropriate way. These can be divided into three categories (which can be partially mapped onto Silzer and Church's (2009a) three dimensions of potential):

Stable (foundational)

These are traits and attributes that do not change. Intelligence and personality are relatively consistent across a person's adult life. Stable traits need to be tested only once, or at very wide intervals. Stable traits lend themselves most to formal, quantitative assessment. For example, self-report personality tests may be appropriate for recruitment, but may not be appropriate for regular assessments or performance reviews.

Variable (growth)

These are attributes or preferences that can change, but are unlikely to change regularly. Job-related skills and career goals will be relatively consistent, but are likely to change in the long term. These should be assessed regularly and typically can be quantified. For example, regular performance reviews should assess performance and abilities. Daily would be too often; once every ten years would not be frequent enough.

Situational

These are preferences or ideas that can change regularly. Day-to-day moods, desires and needs may change. A person's life circumstances can change frequently, or regularly but not at predictable intervals. These are difficult to assess formally and may be difficult to quantify – but are still important. For example, regular conversations can keep a good leader informed but a daily, written report about mood and personal circumstances test would be excessive.

Then, that assessment can be used to make (in the most simplified sense) one of three retention decisions. *First,* keep and develop that person into future positions. *Second,* keep the person in their current job and maximize job performance and/or satisfaction. *Third,* if they are not suited to their current position or other positions in the organization, take the necessary ethical, practical and legal steps to help them leave the company.

Common problems and issues with retention

Individual issues, circumstances and desires can lead people away from the organization. Employee turnover (people leaving) is not bad in itself; people leave or change jobs for all sorts of reasons outside the companies' control. But, retention problems can also be symptomatic of a dysfunctional system or leader. People leave bosses, colleagues, situations and systems. It is always easy to point out individual reasons why people leave work, but the systemic issues are important and can be influenced. There are a few key errors and common misconceptions about retention.

Error 1: Neglecting retention completely

The focus of employers is typically placed on recruitment, where development is an afterthought, and retention is a footnote. The greatest initial human resource/talent management challenge is finding and attracting the right people. The importance of *keeping* those 'right people' is often overlooked (Gully and Phillips, 2012). While selection is essentially a one-off process, it has a single, clear goal with simple success criteria; retention is ongoing and therefore much more challenging.

The excitement that frequently comes with a new job, seeing new possibilities and opportunities, can fade quickly when not cultivated. Or, it can be encouraged and built upon to increase capacity for high performance and high potential. Other activities like development, fair assessment and strong leadership can be used as a tool to improve retention, a key part of the framework of keeping and developing the right people.

Retention is often and misleadingly framed as a matter of individual preference and choice; people are said to leave because they are unsuited, lazy, unskilled, unable to cope with the pressure or had the wrong values. It is rarely said that people leave because of systemic problems in the organization, bosses rarely admit, 'Oh dear, I managed that person very badly', but those systemic and interpersonal factors play a significant role.

Error 2: Believing that turnover (and loyalty) is generational

The belief that young people are who are fundamentally different from previous generations is nothing new. It is typical for people to make broad, sweeping statements about generations. Take these two examples from a few thousand years apart.

> Our youth now love luxury. They have bad manners, contempt for authority; they show disrespect for their elders and love chatter in place of exercise; they no longer rise when elders enter the room; they contradict their parents, chatter before company; gobble up their food and tyrannize their teachers. (Attributed to Socrates in Patty and Johnson, 1953, p. 277)
>
> They're 'Millennials' (also known as Generation Y), and many will want to wear flip-flops to work, don't care about spelling, have zero discipline, and expect the keys to the C-Suite. Despite the fact that their managers likely raised Millennial children of their own, those managers frequently find themselves at a loss as to how to train and retain Millennial malcontents. (Mayhew, 2013)

Each quotation introduces the point like it is a current, new and pressing challenge to the world. The reality, though, is there is no evidence to support the latest cohort of young people is any more disrespectful, indolent or impatient than any previous generation (Becton et al., 2014). Scales (2011) reviews the research, and finds no evidence that there has been any major change in the behaviour or performance of young people: 'there is no research which would provide us with evidence that pupil behaviour is becoming worse, or better for that matter' (p. 229). Findings from MacRae and Furnham (2017a, b) also show that there is no truth behind the myths of generational differences in factors like workplace motivation or values.

There have been large-scale changes, however, in organizational culture of work, and the commitments organizations make to hiring. The reverse issue is that of work stability and commitments to employees such as 'zero hour contracts'. Estimates suggest between 250,000 and one million people in the UK have zero hour contracts (CIPD, 2013; ONS, 2013), with the most rapid increase in zero hour contracts for those between the ages of 16 and 24. A zero hour contract means the employee has an employment agreement with no guarantee of work. The *zero hours* refer to the amount of work the employer is required to provide for the employee. The reality is these changes are not objectively good or bad, but understanding these changes makes understanding individual differences more important, particularly for retention (MacRae, 2017).

Attributing blame is not helpful, but realizing the employment climate is different than decades past is essential, and should not be surprising to either employees or employers. Loyalty and mutual respect is something that can develop between employees, managers and corporations when it is deserved, but commitment and work are required on both sides.

Error 3: Assuming that if you find the best, they'll do the rest

A study from the *Harvard Business Review* (Hamori et al., 2012) found that most high-performing young people with records of strong academic and workplace performance regularly and actively looked for new jobs even when they were already employed. A Deloitte survey from 2016 shows that 57 per cent of millennial leaders are likely to leave their current position in the next two years. This was primarily because of a large gap between what development opportunities employers were providing and what employee development opportunities were desired. Training, mentoring and coaching were all highly desired but insufficiently provided (or completely omitted).

Rhetoric about the *war for talent,* although true and of concern, can exacerbate this problem because it creates a sense that poaching high-potential talent from a competitor is a 'tactical victory' in the war for talent. This leads to promises about compensation, benefits and development opportunities in the war to attract talent and can sometimes lead to certain opportunities being exaggerated. Lack of clarity communicating real benefits and opportunities along with obscurantism about the reality of the position can complicate the vicious cycle of employee's development ambitions not being met and hoping for a new employer that can meet those demands.

The problem is that of entitlement on both sides. Both employer and employee want the other to meet their demands and requirements. Employers want loyal, dedicated, reliable and hardworking employees, but may not provide their employees any real motives to stay at the company. The employee who has been identified as high potential (or believes himself to be high potential) is receptive to encouragement and development, but may be less receptive to criticism or putting in the effort required to develop potential into performance. Both sides have to be realistic about their expectations, and *be clear about their expectations* to their employee/employer. If neither can offer what the other is looking for, it is a poor fit. If either the employee or employer continually finds no one is able to meet their expectations, perhaps it is time for some self-reflection, on both parts.

The most skilled, intelligent, driven, conscientious and desirable people are the most 'in demand', yet are the most able to seek a different position that fits their own high goals, or their own definition of success. High flyers are the *right people* with the *right stuff*, and are consequently the least likely to stay in the *wrong position*. They know they have considerable occupational mobility.

Retention, development and recruitment are involved in an intimate circle. Recruiting the right people increases development opportunities. Development opportunities mean retaining the right people. Retaining the right people reduces the need for recruitment. It is also important to distinguish between retention efforts for general employee retention for mastery potential, and retaining those with high-flying or leadership potential.

Retaining mastery potential

Retaining mastery potential is relatively straightforward. These are the people who want to excel in a single position: a brilliant physicist, top athlete, discontented mother or a regimental wife, a clever innovator or creative designer. Being flexible with work schedules, good leadership, clear direction, fair reimbursement and tailored development paths can be important to ensure those with talent/expertise, but who also want to master their current skill set and remain with the organization. They likely want to stay in the same position, and will want to just 'get the job done'. They are frequently technical experts wanting to do what they are best at and not take on administrative or supervisory responsibilities.

Retaining high leadership potential

Retaining leadership and high-flying potential is much different, and requires a much greater emphasis on adaptation. High flyers are, by nature (and nurture), those who are most likely to search for new challenges, pursue new ideas and be their own advocates for working in new capacities. This characteristic should be cautiously encouraged. To retain this proactive behaviour, taking on new responsibilities should be rewarded, loosely monitored and supported.

Corporate and personal characteristics, of course, will dictate the creative and ambitious freedom that potential high flyers should be given. The consequences of success and failure should always be in the mind for the potential high flyer and those supervising/coaching/leading the team. While ingenuity is desirable, reckless pursuit of the new and different or unfocused dabbling may be a concern. Excessive risk taking at work, a constant focus on their own public persona or rash thrill seeking may be a sign of something darker. Thus, retention involves being on the lookout for the desirable traits of a high flyer, and adapting roles and responsibilities to particular skills and attributes – it also involves being on guard for characteristics that may have led to early success, but are derailment indicators.

Training and developing the right people

Some managers and leaders fear that the price of training people will be losing those people. There is an element of truth in this – the most skilled and experienced are the most able to find other jobs, and may be rewarded for doing so. However, when people are connected with their colleagues and leaders in the organization, feel the values of their current organization match their own, are engaged in their work and believe there are further opportunities for development and advancement by remaining with their current company, it is, for the most part, far more desirable than switching jobs.

Talent (ability and motivation) alone is not enough to ensure competence. What is also required is appropriate learning experiences. McCall (1998) argues that 'leadership ability can be learned, that creating a context that supports the development of talent can become a source of competitive advantage, and that the development of leaders is itself a leadership responsibility' (p. xii). Leaders will be expected to grow and lead their groups in a climate which is highly competitive, increasingly accountable and performance-driven (Browning et al., 2017). Survival of the fittest models do not translate well into good retention methods and do little to develop many of those who *could* be strong performers.

McCall stresses that continual growth, transition and transformation are as important for success as 'natural ability'. Organizations need to strengthen and polish what already exists but also bring potential into being. He also distinguished between two models:

- *The Darwinian Model*: which attempts to identify less/more successful executive traits, search for the latter, then give people tests/experience to polish these skills. On-the-job challenges reveal actual talent;

- *The Agricultural Model*: this attempts to identify strategic challenges that are likely to occur, search for people who can learn from the experiences, then help them to succeed. 'Grow' leaders instead of forcing people to fight their way to the top.

In a sense McCall argues from *survival* of the fittest to the *development* of the fittest; from being a corporate Darwinist to a managerial developer. The survival of the fittest model falls down under any serious scrutiny. Not least because attempting to translate survival of the fittest to individual performance in the workplace is a misnomer: evolution through the process of natural selection is not observable in an individual person (organism).

Survival of the fittest is not a good model for describing individual performance or values in people when we have culture, social structures, higher intelligence and empathy (Dawkins, 2004). The Darwinian model also has repercussions for retention. A model of natural selection would mean hiring as many different people as possible, waiting for a majority to fail and just promoting those 'survivors'.

Developmental opportunities arise from being given *new assignments* (project, task force), dealing with *hardships/setbacks* (business failure), *other people* (who are role models) and 'other events'. Clearly, people who take on continuous, realistic challenges with occasional changes of function will learn the most. International assignments and training can all enhance this process. Some organizations also choose to create and fund company schools and universities. Whether deliberate or serendipitous, organizations can provide powerful experiences that become opportunities to learn.

Ultimately the question remains about how organizations can provide the learning experiences that their potential leaders need to develop and will encourage them to stay with the company. Most companies insist that managers are accountable for results and not development, and, hence, ignore the development aspects of job assignments. Poorly planned job rotation focuses on exposure rather than task, performance or evidence of learning. Managers need incentives, resources and support in order to change. There should also be a framework for measuring the impact of development opportunities: some combination of the elements discussed in Part Two.

There are powerful reasons for, and arguments why, management training is not a *luxury* but a *necessity* for organizations in the new millennium. The increased global competition, as well as rapid changes in technology and the workforce, demands ever more numerous, ever more subtle and higher-level (but trainable) skills. There are inevitably greater demands on management time and the need for well-informed and accurate plans and decisions. Further, the high-potential people *want* this training. They are often motivated, interested in complex systems and ambiguous environments, and are clever enough to learn to navigate and manage them. Nobody begins fully trained and experienced. As a consequence, all organizations have to educate and train staff to improve their performance. This may be achieved by providing new and relevant knowledge and information, by teaching new skills, or by changing attitudes, values and motives. Typically it requires a combination of all the above.

The purpose of training is to enhance skill and knowledge. Good training can, and should, provide a focus for aligning the capabilities of the workforce with the company strategy. It can also ensure that workforce skill levels are up to, or even better than, national or industry levels. Good training can be a powerful individual motivator and a good catalyst for change.

Employee support

People need to be supported at a range of levels not just to feel satisfied at work, but to get their job done properly. The culture of an organization influences supports at all levels: a highly competitive or mistrustful culture means people are less willing to share ideas and information and help colleagues out. When people feel they are working *against* the organization or their leaders, the work can feel like a constant battle which dampens motivation and lowers job satisfaction.

Colleague support

People, quite simply, need to be able to work together. Challenging relationships with colleagues is one of the main reasons people choose not to remain in their job (Gully and Phillips, 2012). It is not *the* reason, but it is an important one. No matter how enjoyable or engaging a job is, no matter how good the leadership is, other people can make the job a joy or a misery. Conversely great colleagues who are interested, passionate and talented can be worth staying with.

Supervisor or leader support

The supervisor or team leader needs to actively and visibly support those they are working with. The behaviour of employees' direct supervisors are one of the greatest impacts on their job satisfaction, and poor supervision is one of the most common reasons employees leave. All supervisors or team leaders should be trained to do a few important, but relatively straightforward, key things (Gully and Phillips, 2012):

Have personal contact and be present

Just being there, asking questions and having meaningful conversations are essential for supporting employees. It is important for knowing what is going on, developing a positive working relationship and showing involvement and interest in the work. Even the highest levels of leadership should meet with people across the organization, not just the senior leadership team. A good leader can motivate many people, but will also learn much more by having conversations and asking good questions at the top and bottom of the pyramid.

Gain and earn trust

Being present and involved in the work people are doing is important, but not if being present means standing, watching, silently. The objective of being present is not surveillance, but about asking questions about what people are doing, if things are going well, and relating to employees and the work they are doing. Many people will bring issues and concerns to their supervisor *if they have established trust*. Employees who can trust their supervisor or team leader will be more honest about their problems, challenges, ambitions and goals. But it requires effort and honesty, and must be mutual.

Be available

Better supervisors are those who are present, who have personal contact and who will hear the stories that help them make better decisions. It is a professional relationship; neither a best friend, nor a blog, nor a psychiatrist, but someone who is available and listening when there is something important. When an opportunity or a challenge arises, the supervisor should be available (when important), be confidential (where appropriate) and will act (when necessary).

Organizational support

The policies, procedures, the organizational culture and values affect supervisor and colleague support, and have a direct effect on how likely a person is to stay with the organization. Complex and byzantine procedures frustrate people or beliefs – that senior leaders or the company disdain front line employees, for example, increases people's intention to leave.

Provide equitable rewards and appropriate consequences

This is a responsibility shared by the manager, company policy and possibly an HR department. People need to be treated, compensated and disciplined equitably and fairly. As we will discuss in the next section of this chapter, people have keen senses of what they believe to be fair and unfair, and it will drastically affect their motivation, performance and, in turn, desire to leave or stay. First, people should be compensated in similar ways for similar types of work and responsibility. Large pay disparities make people uncomfortable or angry, and more likely to look for work elsewhere. Favouritism: promotions, rewards or punishments that are not visibly or clearly linked to performance heighten sense of injustice, and people who see themselves outside the group of favourites quickly become unsatisfied. If the group of favourites appears to align with ethnicity, gender, class or other attributes, a concern about unfairness can quickly change into a legal issue.

Equity and the perception of fairness

People are deeply sensitive to equity. As soon as they detect a system or manager as being unfair they leave. Equity needs to describe the proximity or gap between what a person believes is fair, and what actually happens. A prime example from the workplace is the gap between needs for equity and perceptions about fair treatment.

Perceptions about equity and fairness can be one of the greatest motivators of 'revenge' behaviour. One of the authors knew a very intelligent young woman who worked briefly in a large American retail chain as a cashier. She felt that she (along with most other staff) was consistently mistreated and mismanaged. She found herself 'accidentally' giving back extra change to customers who were kind or polite. She quickly learned the systems, processes, and how to avoid getting caught. It was not a matter of stealing, or personal gain, but a small act of rebellion. She was *motivated* to sabotage the company (in a relatively minor way), clever enough not to get caught, and *motived* to 'reward' the good behaviour she saw, or the kindness of strangers. It's an interesting case of money going astray, but redistributed to many instead of being pocketed for personal profit.

Equity theory suggests people compare themselves socially with others, making a quantity judgement (more, less, equal) on two factors outcomes (benefits, rewards) and inputs (effort, ability). Outcomes are what workers believe they take out of their work such as pay, prestige, satisfaction, accomplishment or accolades. Inputs are what people believe they put into their job, such as hours of work, effort, social capital or qualifications and experience they bring to the job. However, perceptions of equity are based on what people believe the inputs and outcomes are, not what they necessarily are. Equity theory is entirely about subjective matters, not to be confused with employment equity which can be objectively quantified (e.g. equal pay for equal performance).

One way of thinking of equity and the results of equity as a motivator is that when people believe there is an imbalance (see Figure 22.1) they have essentially six options or potential reactions to perceived inequality:

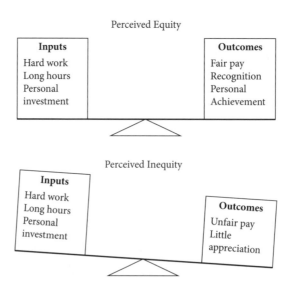

FIGURE 22.1 *Perceived weight of equality vs. inequality.*

- change their inputs (e.g. exert less or more effort);

- change their outcome (e.g. provide performance bonus that is tied to inputs);

- modify perceptions of self (e.g. 'I used to think I worked the hardest, but I never realized how much time and energy my supervisor put in');

- modify perceptions of others (e.g. 'No amount of money is worth it for such a tireless and thankless job');

- choose a referent (e.g. 'I earn less than most of my friends, but I'm paid more than most of my colleagues');

- leave the field (e.g. quit the job; take early retirement).

An analogous set of behavioural and psychological reactions can be identified for overpayment inequity. Specifically, employees who lower their own outcomes by not taking advantage of company-provided fringe benefits may be seen as redressing an overpayment inequity.

The concept of justice and fairness, which is at the heart of equity theory, is a powerful motivator for everyone. People have a keen sense of fairness (even when their perceptions do not match up to reality). People are motivated to match their inputs with their outcomes, whether it's working harder to earn a pay raise, working harder to see the results of their charitable work, slacking off or even thieving to personally rebalance the system of inputs and outcomes.

Those with high potential may have particularly keen senses of equity. High flyers will be willing to put in greater time, energy and effort into their work. They will try to maximize their inputs and expect commensurate outcomes in return in the form of specialized training, acknowledgement, advancement or financial compensation. Those with the intellectual tools and high-potential characteristics can also be the most able to lean on either side of the input/outcomes balance in the way they see fit when they perceive injustice.

Conclusion

Self-evidently people stay with an organization when they are happy: happy with the way they are managed and rewarded. They stay with organizations and the people in them which they like, respect and trust. They stay in organizations where they see a future for themselves and a way of achieving their ambitions.

It is often healthy for a high flyer to 'move on'; to gain experience in different organizations and different sectors. Whilst many managers seem particularly reluctant to 'let go' of a highly productive 'high flyer', it is probably best for both parties as people who felt well treated not only to act as goodwill ambassadors for an organization but they may choose to return to it.

NOTES

Chapter 3

1   Banker is the odd one out; others are chapter titles from the first section of Chaucer's *Canterbury Tales*.

BIBLIOGRAPHY

Ajzen, I. (1991). 'The theory of planned behaviour'. *Organisational Behaviour and Human Decision Processes*, 50, 179–211.

Ajzen, I. and Fishbein, M. (1980). *Understanding attitudes and predicting social behaviour.* Englewood Cliffs, NJ: Prentice Hall.

Allen, D. and Bryant, P. (2012). *Managing employee turnover: Myths to dispel and strategies for effective management.* Business Expert Press.

Allen, L. G., Siegel, S. and Hannah, S. (2007). 'The sad truth about depressive realism'. *The Quarterly Journal of Experimental Psychology*, 60(3), 482–495.

Amichai-Hamburger, Y. and Vinitzky, G. (2010). 'Social network use and personality'. *Computers in Human Behavior*, 26, 1289–1295.

Anderson, N., Lievens, F., van Dam, K. and Ryan, A. (2004). 'Future perspectives on employee selection: Key directions for future research and practice'. *Applied Psychology*, 53, 487–501.

Applebaum, S. H., Roberts, J. and Shapiro, B. T. (2009). Cultural strategies in M&As: Investigating ten case studies. *Journal of Executive Education*, 8(1), 33–58.

Argyle, M. (2001). *The psychology of happiness.* London: Routledge.

Arnold, J., Randall, R. and Patterson, S. (2005). *Work psychology: Understanding human behaviour in the workplace.* Harlow: Prentice-Hall.

Arvey, R. D., Rotundo, M., Johnson, W., Zhang, Z. and McGue, M. (2006). 'The determinants of leadership role occupancy: Genetic and personality factors'. *The Leadership Quarterly*, 17, 1–20.

Corrice, A. (2009). 'Unconscious bias in faculty and leadership recruitment: A literature review'. *Analysis: In Brief. Assocation of American Medical Colleges*, 9(2), 1–2.

Athey, R. (2005). 'The talent crisis: How prepared are you?' *Strategic HR Review*, 4, 3.

Babiak, P. and Hare, R. (2006). *Snakes in suits.* New York: Regan Books.

Baron, J. (1985). 'What kinds of intelligence components are fundamental'? In J. W. Segal, S. F. Chipman and R. Glaser (Eds.), *Thinking and Learning Skills*, Vol. 2: Research and open questions (Chapter 16). London: Lawrence Erlbaum Associates.

Barrick, M. R., Mount, M. K. and Judge, T. A. (2001). 'Personality and performance at the beginning of the new millennium: What do we know and where do we go next?' *International Journal of Selection and Assessment*, 9(1/2), 9–30.

Bartholomew, D. J. (2004). *Measuring intelligence: Facts and fallacies.* Cambridge, UK: Cambridge University Press.

Becton, J. B., Walker, H. J. and Jones-Farmer, A. (2014). 'Generational differences in workplace behavior'. *Journal of Applied Social Psychology*, 44(3), 175–189.

Beechler, S. and Woodward, I. (2009). 'The global "war for talent"'. *Journal of International Management*, 15, 273–285.

Bent, S. A. (1887). *Familiar short sayings of great men: With historical and explanatory notes*. Boston: Ticknor and Co.

Benning, S., Patrick, C., Bloniger, D., Hicks, B. and Iacono, W. (2003). 'Estimating facets of psychopathy from normal personality traits'. *Assessment*, 12, 3–18.

Berger, L. (2004). 'Creating a talent management system for organisation excellence'. In L. Berger and D. Berger (Eds.), *The Talent Management Handbook*. New York: McGraw-Hill, 3–21.

Berger, L. and Berger, D. (2004). *The Talent Management Handbook*. New York: McGraw Hill.

Berson, A. S. and Stieglitz, R. G. (2013). *Leadership Conversations: Challenging high potential managers to become great leaders*. San Francisco, CA: Jossey-Bass.

Bertua, C., Anderson, N. and Salgado, J. F. (2011). 'The predictive validity of cognitive ability tests: A UK meta-analysis'. *Organizational Psychology*, 78(3), 387–409.

Block, J. (2010). 'The five-factor framing of personality and beyond: Some ruminations'. *Psychological Inquiry*, 21, 2–25.

Boudreau, J. W., Boswell, W. R. and Judge, T. A. (2001). 'Effects of personality on executive career success in the United States and Europe'. *Journal of Vocational Behaviour*, 58, 53–81.

Brody, L. (2005). 'The study of exceptional talent'. *High Ability Studies*, 16, 87–96.

Brody, L. and Mills, C. (2005). 'Talent search research'. *High Ability Studies*, 16, 97–111.

Brown, R. (1999). 'The use of personality tests: A survey of usage and practice in the UK'. *Selection and Development Review*, 15, 3–8.

Brown, R. and McCartney, S. (2004). 'The development of capability: The content of potential and the potential of content'. *Education + Training*, 46(1), 7–10.

Browning, L., Thompson, K. and Dawson, D. (2017). 'From early career researcher to research leader: Survival of the fittest'? *Journal of Higher Education Policy and Management*, 9(4), 1–17.

Budner, S. (1962). 'Intolerance of ambiguity as a personality variable'. *Journal of Personality*, 30, 29–59.

The Business and Industry Advisory Committee to the OECD. (2012). Putting all our minds to work: Harnessing the gender dividend. http://www.amchamfrance.org/assets/special_business_reports/57055_10721-biac.pdf

Bywater, J. and Thompson, D. (2005). 'Personality questionnaires in a redundancy/restructuring setting – what do we know now?' *Selection and Development Review*, 21, 7–13.

Cacioppo, J. and Petty, R. (1982). 'The need for cognition'. *Journal of Personality and Social Psychology*, 42, 116–131.

Carroll, J. (1993). *Human cognitive abilities*. Cambridge: Cambridge University Press.

Carver, C. S., Sutton, S. K. and Scheier, M. F. (2000). 'Action, emotion, and personality: Emerging conceptual integration'. *Personality and Social Psychology Bulletin*, 26, 741–751.

Cattell, R. (1987). *Intelligence: Its structure, growth and action*. New York: North Holland.

Chamorro-Premuzic, T., Winsborough, D., Sherman, R. A. and Hogan, R. (2016). 'New talent signals: Shiny new objects or a brave new world?' *Industrial and Organizational Psychology*, 1–20.

Chapman, D. and Webster, J. (2003). 'The use of technologies in the recruiting, screening, and selection process for job candidates'. *International Journal of Selection and Assessment*, 11, 113–120.

Chartered Institute of Personnel Development [CIPD]. (2013). Zero hours contracts more widespread than thought. https://yougov.co.uk/news/2013/08/05/zero-hours-contracts-more-widespread-thought/

Cheke, L. G., Loissel, E. and Clayton, N. S. (2012). 'How do children solve Aesop's Fable?' *Plos One.* http://dx.doi.org/10.1371/journal.pone.0040574

Cherrington, D. (1980). *The work ethic.* New York: AMACOM.

Chorley, M. J., Whitaker, R. M. and Allen, S. M. (2015). 'Personality and location-based social networks'. *Computers in Human Behavior*, 46, 45–56.

Clarke, B. (1988). *Growing up gifted.* Columbus, OH: Charles E Merrill.

Clare, D. and Nyhan, R. (2001). 'A grand scan plan'. *Association Management*, 53(1), 73–77.

Cloutier, O., Felusiak, L., Hill, C. and Pemberton-Jones, E. J. (2015). 'The importance of developing strategies for employee retention'. *Journal of Leadership, Accountability and Ethics*, 12(2), 119.

Coast Capital Savings. (2008). 2008 Annual Report. https://www.coastcapitalsavings.com

Cohen, R. J. (2012). *Psychological testing and assessment* (8th edition). New York: McGraw Hill.

Cohen, R. J. and Swerdlik, M. E. (2010). *Test development. Psychological testing and assessment.* New York: McGraw-Hill Higher Education.

Collinson, P. (2016). 'Norway, the country where you can see everyone's tax returns'. *The Guardian.*

Colvin, G. (2008). *Talent is overrated: What really separates world-class performers from everybody else?* London: Nicholas Brealy.

Colvin, G. (2011). *Talent is overrated: What Really separates world-class performers from everyone else?* London: Nicholas Brealy.

Cook, M. (2008). *Personnel selection: adding value through people.* Chichester: Wiley.

Coren, S. (2009). Address: 'How Dogs Think' Session: 3282, 2:00–2:50 PM, Saturday, August 8, Metro Toronto Convention Centre.

Costa, P. and McCrae, R. (1992). 'Four ways five factors are basic'. *Personality and Individual Differences*, 13, 357–372.

Costa, P. and McCrae, R. (2006). 'Reinterpreting the Myers-Briggs Type Indicator from the perspective of the five-factor model of personality'. *Journal of Personality*, 57(1), 17–40.

Csíkszentmihályi, M. (2008). *Flow: The psychology of optimal experience.* New York: Harper Perennial.

da Silveira, A. M. (2013). The Enron scandal a decade later: Lessons learned? Working paper, Corporate Governance at the School of Economics, Management and Accounting at the University of São Paulo.

Dalal, D. and Nolan, K. (2009) 'Using dark side personality traits to identify potential failure'. *Industrial and Organisational Psychology*, 2, 434–436.

Dalbert, C. (2001). *The justice motive as a personal resource.* New York: Plenum Press.

Dawkins, R. (2004). *A devil's chaplain: Reflections on hope, lies, science and love*. Boston, MA: Mariner Books

De Vos, A., Buijen, D. and Schalk, R. (2005). 'Making sense of a new employment relationship'. *International Journal of Selection and Assessment*, 13, 41–52.

de Waal, F. B. M. (2004). 'Peace lessons from an unlikely source'. *PLoS Biology*, 2(4). https://doi.org/10.1371/journal.pbio.0020101

de Wall, F. B. M. and Ren, R. (1988). 'Comparison of the reconciliation behavior of Stumptail and Rhesus Macaques'. *Etiology*, 78(2), 129–142.

de Wall, F. B. M. and Johanowicz, D. (1993). 'Modification of reconciliation behavior through social experience: An experiment with two macaque species'. *Child Development*, 64, 897–908.

Deary, I. J., Penke, L. and Johnson, W. (2010). 'The neuroscience of human intelligence differences'. *Nature Reviews Neuroscience*, 11, 201–211.

Deloitte Survey. (2016). Millennial survey winning over the next generation of leaders. https://www2.deloitte.com/content/dam/Deloitte/global/Documents/About-Deloitte/gx-millenial-survey-2016-exec-summary.pdf

Dey, R., Jelveh, Z. and Ross, K. (2012). Facebook users have become much more private: A large-scale study. 4th IEEE International Workshop on Security and Social Networking (SESOC), Lugano, Switzerland.

Diener, E. (2000). 'Subjective wellbeing'. *American Psychologist*, 55, 34–41.

Dotlick, D. and Cairo, P. (2003). *Why CEOs fail*. New York: Jossey-Bass.

Doyle, C. (2003). *Work and organisational psychology*. Hove: Psychology Press.

Dulewicz, V. and Higgs, M. (2004). 'Design of a new instrument to assess leadership dimensions and styles'. *Selection and Development Review*, 20, 7–12.

Dulewicz, V., Higgs, M. and Slaski, M. (2003). 'Measuring emotional intelligence'. *Journal of Managerial Psychology*, 18, 405–420.

Dragoni, L., Oh, I., Vankatwyk, P. and Tesluk, P. E. (2011). 'Developing executive leaders: The relative contribution of cognitive ability, personality, and the accumulation of work experience in predicting strategic thinking competency'. *Personnel Psychology*, 64, 829–864.

Dries, N. and Peperman, R. (2007). '"Real" high-potential careers: An empirical study into the perspectives of organisations and high potentials'. *Personnel Review*, 37(1), 85–108.

The Economist. (2013). 'Personality testing at work: Can leaders be identified by psychometrics?' *The Economist*.

Economist Intelligence Unit. (2006). *The CEOs role in talent management*. London: Economist.

Edwards, R. (2011). 'So you think you've got what it takes: Measuring potential'. *Strategic HR Review*, 10, 6.

Eggert, M. A. (2013). *Deception in selection: Interviewees and the psychology of deceit*. London: Gower Pub Co.

Ericsson, K. A., Krampe, R. T. and Tesch-Römer, C. (1993). 'The role of deliberate practice in acquisition of expert performance'. *Psychological Review*, 100(3), 363–406.

Farleigh, R. (2007). *Dragons' Den: Success from pitch to profit*. London: Harper Collins.

Feather, N. (1975). *Values in education and society*. New York: Free Press.

Ferwerda, B., Schedl, M. and Tkalcic, M. (2015). Predicting personality traits with instagram pictures. In *Proceedings of the 3rd Workshop on Emotions and Personality in Personalized Systems 2015* (pp. 7–10). ACM.

Fillery-Travis, A. and Lane, D. (2006). 'Does coaching work or we asking the wrong question?' *International Coaching Psychology Review*, 1(1), 24–36.

Fogel, J. and Nehmad, E. (2009). 'Internet social network communities: Risk taking, trust and privacy concerns'. *Computers in Human Behaviour*, 25, 153–160.

Frauendorfeer, D. and Mast, M. S. (2015). 'The impact of nonverbal behavior in the job interview'. In A. Costik and D. Chaddee (Eds.), *The social psychology of nonverbal communication*. London: Palgrave Macmillan, 220–247.

Fredrickson, B. L. (2001). 'The role of positive emotions in positive psychology: The broaden-and-build theory of positive emotions'. *American Psychologist*, 56, 218–226.

Frenkel-Brunswick, E. (1949). 'Tolerance toward ambiguity as a personality variable'. *American Psychologist*, 3, 268.

Furnham, A. (1994). 'A content, correlational and factor analytic study of four tolerance of ambiguity questionnaires'. *Personality and Individual Differences*, 16(3), 403–410.

Furnham, A. (2003a). 'The Icarus Syndrome: Talent management and derailment in the new millennium'. In M. Effron, R. Gandossy and M. Goldsmith (Eds.), *Human Resources in the 21st century*. New York: Wiley, 99–108.

Furnham, A. (2003b). 'Belief in a just world: Research progress over the past decade'. *Personality and Behavioural Differences*, 34, 795–817.

Furnham, A. (2008a). *Personality and intelligence at work: Exploring and explaining individual differences at work*. London: Routledge.

Furnham, A. (2008b). 'HR Professionals' beliefs about, and knowledge of, assessment techniques and psychometric tests'. *International Journal of Selection and Assessment*, 16, 301–306.

Furnham, A. (2010). *The elephant in the boardroom: The causes of leadership derailment*. Basingstoke: Palgrave Macmillan.

Furnham, A. (2012). *The talented manager*. Basingstock: Palgrave Macmillan.

Furnham, A. (2015). 'Whither talent?' *European Business Review*.

Furnham, A. and Jackson, C. (2010). 'Practitioner reactions to work-related psychological tests'. *Journal of Managerial Psychology*, 26, 549–565.

Furnham, A., Petrides, K. V., Isaousis, I., Pappas, K. and Garrod, D. (2005). 'A cross-cultural investigation into the relationship between personality traits and work values'. *Journal of Psychology*, 139, 5–32.

Furnham, A. and Ribchester, T. (1995). 'Tolerance of ambiguity'. *Current Psychology*, 14, 179–199.

Gagne, F. (2004). 'Transforming gifts into talents'. *High Ability Studies*, 15, 119–147.

Galpin, M. and Skinner, J. (2004). 'Helping high flyers fly high: Their motives and developmental preferences'. *Industrial and Commercial Training*, 36(3), 113–116.

Garavan, T. and Morley, M. (1997). 'The socialization of high-potential graduates into the organization'. *Journal of Managerial Psychology*, 12, 118–137.

Gardner, H. (1983). *Frames of mind: The theory of multiple intelligences*. New York: Basic Books.

Gibney, A., Elkind, P., McLean, B. and Coyote, P. (2005). *Enron: The smartest guys in the room (video file).*

Gladwell, M. (2002). The talent myth. *New Yorker*, July, 28–33.

Gladwell, M. (2008). *Outliers: The story of success.* New York: Little, Brown and Company.

Goff, M. and Ackerman, P. (1992). 'Personality-Intelligence relations'. *Journal of Educational Psychology*, 84, 537–553.

Goldberg, L. R. (1992). 'The development of markers of the Big-Five factor structure'. *Psychological Assessment*, 4, 26–42.

Goodge, P. (2004). 'Capabilities versus competencies'. *Selection and Development Review*, 20, 7–10.

Gottfredson, L. S. (1997a). 'Mainstream science on intelligence: An editorial with 52 signatories, history and bibliography'. *Intelligence*, 24, 13–23.

Gottfredson, L. S. (1997b). 'Why g matters: The complexity of everyday life'. *Intelligence*, 24, 79–132.

Gottfredson, L. (2002). 'Where and why g matters: Not a mystery'. *Human Performance*, 15, 25–46.

Gottfredson, L. (2003). 'Dissecting practical intelligence theory: Its claims and evidence'. *Intelligence*, 31, 343–397.

Graen, G. (2009). 'Early identification of future executives'. *Industrial and Organisational Psychology*, 2, 437–441.

Greenberg, J. and Baron, R. (2003). *Behaviour in organisations.* New York: Pearson Educational.

Gross, R. and Acquisti, A. (2005). Information revelation and privacy in online social networks. ACM Workshop on Privacy in the Electronic Society, Alexandria, VA.

Guilford, J. (1980). 'Higher-order structure-of-intellect abilities'. *Multivariate Behavioural Research*, 16, 411–435.

Guinness World Records. (2013). Most garters removed with the teeth in one minute. Retrieved from http://www.guinnessworldrecords.com/world-records/speed/most-garters-removed-with-the-teeth-in-one-minute.

Gully, S. and Phillips, J. (2012). *Managing employee turnover: Dispelling myths and fostering evidence-based retention strategies.* New York: Business Expert Press.

Gurria, A. (May, 2012). All on board for gender equality. Speech Presented at the Launch of Gender reports (OECD and BIAC).

Hamori, M., Cao, J. and Koyuncu, B. (2012). Why young managers are in a nonstop job hunt. *Harvard Business Review: The Magazine*, July–August 2012. Retrieved from http://hbr.org/2012/07/why-top-young-managers-are-in-a-nonstop-job-hunt/ar/1

Hancock, J. I., Allen, D. G., Bosco, F. A., McDaniel, K. R. and Pierce, C. A. (2013). 'Meta-analytic review of employee turnover as a predictor of firm performance'. *Journal of Management*, 39, 573–603.

Hannah, S., Sweeney, P. J. and Lester, P. B. (2007). 'Toward a courageous mindset: The subjective act and experience of courage'. *The Journal of Positive Psychology*, 2(2), 129–135.

Hare, P. (1999). *Without conscience.* New York: Guilford Press.

Henson, R. (2009). 'Key practices in identifying and developing potential'. *Industrial and Organisational Psychology*, 2, 416–419.

Herman, J. L., Stevens, M. J., Bird, A., Mendenhall, M. and Oddou, G. (2010). 'The tolerance for ambiguity scale: Towards a more refined measure for international management research'. *International Journal of Intercultural Relations*, 24, 58–65.

Herrmann, E., Call, J., Hernández-Lloreda, M. V., Hare, B. and Tomasello, M. (2007). 'Humans have evolved specialized skills of social cognition: The cultural intelligence hypothesis'. *Science*, 317, 1360–1366.

Herzberg, F., Mausner, B. and Snyderman, B. (1959). *The motivation to work*. New York: Wiley.

Heslin, P. (2009). '"Potential" in the eye of the beholder: The role of managers who spot rising stars'. *Industrial and Organisational Psychology*, 2, 420–424.

Higgens, C. A. and Sekiguchi, T. (2006). *A dynamic model of person-group fit. Power and influence in organizations: New empirical and theoretical perspective*. Charlotte, NC: Information Age Publishing.

Higgs, M. and Aitken, P. (2003). 'An exploration of the relationship between emotional intelligence and leadership potential'. *Journal of Managerial Psychology*, 18, 814–823.

Hogan, M. (2009). *Personality and the fate of organisations*. New York: LEA.

Hogan, M. (2012). In One Lifespan: From critical thinking to creativity and more. *Psychology Today*.

Hogan, H. and Hogan, J. (2004). 'Assessing leadership: A vision from the dark side'. *Selection and Development Review*, 20. 3–15.

Holland, J. (1973). *Making vocational choices*. Englewood Cliffs, NJ: Prentice Hall.

Huffcutt, A. I., Culberston, S. S. and Wehyrauch, W. S. (2013). 'Employment interview reliability: New meta-analytic estimates by structure and format'. *International Journal of Selection and Assessment*, 13, 264–276.

Human Resources and Skills Development Canada. (2011). National occupational classification 2011. Retrieved from http://www5.hrsdc.gc.ca/NOC/English/NOC/2011/Welcome.aspx

Hunter, J. (1986). 'Cognitive ability, cognitive aptitudes, job knowledge and job performance'. *Intelligence*, 29, 340–362.

Hunter, J. and Hunter R. (1984). 'Validity and utility of alternative predictors of job performance'. *Psychological Bulletin*, 96, 2–98.

Huppert, F. A., Baylis, N. and Keverne, B. (2005). *The science of well-being*. Oxford: Oxford University Press.

Industry Training Authority. (2013a). *Program outline: Aircraft structural technician*. Victoria, Canada: Crown Publications.

Industry Training Authority. (2013b). *Program outline: Utility arborist*. Victoria, Canada: Crown Publications.

Ingold, P. V., Cornelius, M. K., König, J., Melchers, K. G. and Van Iddekinge, C. H. (2016). 'Why do Situational Interviews Predict Job Performance? The Role of Interviewees' Ability to Identify Criteria'. *Journal of Business and Psychology*, 30(2), 397–398.

Jeanneret, R. and Silzer, R. (2000). 'An overview of individual psychological assessment'. In R. Jeanreret and R. Silzer (Eds.), *Individual psychological assessment*. San Francisco, CA: Jossey Bass, 3–26.

Jones, G. (1988). Investigation of the efficacy of general ability versus specific abilities as predictors of occupational success. Unpublished thesis, St. Mary's University of Texas.

Judge, T. A., Higgins, C. A., Thoresen, C. J. and Barrick, M. R. (1999). 'The big five personality traits, general mental ability, and career success across the lifespan'. *Personnel Psychology*, 52(3), 621–652.

Judge, T. A. and Illies, R. (2002). 'Relationship of personality to performance motivation: A meta-analytics review'. *Journal of Applied Psychology*, 87, 797–807.

Judge, T. A. and Locke, E. A. (1992). The effect of dysfunctional thought processes on subjective well-being and job satisfaction. CAHRS Working Paper Series.

Judge, T. A., Martocchio, J. J. and Thoresen, C. J. (1997). 'Five-factor model of personality and employee absence'. *Journal of Applied Psychology*, 82(5), 745–755.

Karl, K., Peluchette, J. and Schaegel, C. (2010). 'Who's posting Facebook faux pas? A cross-cultural examination of personality differences'. *International Journal of Selection and Assessment*, 18, 174–186.

Keenan, A. and McBain, G. D. M. (2011). 'Effects of Type A behaviour, intolerance of ambiguity, and locus of control on the relationship between role stress and work-related outcomes'. *Journal of Occupational Psychology*, 52(4), 227–285.

Keith, N. and Frese, M. (2008). 'Effectiveness of error management training: A meta-analysis'. *Journal of Applied Psychology*, 93(1), 59–69.

Kerr-Phillips, B. and Thomas, A. (2009). 'Macro and micro challenges for talent retention in South Africa'. *South African Journal of Human Resource Management*, 7(1), 1–10.

Kluemper, D. H., Rosen, P. A. and Mossholder, K. W. (2012). 'Social networking websites. Personality ratings, and the organizational context: More than meets the eye?' *Journal of Applied Psychology*, 42(5), 1143–1172.

Kosinski, M., Stillwell, D. and Graepel, T. (2013). 'Private traits and attributes are predictable from digital records of human behavior'. *Proceedings of the National Academy of Sciences of the United States of America*, 110(15), 5802–5805.

Kouzes, J. M. and Posner, B. Z. (1998). *The leadership challenge*. San Fransisco: Jossey Bass.

Kuncel, N., Hezlett, S. and Ones, D. (2004). 'A comprehensive meta-analysis of the predictive validity of the graduate record examinations: Implications for graduate student selection and performance'. *Journal of Personality and Social Psychology*, 86, 148–161.

Kwaitkowski, R. (2003). 'Trends in organisations and selection'. *Journal of Managerial Psychology*, 18, 382–394.

Laland, K. N. and Hoppitt, W. (2003). 'Do animals have culture'? *Evolutionary Anthropology*, 12, 150–159.

Lapowsky, I. (2016). 'A lot of people are saying Trump's new data team is shady'. *Wired*.

Levishina, J., Hartwell, C. J., Morgeson, F. P. and Campion, M. A. (2013). 'The structured employment interview: Narrative and quantative review of the research literature'. *Personnel Psychology*, 67, 241–293.

Lewis, C. S. (2008). *Studies in words*. Cambridge: Cambridge University Press.

Lewis, C. S. (2009). *An experiment in criticism*. Cambridge: Cambridge University Press.

Lewis, R. E. and Heckman, R. J. (2006). 'Talent management: A critical review'. *Human Resource Management Review*, 16, 139–154.

Lievens, F., van Dam, K. and Anderson, N. (2002). 'Recent trends in challenges in personnel selection'. *Personnel Review*, 31, 580–601.

Lilico, A. (2016). 'What if everyone in Britain had to publish their tax returns?' *The Telegraph*.

Linden, D., Nijenhuis, J. and Bakker, A. B. (2010). 'The general factor of personality: A meta-analysis of Big Five intercorrelations and a criterion-related validity study'. *Journal of Research in Personality*, 44(3), 315–327.

Lombardo, M. (2005). 'Developing talent: The magic bullets'. *Strategic HR Review*, 4(2), 3–3.

Lievens, F., DeCorte, W. and Brysse, K. (2003). 'Applicant perceptions of selection procedures'. *International Journal of Selection and Assessment*, 11, 67–71.

Lynch, G. and Granger, R. (2009). *Big brain: The origins and future of human intelligence*. Basingstoke: Palgrave Macmillan.

MacFarlane, S. and Roach, R. (1999). Great expectations: The ideal characteristics of non-profits. *Alternative Service Delivery Project Research Bulletin*, Canada West Founation.

MacRae, I. (2010). Organizational well-being and communication in a medical setting. (Undergraduate dissertation). Retrieved from cIRcle (http://hdl.handle.net/2429/27006)

MacRae, I. (2012). Success, potential and validating a measure of High Flying Personality Traits in Organisations. Unpublished Masters Dissertation, University College London.

MacRae, I. (2014). 'Assessing and developing value(s) in the financial sector: A case study'. *Assessment and Development Matters*, 6(1), 15–17.

MacRae, I. (2016). 'What is the profile of an effective senior leader'. *Thomas International*.

MacRae, I. (2017). 'Global Masterclass: Don't generalise the generations'. *HR Future Magazine*.

MacRae, I. (2017). 'Money talks: Understanding the role of money in motivation'. *Irish Tech News*.

MacRae, I. (2017). 'Zero hours contracts for SMEs: A problem or an opportunity'? *SME Magazine*.

MacRae, I. and Furnham, A. (2014). *High potential: How to spot, manage and develop talented people at work*. Bloomsbury: London.

MacRae, I. and Furnham, A. (2017a). *Motivation and performance: A guide to motivating a diverse workforce*. London: Kogan Page.

MacRae, I. and Furnham, A. (2017b). *Myths of work: The stereotypes and assumptions holding your organisation back*. London: Kogan Page.

Martin, J. and Schmidt, C. (2010). How to keep your top talented. *Harvard Business Review*, May, 54–61.

Mayhew, B. (2013). Eight tips for managing millennials at the office. *The Huffington Post*.

Mayrhofer, W. (1997). 'Of dice and men: high flyers in German-speaking countries'. *Career Development International*, 2, 331–340.

McCall, M., Lombardo, M. and Morrison, A. (1990). *The lessons of experience: How successful executives develop on the job*. Lexington, MA: Lexington Books.

McCall, M. W. (1998). *High Flyers: Developing the next generation of leaders*. Boston, MA: Harvard Business School.

McCall, M. W. (2010). 'Recasting leadership development'. *Industrial and Organizational Psychology: Perspectives on Science and Practice*, 3(1), 3–19.

McClelland, D. C. (1965). 'Toward a theory of motive acquisition'. *American Psychologist*, 20, 321–333.

McClelland, D. C. (1973). 'Testing for competence rather than "intelligence"'. *American Psychologist*, 28(1), 1–14.

McClelland, D. C. and Burnham, D. H. (1976). 'Power is the great motivator'. *Harvard Business Review*, 54(2), 117–126.

McCrae, R. R. and Costa, P. T. (1987). 'Validation of the five-factor model of personality across instruments and observers'. *Journal of Personality and Social Psychology*, 52, 81–90.

McDonnell, A., Lamare, R., Gunnigle, P. and Lavelle, J. (2010). 'Developing tomorrow's leaders-Evidence of global talent management in multinational enterprises'. *Journal of World Business*, 45, 150–160.

McLean, B. and Elkind, P. (2004). *The smartest guys in the room: The amazing rise and scandalous fall of Enron*. London: Penguin.

Messick, S. (1976). *Individuality and learning*. San Francisco, CA: Jossey-Bass.

Michaels, E., Handfield-Jones, H. and Axelrod, B. (2001). *The war for talent*. Boston, MA Harvard Business School.

Mintzberg, H. (1994). *The rise and fall of strategic planning*. New York: The Free Press.

Moss-Racusin, C. A., Dovidio, J. F., Brescoll, V. L., Graham, M. J. and Hanelsman, J. (2012). Science faculty's subtle gender biases favour male students. Proceedings of the National Academy of Sciences of the United States of America.

Murphy, K. (2002). 'Can conflicting perspectives on the role of g in personnel selection be resolved?' *Human Performance*, 15, 173–186.

Myers, D. (1992). *The pursuit of happiness*. New York: Avon.

Nettle, D. (2005). 'An evolutionary approach to the extraversion dimension continuum'. *Evolution and Human Behaviour*, 26, 363–373.

Nettle, D. (2006). 'The evolution of personality variation in human and other animals'. *American Psychologist*, 61, 622–631.

Nettlebeck, T. and Wilson, C. (2005). 'Intelligence and IQ: what teachers should know?' *Educational Psychology*, 25, 609–630.

Newby, L. and Howarth, C. (2012). 'How Specsavers attracts and nurtures outstanding talent'. *Strategic HR Review*, 11, 193–198.

The New York Times. (2001). The rise and fall of Enron. *New York Times*.

Nezami, E. and Butcher, J. N. (2000). 'Personality Assessment'. In G. Goldstein and M. Hersen (Eds.), *Handbook of psychological assessment*. Amsterdam, The Netherlands: Elsevier.

Nijenhuis, J., Voskuijl, O. and Schijive, N. (2001). 'Practice on coaching on IQ tests'. *International Journal of Selection and Assessment*, 9, 302–306.

Nisbett, R. E., Peng, K., Choi, I. and Norenzayan, A. (2001). 'Culture and systems of thought: Holistic versus analytic cognition'. *Psychological Review*, 108(2), 291–310.

Nix, A. [Concordia]. (2016, September 27). The Power of Big Data and Psychographics. [Video File]. Retrieved from https://www.youtube.com/watch?v=n8Dd5aVXLCc.

Nolan, K. P., Langhammer, K. and Salter, N. P. (2016). 'Evaluating fit in employee selection: Beliefs about how, when, and why'. *Consulting Psychology Journal: Practice and Research*, 61, 222–256.

Northern Opportunities. Developed by Heather Stewart and Ian MacRae. (2013). Northern opportunities program: Export model. http://northernopportunities.bc.ca/wp-content/uploads/2013/03/NOP-Export-Model.FINAL_.dec20-2.pdf

Norton, P. J. and Weiss, B. J. (2009). 'The role of courage on behavioral approach in fear-eliciting situations: A proof-of-concept pilot study'. *Journal of Anxiety Disorders*, 23, 212–217.

Norton, R. W. (1975). 'Measurement of ambiguity tolerance'. *Journal of Personality Assessment*, 29(6), 607–619.

Oakland, T. (2004). 'Use of educational and psychological tests internationally'. *Applied Psychology*, 53, 157–172.

Office of National Statistics [ONS]. (2013). Zero hours contract levels and percent 2000 to 2012. https://www.ons.gov.uk/.../zero-hours-contract-levels-and-percent-2000-to-201.xls

Ones, D. S., Viswesvaran, C. and Dilchert, S. (2005). 'Cognitive ability in personnel selection decisions'. In A. Evers, O. Voskuijl and N. Anderson (Eds.), *Handbook of personnel selection*. Oxford, UK: Blackwell, 143–173.

Organisation for Economic Cooperation and Development. (2001). *Public sector leadership for the 21st century*. Paris: OECD Publishing.

Organisation for Economic Cooperation and Development [OECD]. (2015). *Income Inequaliy (indicator)*. doi: 10.1787/459aa7f1-en

Owen, D. (2012). *The Hubris Syndrome: Bush, blair and in intoxication of power* (New Edition). York: Methuen.

Park, G., Schwartz, H. A., Eichstaedt, J. C., Kern, M. L., Kosinski, M., Stillwell, D. J., Ungar, L. H. and Seligman, M. E. P. (2015). 'Automatic personality assessment through social media language'. *Journal of Personality and Social Psychology*, 108(6), 934–952.

Parks, L. and R. P. Guay. (2009). 'Personality, motivation and values'. *Personality and Individual Differences*, 47, 675–684.

Patty, W. L. and Johnson, L. (1953). *Personality and adjustment*. New York: McGraw-Hill.

Paulus, D. and Williams, K. (2002). 'The dark triad of personality'. *Journal of Research in Personality*, 36, 556–563.

Perry, G. (2013, January). *Inside the industry: Grayson Perry visits the LCF*. London: London College of Fashion.

Phillips, J. M. and Gully, S. M. (1997). 'Role of goal orientation, ability, need for achievement, and locus of control in the self-efficacy and goal setting process'. *Journal of Applied Psychology*, 82(5), 792–802.

Posner, G. (2015). *God's Bankers: A history of money and power at the Vatican*. London: Simon & Schuster.

Potosky, D. and Bobko, P. (2004). 'Selection testing via the internet'. *Personnel Psychology*, 57, 1003–1034.

Quinn, R. W. and Quinn, R. E. (2016). Change management and leadership development have to mesh. *Harvard Business Review*.[Online] [Accessed on 8 October 2016]. Retrieved from https://hbr. org/2016/01/change-management-and-leadership-development-have-to-mesh.

Rajagopal, S. (2006). 'The Placebo Effect'. *The Psychiatrist*, 30(5), 185–188.

Ree, M. and Carretta, T. (1998). 'General cognitive ability and occupational performance'. *International Review of Industrial and Organisational Psychology*, 13, 161–189.

Ree, M. and Earles, J. (1994). 'The ubiquitous predictiveness of g'. In M. Rumsey, C. Walker and J. Harris (Eds.), *Personnel selection and classification*. Hillsdale, NJ: Lawrence Erlbaum, 127–135.

Ree, M., Earles, J. and Teachout, M. (1994). 'Predicting job performance: Not much more than g'. *Journal of Applied Psychology*, 79, 518–524.

Ree, M. J. and Earles, J. A. (1992). 'Intelligence is the best predictor of job performance'. *Current Directions in Psychological Science*, 1(3), 86–89.

Rentsch, J. and McEwan, A. (2002). 'Comparing personality characteristics, values and goals as antecedents of organisational attractiveness'. *International Journal of Selection and Assessment*, 10, 225–234.

RHR. (2005). Filling the executive bench: How companies are developing future leaders. Buckingham Gate London.

Riding, R. (2005). 'Individual differences and educational performance'. *Educational Psychology*, 25, 659–672.

Robinson, C., Fetters, Riester D. and Bracco, A. (2009) 'The Paradox of potential'. *Industrial and Organizational Psychology*, 2, 413–415.

Rogers, G., Finley, D. S. and Galloway, J. R. (2001). *Strategic planning in social services organizations: A practical guide*. Toronto, ON: Canadian Scholars' Press and Women's Press.

Rogers, T. B., Kuiper, N. A. and Kirker, W. S. (1977). 'Self-reference and the encoding of personal information'. *Journal of Personality and Social Psychology*, 35, 677–678.

Ryan, A. M. and Sackett, P. (1988). 'Individual assessment: The research base'. In R. Jeanreret and R. Sulzer (Eds.), *Individual psychological assessment*. San Francisco, CA: Jossey Bass, 54–87.

Rydell, S. (1966). 'Tolerance of ambiguity and semantic differential ratings'. *Psychological Reports*, 19, 139–165.

Salgado, J. (2001). 'Some landmarks of 100 years of scientific personal selection at the beginning of the new century'. *International Journal of Selection and Assessment*, 9, 3–8.

Salpukas, A. (1999). *Firing up an idea machine; Enron is encouraging the entrepreneurs within. The New York Times*.

Sapolsky, R. M. (2006). 'Culture in animals: The case of a non-human primate culture of low aggression and high affiliation'. *Social Forces*, 85(1), 217–233.

Scales, P. (2011). *Teaching in the lifelong learning sector*. Maidenhead: Open University Press.

Schaufeli, W. B., Bakker, A. B. and Salanova, M. (2006). 'The measurement of work engagement with a short questionnaire: A cross-national study'. *Education and Psychological Measurement*, 66(4), 701–706.

Schmidt, F. L. (2011). 'The role of general cognitive performance: Why there cannot be a debate'. *Human Performance*, 15, 187–21.

Schmidt, F. L. (2016). The validity and utility of selection methods in personnel psychology: Practical and theoretical implications of 100 years. *Fox School of Business Research Paper*. https://ssrn.com/abstract=2853669

Schreisheim, C. and Neider, L., L. (2006). *Power and influence in organizations: New empirical and theoretical perspectives*. Charlotte, NC: Information Age Publishing.

Schuler, R., Jackson, S. and Tarique, I. (2011). 'Global talent management and global talent challenges'. *Journal of World Business*, 46, 506–516.

Seibert, S. E., Kraimer, M. L. and Liden, R. C. (2001). 'A social capital theory of career success'. *Academy of Management Journal*, 44(2), 219–237.

Shavinina, L. (2004). 'Explaining high abilities of Nobel Laureates'. *High Ability Studies*, 15, 243–254.

Shen, J., Brdiczka, O. and Liu, J. (2015). 'A study of Facebook behavior: What does it tell about your Neuroticism and Extraversion?' *Computers in Human Behavior*, 45, 32–38.

Shirom, A. (2011). 'Vigor as a positive affect at work: Conceptualizing vigor, its relations with related constructs and its antecedents and consequences'. *Review of General Psychology*, 15(1), 50–64.

Shurkin, J. N. (1992). *Terman's kids: The groundbreaking study of how the gifted grow up.* New York: Little, Brown & Co.

Slemrod, K. (2005). Taxation and big brother: Information, personalization, and privacy in the 21st century tax policy. *Lecture given at Annual Lecture to the Institute of Fiscal Studies*, London, September 26, 2005.

Silvia, P. J., Nusbaum, E. C., Berg, C., Martin, C. and O'Connor, A. (2009). 'Openness to experience, plasticity, and creativity: Exploring lower-order, higher-order, and interactive effects'. *Journal of Research in Personality*, 43(6), 1087–1090.

Silzer, R. and Church, A. H. (2009a). 'The pearls and perils of identifying potential'. *Industrial and Organizational Psychology*, 2(4), 377–412.

Silzer, R. and Church, A. H. (2009b). 'Identifying and assessing high potential talent: Current organizational practices'. In R. F. Silzer and B. E. Dowell (Eds.), *Strategy-driven talent management: A leadership imperative*. New Jersey: Wiley.

Silzer, R. and Jeanneret, R. (2000). 'Anticipating the Future: Assessment Strategies for tomorrow'. In R. Jeanreret and R. Silzer (Eds.), *Individual psychology assessment*. San Francisco, CA: Jossey Bass, 445–477.

Skowron, M., Tkalčič, M., Ferwerda, B. and Schedl, M. (2016). Fusing social media cues: personality prediction from twitter and instagram. In *Proceedings of the 25th international conference companion on world wide web* (pp. 107–108). International World Wide Web Conferences Steering Committee.

Sloan, E. (2001). 'Identifying and developing high potential talent: A succession management methodology'. *The Industrial-Organisational Psychologist*, 38, 84–90.

Smith, M. and Robertson, I. (1989). *Advances in selection and assessment*, Chichester: John Wiley.

Spangler, W. D. (1992). 'Validity of questionnaire and TAT measure of need for achievement: Two meta-analysis'. *Psychological Bulletin*, 112(1), 140–154.

Spector, P. (1982). 'Behaviour in organisations as a function of employees' locus of control'. *Psychological Bulletin*, 91, 482–497.

Spector, P. (2006). *Industrial and organisational psychology: Research and practice*. New Jersey: John Wiley.

Spreitzer, G. M., McCall, M. W. and Mahoney, J. D. (1997). 'Early identification international executive potential'. *Journal of Applied Psychology*, 82(1), 6–29.

Sternberg, R. (1997). *Successful intelligence*. New York: Plume.

Subotnik, R. F., Olszewski-Kubilius, P. and Worrell, F. C. (2011). 'Rethinking giftedness and gifted education: A proposed direction forward based on psychological science'. *Psychological science*, 12(1), 3–54.

Swami, V., Knight, D., Tovée, M. J., Davies, P. and Furnham, A. (2007). 'Preferences for demale body size in Britain and South Pacific'. *Body Image*, 4(2), 219–223.

Tanaka, J. S., Panter, A. T. and Winborne, W. C. (1988). 'Dimensions of the need for cognition: Subscales and gender differences'. *Multivariate Behavioural Research*, 23(1), 35–50.

Tanner, R. and Gore, C. (2013). *Physiological tests for elite athletes* (2nd Edition) Canberra: Australian Institute of Sport.

Tansley, C. (2011). 'What do we mean by the term "talent" in talent management'. *Industrial and Commercial Training*, 43, 266–274.

Teasdale, T. W. and Owen, D. R. (2008). 'Secular declines in cognitive test scores: A reversal of the Flynn Effect'. *Intelligence*, 36, 121–126.

Teodorescu, A., Furnham A. and MacRae, I. (2017). 'Trait correlates of success at work'. *International Journal of Selection and Assessment*, 25, 35–40.

Tett, R. P., Jackson, D. N., Rothstein, M. and Reddon, J. R. (1999). 'Meta-analysis of bidirectional relations in personality-job performance research'. *Human Performance*, 12, 1–9.

Theeboom, T., Beersma, B. and van Vianen, A. E. M. (2013). 'Does coaching work? A meta analysis on effects of coaching on individual level outcomes in an organisational context'. *The Journal of Positive Psychology*, 9.

Thomason, S., Weeks, M., Bernadin, H. and Kane, J. (2011). 'The differential focus of supervisors and peers in evaluations of managerial potential'. *International Journal of Selection and Assessment*, 19, 81–92.

Thornton, B., Ryckman, R. M. and Gold, J. A. (2011). 'Competitive orientations and the Type A behaviour pattern'. *Psychology*, 2(5), 411–415.

Thunnissen, M., Boselie, P. and Fruytier, B. (2013). 'A review of talent management: "Infancy or adolescence?"'. *The International Journal of Human Resource Management*, 24(9), 1744–1761.

Tiedemann, J. (1989). 'Measures of cognitive styles: A critical review'. *Educational Psychologist*, 24, 261–275.

Transparency International. (2015). *Corruption Perceptions Index 2015*. Transparency International.

Triandis, H. C. and Suh, E. M. (2002). 'Cultural influences on personality'. *Annual Review of Personality*, 53, 133–160.

Truxillo, D., Steiner, D. and Gilliland, S. (2004). 'The importance of organisational justice in personnel'. *International Journal of Selection and Assessment*, 12, 39–53.

UK Fire Services. (2011). The physical tests: UK fire service resources. Retrieved from http://www.fireservice.co.uk/recruitment/physical

Ulrich, D., Younger, J., Brockbank, W. and Ulrich, M. (2012). 'HR talent and the new HR competencies'. *Strategic HR Review*, 11, 217–222.

Uren, L. (2011). 'What talent wants: the journey to talent segmentation'. *Strategic HR Review*, 10, 31–37.

Vaeyens, R., Güllich, A., Warr, C. R. and Philippaerts, R. (2009). 'Talent identification promotion programmes of Olympic athletes'. *Journal of Sports Sciences*, 27(13), 1367–1380.

Vallerand, R., Mageau, G., Elliot, A., Dumais, A., Demers, M-A. and Rousseau, F. (2008). 'Passion and performance attainment in sport'. *Psychology of Sport and Exercise*, 9, 373–392.

Van de Vijver, F. (2008). 'Personality assessment of global talent'. *International Journal of Testing*, 8, 304–314.

Van de Vijver, F. and Phalet, K. (2004). 'Assessment in Multicultural Groups'. *Applied Psychology*, 53, 215–236.

Van Maanen, J. and Schein, E. H. (1979). 'Toward a theory of organizational socialization'. *Research in Organizational Behaviour*, 1, 209–264.

Vincent, C. and Furnham, A. (1997). *Complementary medicine*. Chichester: Wiley.

Visweswaran, C., Ones, D. and Schmidt, F. (1996). 'Comparative analysis of the reliability of job performance ratings'. *Journal of Applied Psychology*, 81, 557–574.

Vlasic, B. and Stertz, B. A. (2000). *Taken for a ride: How Daimler-Benz drove off with Chrysler*. Hoboken, NJ: John Wiley & Sons.

Vygotsky, L. S. (1978). *Mind in society: The development of higher psychological processes*. Interaction between learning and development. Cambridge, MA: Harvard University Press, 79–91.

Wang, G. and Netemeyer, R. G. (2002). 'The effects of job autonomy, customer demandingness, and trait competitiveness on salesperson learning, self-efficacy and performance'. *Journal of the Academic Study of Marketing Science*, 30, 217–227.

Wareing, B. and Fletcher, C. (2004). 'Ethnic minority differences in self-assessment'. *Selection and Development Review*, 20, 7–10.

Weber, M. (1905). 'Die Protestantische Ethik und der "Geist" des Kapitalismus'. *Archib fur Sozialwissenschaft und Sozialpolitik*, 20, 1–54.

Whitmore, J. (2009). *Coaching for performance* (4th Edition). Lonson: Nicholas Brealey Publishing.

Wille, B., Beyers, W. and De Fruyt, F. (2012). 'A transactional approach to person-environment fit: Reciprocal relations between personality development and career role growth across young to middle adulthood'. *Journal of Vocational Behavior*, 81, 307–321.

Wilson, R. E., Gosling, S. D. and Graham, L. T. (2012). 'A review of facebook research in the social sciences'. *Perspective on Psychological Science*, 7(3), 203–220.

Winterton, J. and Winterton, R. (1999). *Developing managerial competence*. London: Routledge.

Wood, D. and Brumbaugh, C. C. (2009). 'Using revealed mate preferences to evaluate market force and differential preference explanations for mate selection'. *Journal of Personality and Social Psychology*, 96, 1226–1244.

Wood, P. (2016). 'The British data-crunchers who say they helped Donald Trump to win: Are Cambridge Analytica brilliant scientists or snake-oil salesmen'? *The Spectator*.

Yang, Y. and Green, S. B. (2011). 'Coefficient alpha: A reliability coefficient for the 21st century?' *Journal of Psychoeducational Assessment*, 29(4), 377–292.

Yost, P. R. and Chang, G. (2009). 'Everyone is equal, but some are more equal than others'. *Industrial and Organizational Psychology*, 2(4), 442–445.

Young, D. Hamilton, C. and Kirk, A. (2004). 'Web-based coaching – lessons from a practical experience'. *Selection and Development Review*, 20, 18–23.

Zimbardo, P. (2008). *The Lucifer effect: How good people turn evil*. London: Rider Books.

INDEX